MOTOR
RACING
CIRCUITS

IN ENGLAND
THEN & NOW

MOTOR RACING CIRCUITS IN ENGLAND
THEN & NOW

Peter Swinger

Ian Allan PUBLISHING

DEDICATION

Cyflwni'r llyfr hwn fel cofeb i'm ffrind

THOMAS MALDWYN PRYCE

oedd wedi ei fendithio a dawn mor ddwfn a phyllau glo Hen Wlad fy Nhadau. Fe'i gymerwyd oddi wrthym trwy ddamwain anghyffredin, ac onibai am hyn, nid oes amheuaeth mai ef fuasai'r Cymro cynta i fod yn Bencampwr Rasio Ceir y Byd.

This book is dedicated to the memory of my friend

THOMAS MALDWYN PRYCE

who was blessed with a talent as deep as the mines of the Land of our Fathers. He was taken from us by a freak accident but for which he would, undoubtedly, have been the first Welsh Motor Racing World Champion.

First published 2001
This paperback edition first published 2005
Reprinted 2007

ISBN (10) 0 7110 3104 5
ISBN (13) 978 0 7110 3104 3

Published by Dial House
an imprint of Ian Allan Publishing Ltd, Hersham,
Surrey KT12 4RG.
Printed in England by Ian Allan Printing Ltd, Hersham,
Surrey KT12 4RG.

Code: 0705/A1

Visit the Ian Allan Publishing website:
www.Ianallanpublishing.com

ACKNOWLEDGEMENTS

This project would not have been possible without a great deal of help from many kind people involved in the sport and the list will be long.

My grateful thanks to Nicola Fulston for permission to use the maps and programme information from the Brands Hatch group of circuits (now Octagon Motor Sports Ltd), Dave Fern of Two Four Sports Ltd at Donington Park, Roger Etcell and Katie Tyler at Silverstone, Lord March and Rob Widdows for information on Goodwood and granting me press accreditation to the Festival of Speed and the Motor Circuit Revival Meeting, Tom Dooley (who has probably forgotten more about Oulton Park than most of us will ever know), Howard Strawford and Rodney Gooch of Castle Combe and the archivist Peter Stowe, my old friend John Aley for finding the maps of the original airfields on which so many of our circuits were built and for remembering so many snippets, John Granger and M. H. Goodall of the Brooklands Museum, everyone who works in the Library at the National Motor Museum at Beaulieu, Michelle Burley, Barbara Robinson and Chris Meek of Mallory Park, Enid Smith of the British Automobile Racing Club's Press Office at Thruxton, Martyn Hadwyn of the Motor Racing Archive, Jerry Millington for the loan of his precious photographs and information on the early circuits in the south, and C. M. S. (Bunny) Abbot of the Eastern Counties Motor Club. To Mike Dixon, Richard Styles, Tony Bancroft, Fred Scatley and Robert Davidson for their photographs, Alan Rawlinson for the loan of priceless programmes from the early days, Mrs Anne Harris of the Jaguar Daimler Heritage Trust, Herr Langer of Daimler Benz Classic Archiv, Herr L. Franz of Archiv Auto Union, Ted Walker of the delightfully named Ferret Fotographics, Steve Quilter of Quilter House, John Aldington, Doug Linton and David Saunders.

A special word of thanks to the Editor of *Motor Sport* who was kind enough to print an appeal which produced so much information from so many people — I just hope that I have not missed anyone: Doug Stephens, Barry Newton, Gavin Ross, Brian Wylie, J. E. Robinson, David Gee, Roland Holt, Brian Joscelyne, Raymond Proctor, Jim Evans, John Frankland, Pat Davies (who wrote from France), Tony Hodgetts, Graham Heath, Alan Broadbent, Barry Newton, B. Woodsford, John Frankland, Julian Roberts, R. R. Davidson and Gavin Ross.

And finally to a man who I am proud to call a friend who has agreed to write the Foreword — Martin Donnelly.

CONTENTS

FOREWORD

The beauty about racing in the UK is the incredible variety of circuits. Anyone coming through the ranks in this country will have the opportunity to develop their skills on just about every kind of corner and bend you could wish to find. Having said that, I thought I knew them all – until I opened this book! Peter Swinger's meticulous research has unearthed tracks I had never heard of, never mind seen. It's a fascinating study; a reference book which no student of British motor racing should be without.

This is no surprise. Along with many racing people, I have known Peter for nearly 20 years and relied heavily on his advice in financial matters. *Motor Racing Circuits in England Then and Now* is yet another example of his incredible eye for detail.

Martin Donnelly on his way to victory in the Brands Hatch round of the International F3000 Championship on 20 August 1989 at the wheel of the Eddie Jordan Racing Reynard 89D-Mugen. *Mike Dixon*

INTRODUCTION

As these words are written, the motorcar is a little over 100 years old and, from a date very shortly after its invention, men have been inspired to compete against one another in them. However, prospective racing motorists were hampered in mainland Great Britain by legislation that required any vehicle powered by steam or internal combustion engine to be preceded by a man bearing a red flag, and to be restricted to a maximum speed of 4mph. This speed limit was later raised to 12mph, with the flag being abandoned, and this advance was marked by the Emancipation Run from London to Brighton on 14 November 1896 and commemorated ever since. The maximum speed was later raised to the ludicrously high figure of 20mph, this limit remaining in force until 1930.

Such nonsense did not impede motorists on the Continent and it was in France that motor racing was first taken seriously. It was also the French of course who coined the term 'Grand Prix' and ran the first such race, and as a result, French became the international language of motor racing. From the very earliest days of motoring, Continental countries allowed public roads to be closed to allow competitive motoring. However, such civilities were always denied within the shores of the United Kingdom — but it is perfectly permissible to close public roads for bicycle races! — so the sport came late to Great Britain.

The first competitive motoring event took place at Bexhill-on-Sea, but the very first motor *race* within the British Isles took place on the Isle of Man where the Manx Government adopted a much more relaxed attitude than did Westminster — as it does to this day. Public roads have been closed on only five occasions in mainland Britain to allow motor racing to take place and an Act of Parliament was required before it could happen. The subsequent races have been staged in the same city, Birmingham, on each occasion. How fortunate, by comparison, are our Continental and Irish cousins, who have been able to close public roads in order to create some truly superb circuits. By contrast, circuits on the British mainland have been purpose-built or converted from redundant airfields.

I have had the great good fortune to be involved in this glorious sport of ours for nigh on 40 years and would not have missed a moment of it. However, in so saying, I must add the rider that I know of no other activity devised by man which takes away one's friends for ever, but which still keeps one coming back for more. Starting as a humble spectator marshal, shortly after I completed National Service, I have passed through the ranks and now have the privilege of being a steward for the Royal Automobile Club Motor Sports Association, the British Racing & Sports Car Club and the Historic Sports Car Club. Somewhere in the middle, lost in the mists of time, I raced my own cars for five years.

When Publishing Manager Peter Waller offered me the opportunity of writing this book I jumped at it, little knowing just what I was taking on. Early research identified in excess of 50 circuits which had been used for motor racing within the British Isles, so something had to go if justice was to be done to those which were to be included. Without in any way wishing to cause offence, the Emerald Isle had to go together with the Channel Islands and the Isle of Man. These have been followed by those of Scotland and Wales so as to leave just England. It is my earnest hope that a second volume can be produced to cover the circuits in these parts of the British Isles, of which there are 26 locations.

This book is concerned with *motor* racing circuits — those intrepid gentlemen (and ladies) who race on two and three wheels have produced a different story from the one told here and it deserves to be written by one steeped in the lore of the motorcycle which I am not. I enjoy watching them in action but I am not an aficionado. Neither does it include sprint and hill-climb venues, since these would occupy another book as long as this one. I have endeavoured to include every circuit venue where cars have competed, if only on one occasion; just one thing concerns me — on the day of publication someone will phone me with details of an obscure circuit of which I have never heard!

The circuit diagrams have been standardised to exclude everything but the outline of the circuit (which has changed often in some cases) and the start/finish line and, unless otherwise stated, all are or were run in a clockwise direction.

Like Topsy, this project 'just growed' and the manuscript will be rather more than a year late to the Publishers; to them and Peter Waller I am most grateful for their forbearance. I hope you will think it has been worth it.

Peter Swinger MIMI
Stowmarket
February 2001

AINTREE
HORSES FOR COURSES

Above: In 1955 Daimler-Benz dominated the British Grand Prix, the Mercedes-Benz W196s filling the first four places. Here, Juan Manuel Fangio appears to be discussing the finer points of the rear view mirror of his car with his mechanics. *Daimler-Benz Classic Archives*

Above right: Fangio driving No 10 and Moss at the wheel of No 12 seen rounding Tatts Corner and passing the packed grandstands in the Mercedes-Benz W196s en route to their dominant victory in 1955, which was in reverse order to that seen here.
National Motor Museum Photographic Library

Aintree, near Liverpool, is best known as the venue of the Grand National horse race but, between 1954 and 1982, it had a short but glorious career as a major motor racing circuit. Between 1955 and 1962 it shared the British Grand Prix with Silverstone in alternate years.

Struggling to keep the 270-acre Aintree course viable on the strength of a few days' horse racing each year the course's larger-than-life owner, Mrs Mirabel Topham, paid a visit to the Duke of Richmond and Gordon to see how he ran cars and horses on adjacent tracks at Goodwood. As a result of that visit, she invested £100,000 in creating an interesting, if flat, circuit measuring exactly three miles within the Grand National course, and formed the Aintree Automobile Racing Co. The building of the circuit employed 2,000 people and was completed in just three months.

Mrs Topham then offered the British Automobile Racing Club (BARC) the exclusive rights to manage motor racing at Aintree and the club officially opened the new track with a meeting on 29 May 1954. The first meeting was run anticlockwise but, from the start of the 1955 season, the more conventional approach was adopted.

From the start/finish line in front of the grandstand the circuit ran to a right-hand sweep called Waterways followed by a short straight before the right-hand Anchor Crossing. Another straight led to the left-hand Cottage and Country corners which were separated by a short straight; after another straight came the sharp right-hand Village leading to Bechers which started as a sharp right-hand and eased at its exit. Now came the longest straight leading to a left flick, short straight, right flick and Tatts and the end of the lap; Stirling Moss maintained that Aintree involved as much gear-changing as Monaco.

Given the geographic and demographic situation of Aintree, the first race meeting attracted a somewhat disappointing crowd of 25,000 who saw Stirling Moss take the first of many victories on the Merseyside circuit when he won the 200-mile Formule Libre event at the wheel of a Maserati 250F. Notwithstanding the disappointing first attendance, Aintree proved to be an excellent spectator circuit, for its permanent grandstands gave a fine view over the whole of the course and

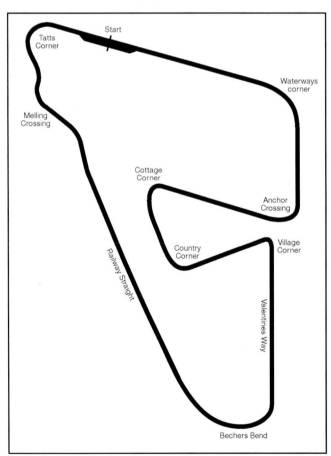

The original Aintree Grand Prix circuit. Whilst it was very flat, it was, none the less, a very interesting circuit and demanding on the drivers. The main grandstands were alongside the start/finish straight, thus making good use of the facilities already in place for horse racing. At the very first meeting for Formula III cars it was used anticlockwise.

Above: The 1955 British GP was run on 16 July and Maserati 250F No 8 (chassis number 2514) driven by Andre Simon is seen being followed by Gordini Type 166 No 26 in the hands of Mike Sparken who is in turn followed by another Gordini. Three of the little French cars had been entered: Manzon retired on lap five with transmission failure so the second one seen here is driven by Hernano da Silva Ramos and he is pursued by Maserati 250F (No 2515) driven by Argentinian Roberto Mieres. Of these four, Simon retired on lap 10 with gearbox troubles, da Silva Ramos retired 17 laps later with engine failure, and Mieres departed on lap 48 when a piston gave up; Sparken brought his Gordini home in seventh place. Apart from the Mercedes-Benz domination the race was notable in that it saw the first appearance of a rear-engined Grand Prix car in England since the Auto Unions at Donington Park in the 1930s; the car in question was something of a lash-up, being a Manx-tailed Cooper central-seat sports car into which had been shoe-horned a 2.2-litre Bristol engine. It was in reality a 1.97-litre unit but Grand Prix regulations stipulated a 2-litre minimum cylinder capacity. It was driven by Jack Brabham and was painfully slow, being lapped on lap five and expiring on lap 31 with a dropped valve. *Liverpool Daily Post and Echo plc*

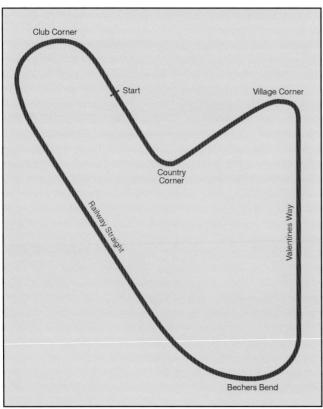

Above: This scene comes from the British Grand Prix at Aintree on 20 July 1957: the BRM P25 No 24 driven by Jack Fairman is having one of the outfield and infield excursions of which he enjoyed several during the race due to some brake problems, while the Argentinian, Carlos Menditèguy, driving No 8 (the very first Maserati 250F (chassis number 2501), looks on in amazement as he passes followed by Stirling Moss in Vanwall No 21 on his way to victory. Moss had started the race driving VW 1 taking over Tony Brooks' car (VW 4) when his own cried 'enough' on lap 21. *Liverpool Daily Post and Echo plc*

Left: Following the loss of the Grand Prix (though not because of it), the Aintree circuit was reduced by inserting a new corner where Cottage Corner used to be and the start/finish line was moved to a point between the new Club Corner and Country Corner.

Mercedes-Benz had been involved in the accident at the Sarthe, which had claimed the lives of more than 80 spectators and the powers that be at Unterturkheim were more than usually concerned with safety. However, after visiting Aintree, they expressed themselves satisfied and a full team of four cars was entered. The drivers were Juan Manuel Fangio, Karl Kling, Piero Taruffi and Stirling Moss. The three-pointed star dominated the race with Mercedes-Benz recording the only one-two-three-four finish in its racing history. After a race-long duel, victory went to Moss from Fangio by just 2sec. However, to this day Moss does not know whether the great Argentinian let him win, as Fangio never revealed if it had been suggested to him that he should do so.

We shall never know. What matters is that Stirling Moss won his first World Championship Grand Prix and became the first Englishman to win his home Grand Prix. Moss completed the 270 miles in 3hr 7min 21.2sec at 86.47mph and set fastest lap at 2min 0.4sec at 89.7mph. Kling was third and Taruffi finished a lap down followed by Luigi Musso in the prototype Maserati 250F number 2501 and Mike Hawthorn for Ferrari driving 625 number 6.

When the Grand Prix returned to Merseyside in 1957, history was again written for the northern circuit was destined to witness the first British Grand Prix win for a British car driven

it was to see British motor racing history made on two occasions. Following on the success of the early meeting, the RAC gave the BARC its opportunity of staging the British Grand Prix at Aintree in 1955. The race took place in the wake of the Le Mans disaster which had resulted in a number of countries cancelling their Grand Prix as a consequence of the accident. Switzerland went as far as to ban all motor racing within its borders for all time and that decision has yet to be rescinded. A

by British drivers. Driving now for Tony Vandervell's Vanwall team, Moss repeated his 1955 victory, having switched from his own ailing car to that of Tony Brooks and after 60 laps was on the tail of team-mate Stuart Lewis-Evans in fourth place. Moss passed Lewis-Evans which left Hawthorn ahead of him in the Ferrari with Jean Behra leading in Maserati 250F number 2528. The clutch of the Maserati exploded, the Ferrari punctured a tyre on the debris and Moss went on to write another page of motor racing history. While no one realised it at the time, the race was a watershed as British manufacturers were on the brink of dominating Formula One for, at last, Tony Vandervell's team had beaten 'those bloody red cars'.

The Moss/Brooks Vanwall completed the race in 3hr 6min 37.8sec at 86.8mph from the three Lancia-Ferraris of Luigi Musso, Mike Hawthorn and Maurice Trintignant who was two laps down. A further three laps adrift in fifth place was Roy Salvadori driving a Cooper-Climax from Bob Gerard in a Cooper-Bristol on 82 laps.

The 1959 race was held on 18 July and saw victory going to Jack Brabham in the diminutive works Cooper from Moss in the British Racing Partnership's beautiful pale green P25 BRM (chassis number 2510 — it can be confusing when BRMs and Maseratis have the same chassis numbers!), and Bruce McLaren in the second works Cooper. Brabham completed the 225-mile race in 2hr 30min 12sec at a speed of 89.88mph. Harry Schell brought his BRM (chassis number 257) home fourth from Maurice Trintignant in Rob Walker's Cooper, and Roy Salvadori gave the lovely but too-late-on-the-scene Aston Martin DBR 4/250 a rare points-scoring sixth place. Of the 18 starters, only nine finished and some of the non-finishers were as worthy of note as those who completed the course. Amongst the latter was Brian Naylor who retired his JBW-Maserati on the 19th lap with transmission problems; not only was he a private entrant, but he actually built and raced his own Formula One cars!

The cars to which Mr Vandervell had referred so disparagingly finished first, second and third in the British Grand Prix at Aintree on 15 July 1961 when the 1.5-litre Formula One cars contested the World Championship for the first time, the cars in question being the Ferrari 156 'shark nose', arguably one of the prettiest Grand Prix cars ever built. The race was run in truly awful weather, the rain starting shortly before the race began, and was won by Phil Hill from Wolfgang ('Taffy') Count (Graf) Berghe von Trips of Cologne and Richie Ginther, the first and, so far, only time that two Americans have finished in the top three of a World Championship Grand Prix.

Perhaps controversially the RAC awarded the Grand Prix to Aintree again in 1962 so the circus arrived to run the race on 21 July; whatever the reasons for the consecutive running, it was to be the last Grand Prix staged on Merseyside. Jim Clark had a copy-book weekend taking pole position, setting fastest lap and winning by the handsome margin of 50sec from John Surtees' Lola with Bruce McLaren third for Cooper and Graham Hill fourth in the BRM. There were 21 starters and 16 finishers for the 225-mile race which Clark completed in 2hr 26min 21sec at an average speed of 92.96mph.

The end of the venue as a Grand Prix circuit came three months after Jack Brabham won the Aintree 200 (a regular

The programme
from the 12th RAC British
Grand Prix, held at Aintree on 18 July 1959,
featuring the then all-conquering Vanwall with sponsorship
from British Petroleum. Organisation of the meeting was entrusted to
the British Automobile Racing Club. *Fergus Whatling*

Formula One fixture in those halcyon days when Grand Prix cars did not just compete in World Championship events) from Jim Clark, when Mrs Topham announced the racecourse was to be sold for building land. Of course, the developers never moved in, but Mrs Topham's loss of interest started a long-running saga over the ownership of Aintree and its financial viability. In the fullness of time the Grand National was to survive but the demise of international motor racing came at the end of the year when the full circuit was closed. Motor racing was destined to continue until the middle of 1982 on a shortened 1.64-mile circuit which was created by inserting a hairpin to link Railway Straight and Cottage Corner. In the late 1970s, the Jockey Club began to assume control and it became progressively more difficult for cars and 'hay burners' to live side by side. At a club meeting in July 1982 (jointly organised by the British Racing & Sports Car Club and the 750 Motor Club) five cars went off, damaging fences and on the Monday morning the Jockey Club decreed that all motor racing should cease.

At the start of the 21st century, sprints still take place at Aintree, the RAC Rally has held a Stage there and racing schools have been based at the circuit, but the glory days have gone — probably for ever.

BIRMINGHAM
REAL STREET RACING

The Birmingham circuit is unique in that it is the only motor racing track that has ever been authorised on public roads in mainland Britain, and for the fact that the races were run in an anticlockwise direction. Most of the credit for the organisation of the Birmingham Super Prix must go to Martin Hone who spent many years cajoling the City Council into taking the necessary actions, and organising 'demonstrations' in the city centre. The matter was then put to the populace of Birmingham who voted 93% in favour of running a motor race through their streets. It was then necessary to obtain an Act of Parliament before anything could proceed further, but in due course the requisite Act was obtained. Once the legislation was in place the British Racing & Sports Car Club was brought into the picture and under the auspices of the late John Nicol persuaded the FIA to sanction the running of a round of the Intercontinental F3000 Championship through the streets of England's second city. Sadly, the race was run on only five occasions (with supporting programme) in August from 1986 to 1990.

The first race, on 25 August 1986, was run over 24 laps of the city circuit, a race distance of 59.272 miles at a speed of 84.105mph; the winner was Luis Perez Sala at the wheel of a Ralt RT20 from Pierluigi Martini in a similar car with Michel Ferté third driving a March 86B. In fourth and fifth places were Eliseo Salazar and Pascal Fabré in Lola T86/50s, with Russell Spence sixth in another March 86B.

The second running of the Birmingham Super Prix, on 1 September 1987, saw the race distance more than doubled to 51 laps making it 126 miles long. It was won by Stefano

Modena at 105.35mph at the wheel of a March 87B, with Roberto Moreno second in a Ralt RT21. Another Ralt was third, piloted by Mauricio Gugelmin, and Lolas took the next three places driven by Luis Perez Sala, Andy Wallace and Olivier Grouillard.

The 1988 race was run on 29 August, a week after an event at Brands Hatch and was 106 miles long over 43 laps. The Ralt chassis had all but disappeared, the preponderance being Lola, March and Reynard, and as before, all were Cosworth-powered. Reynard and March secured the first five places, the former taking the first two places in the hands of Roberto

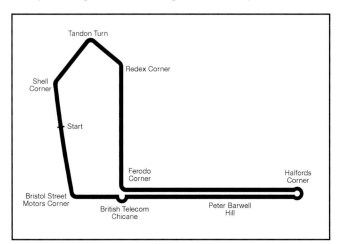

The only street circuit ever used in mainland Britain is the Birmingham city centre circuit: no gentle curves here, just flat out blinds and some very demanding corners. It was run anticlockwise and is probably the only circuit where the names of corners have changed over the years in order to accommodate different sponsors.

Moreno and Martin Donnelly, followed by Martini and Volker Weidler in March 88Bs, with Bertrand Gachot fifth in a Reynard. Eric Bernard was sixth on the road but was disqualified for the second time in England that year which let Ferté's Lola into the points. Moreno's winning speed was 106.21mph.

The F3000 brigade once again took to the streets of Birmingham on 28 August 1989 to race for 126 miles and it was something of a Reynard benefit with 89Ds filling five of the first six places. Jean Alesi won for Eddie Jordan Racing at 105.25mph in a Mugen-engined car with Marco Apicella (First Racing) second, relying on a Judd engine, while Alesi's team-mate Martin Donnelly was third. Bernard was fourth (avoiding disqualification this year) for DAMS Motorsport driving a Mugen-engined Lola T89/50, with Eddie Irvine taking the last point with Cosworth power for Pacific Racing.

The final running of the Birmingham Super Prix was on 27 August 1990 and was once more over 51 laps of the city circuit — 126 miles. Eric van de Poele won at 106.65mph in a Cosworth-powered Reynard 90D in 1hr 11min 47sec, with a Lola T90/50 with Mugen power second in the hands of Andrea Chiesa. The rest of the points-scoring positions were filled by Reynard 90Ds driven by Artzet (Cosworth), Gounon, Giovanardi and Naspetti, all with Mugen engines.

Thus ended the Birmingham Super Prix. It is a great shame that the races did not enjoy a longer life, for those involved in the organisation had accomplished something which British motoring enthusiasts had been striving to achieve since the very dawn of motorsport — to race on closed public roads instead of being confined to purpose-built tracks or converted airfields.

The finish of the 1989 Birmingham Super Prix: Frenchman Jean Alesi takes the flag at the wheel of his Eddie Jordan Racing Reynard 89D-Mugen half a second ahead of Marco Apicella in his First Racing Reynard 89D-Judd. The Birmingham city centre circuit was the only true road circuit ever used in England and the crowds are evidence of the popularity of the event with the city's inhabitants. A brave effort which is unlikely to be repeated. *Motor Racing Archive*

BLANDFORD
THANKS BE TO THE ARMY

Blandford circuit was based at Blandford Camp, a military establishment in Dorset (home of the Royal Electrical & Mechanical Engineers) situated on downs near Salisbury Plain.

The very first post-World War 2 car *road* races in England were staged at Blandford on Saturday, August 27 1949. There had been competition on closed roads in Jersey but this was the first time that racing on a true road circuit had taken place on the mainland; an earlier meeting had been run at Gransden Lodge but that venue was an airfield. The Blandford meeting was sanctioned by Headquarters Southern Command, by kind permission of Lt-Col H. G. Herbert REME and with the co-operation of Lt-Col J. M. Grant MBE, RASC.

The Guide to the Meeting in the programme said, 'Today's Road Race Meeting is an experiment. It is the first time that cars have been raced at Blandford and it is the first time that the West Hants & Dorset Car Club has organised a Race Meeting.' Flag signals were as used as today with the exception that the winner received the chequered flag with his number, and a white flag then signalled the end of the race to the rest of the competitors.

The first meeting consisted of three sports car races, one for Formula III cars divided into two heats and a final, and the Blandford Trophy for Formula Two cars, again divided into two

Following the first Blandford race meeting on Saturday 27 August 1949, the organisers of the meeting, the West Hants & Dorset Car Club, produced a souvenir programme with a card cover which was bound with a green cord and contained all the results. It was distributed within the Club.

heats and a final. The Formula Two event had been intended as a single 100-mile race but the number of entries necessitated two 10-lap heats and an 80-lap final. Part of the reason for this was that RAC had stipulated that no more than 15 cars could start at once and that there could not be more than 20 cars on the track at any one time. There were 20 entries for the 1500cc and 2000cc sports car races so these were run as a single race with the larger-engined cars starting a minute ahead of their smaller-engined brethren. Some of the grids were decided by ballot and some by practice times which had taken place on the Friday preceding race day; the fastest 15 from the heats for the Formula III and Formula Two went through to their respective finals, with the grids being determined by the competitors' race times in the heats.

The track was 3 miles 220yd long and only 20ft wide throughout, with Army buildings close to the road on both sides at one point. The start was situated along the longest straight (roughly 600yd) but after about 250yd it was necessary to change down for Cuckoo Corner, which was a sharp right which eased into a continuous right bend, running downhill at one in 10 until it reached the long left-handed 100mph Valley

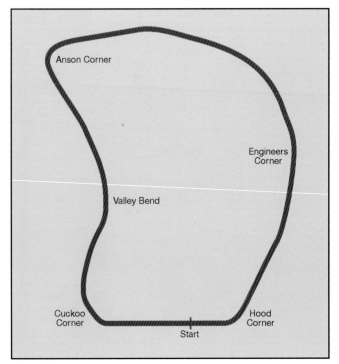

The map of the circuit at Blandford Camp.

Bend; the track then began almost immediately to climb a straight leading to Anson Corner, which was almost a hairpin right, followed by a section which was not quite straight but was certainly not a bend. Then came a continuous right-hand unnamed bend which led to the most challenging and spectacular feature on Blandford, Engineers Corner, a very fast right-hand bend which some cars took at 120mph (the site of the accident which blocked the track and caused the abandonment of the Blandford Trophy, the last race at the first meeting). The following straight brought the course to the right-hand Hood Corner and back to the start and finish line. It was a circuit of considerable character but no more than four or five meetings in all were staged at Blandford on both two and four wheels.

The first meeting was unquestionably a great success but the organisers lost money on it: all cars had to run on fuel which was available to the public which meant Pool petrol (petrol companies at the time were required to sell their products through a 'pool', without branding) to which up to 50% Benzol could be added if required. The entry list was wide and varied and included Ken McAlpine and Rodney Clarke in Connaughts in the Unsupercharged Sports Car race, a Cisitalia, and Stirling Moss and John Cooper himself in Cooper-Vincents in the Blandford Trophy.

The *Bournemouth Daily Echo* carried a full-page report on the following Monday but without any results! There were some crashes, one resulting in the stopping of the Blandford Trophy (as mentioned above) and a spectacular one when P. K. Braid left the road between Engineers Corner and Hood Corner, demolished a bus stop, launched himself off a pine sapling and parked his Formula III Cooper on the roof of Battalion Headquarters. Sadly, Gordon Woods crashed his Frazer-Nash BMW in the same area, receiving head injuries from which he later died.

Winner of the Formula III Final was R. M. Dryden in a Cooper at 73.65mph from K. E. Carter and Alan Brown, who were also Cooper mounted; Carter set the fastest lap in 2min, 27.6sec at 76.6mph. The Blandford Trophy went to G. S. Shillito who drove a Riley, his winning speed being 80.16mph from Jack Fairman's Riley and E. Winterbottom's 996cc Cooper. Following the Fairman/Baird crash, the race was declared to have ended at the end of the 18th of the scheduled 25 laps. Stirling Moss had been a non-starter and John Cooper won his heat but retired on the ninth lap of the Final. Fairman set the fastest lap at 83.87mph in 2min 14.8sec and this appears to be the outright, all-time lap record.

The second race meeting at Blandford took place on Whit Monday, 29 May 1950 and ran to much the same format as the first one, starting with two five-lap heats for Formula III cars, a 15-lap race for production cars, 10 laps for the Lombard Trophy for racing cars up to 1100cc, a 20-lap Final for Formula III, the meeting again being rounded off with the Blandford Trophy Race for Formula 2 cars.

This meeting saw the first postwar race in England to have a rolling start, for the Formula III cars were led around on a parade lap by an 'official car' which pulled off before the Union Flag was dropped. The fastest 20 cars from the heats qualified for the Final which was broadcast by the BBC (with two commentators) on the Light Programme from 3.10pm to 3.25pm and from 4pm to 4.15pm. There appears to be an anomaly for only 15 cars were allowed to start at a time in the Production Car Race but 20 were allowed on the circuit at a time, which led to a strange arrangement at the start; the odd-numbered competitors started first followed 90sec later by the even numbers!

There were further fatalities at later meetings resulting in the authorities withdrawing approval of Blandford as a race circuit and racing appears to have ceased at the end of 1950. The track surface consisted of granite chips and some of the bends were very loose on the outside which may have been a contributory factor in the accidents but the surface was said to give good grip even in the wet. With the loss of Blandford the West Hants & Dorset Car Club Club's Committee, who had organised all of the meetings, turned its attention to Ibsley.

Fastest lap at the 1950 meeting was set jointly by W. Aston and Eric Brandon in 1-litre Cooper single-seaters at 82.76mph.

At Whitsun in the following year, 1950, the club organised its second race meeting. The front cover of the programme on Whit Monday, 29 May, carries a picture from the inaugural meeting. Perusal of the earlier programme indicates that the cars portrayed are competing in the third event of that day, a five-lap race for unsupercharged sports cars from 1101 to 1500cc; leading is No 7, W. P. Uglow's 1496cc HRG, driven by W. A. Cleave, followed by the similar car of G. A. Rudduck (No 1). Third is R. C. C. Palmer's Frazer-Nash ahead of the MG T Types of R. E. Molyneaux (No 4) and J. C. C. Myers (No 6). Two of the cars pictured featured in the results, the race being won by R. C. Willis' Frazer-Nash BMW in 13min 35.2sec at 69.34mph from Ruddock and Uglow, who set the fastest lap in 2min 37.2sec at 71.91mph. *Author's collection*

BOREHAM
MOTOR RACING IN ESSEX

The airfield at Boreham was created on 630 acres of Essex countryside in 1943-4 and involved the clearance of a considerable amount of woodland by the 861st Engineers of the United States Army Air Force in preparation for the arrival of the Martin Marauders of the 394th Bombardment Group of the 9th USAAF. Some 130,000 tons of concrete were laid along with 50 miles of cable and conduit. What emerged was a three-runway airfield (one a mile long) with a three-mile perimeter track and which bore a striking resemblance to Silverstone, but it was destined to have one of the shortest operational careers of any of the wartime airfields. March 1944 saw the commencement of operations with 'Ramrods' to France, Holland and Belgium, the targets including airfields, marshalling yards, gun emplacements, V-weapon sites and bridges. These attacks were short-lived as they were moved to Holmsley South near Bournemouth in July.

During the USAAF use of RAF Boreham, 61 aircrew lost their lives. The airfield remained in American hands although it was earmarked for 38 Group RAF but in the event the station was not needed and it closed in 1945. The local council could see that the redundant site would be ideal as temporary accommodation for families awaiting better housing, and in the early 1950s, some 600 people made short-term homes in the converted Nissen huts. As these people moved into their new homes in the mid-1950s the Nissen huts were gradually demolished but the ex-aerodrome did not return to its former quiet rural atmosphere.

Motorsport arrived in 1949 but, sadly, the motor racing career of Boreham was not much longer lived than its career as an operational airfield. In the autumn of 1949 a driving test was held at the airfield at the conclusion of the Chelmsford Rally and motorcycle racing took place in 1950. The following year was a busy season; the first car meeting was held in April and was dominated by Archie Butterworth driving his AJB — a single-seater four-wheel-drive device of his own design powered by a 4-litre engine. The next meeting was on 26 May when Reg Parnell handed victory in the main event to Dennis Poore's Alfa Romeo when he lost control and deposited his car amongst the straw bales. There were two further meetings in 1951, the August one attracting a crowd of 20,000 in wet conditions, but

Above: The Le Mans-type start of the sports car race at the *Daily Mail* International Festival of Motor Sport at Boreham on 2 August 1952; Stirling Moss had set fastest lap in practice so his car was at the head of the line at the pits. Contemporary reports of the race describe his mount as a Jaguar XK120C but this version of the Jaguar is now known as the C-type,: his car was disc-braked and as he leads the field away to Hangar Bend he is followed by Reg Parnell in the Aston Martin DB3 and his team-mate Duncan Hamilton in a drum-braked version of the C-type. The race was run over 34 laps/100 miles and divided into classes 2 litres to 3 litres, and over 3 litres. Moss won at 88.09mph in 1hr 9min 28sec from Hamilton and a Jaguar XK120 driven by W. Dobson. The smaller class went to Reg Parnell from two Ferraris driven by Roy Salvadori and Tom Cole. *Ford Motor Co Ltd*

Above: Reg Parnell at the wheel of the works Aston Martin DB3 which he took to a class win at Boreham on 2 August 1952. *Ford Motor Co Ltd*

many of them gained admittance without paying. The meeting attracted some top-name drivers including Roy Salvadori, Reg Parnell, Duncan Hamilton, Tony Rolt and Sidney Allard. Victory in the main race went to Brian Shawe-Taylor in an ERA.

The circuit was equally active in 1952 with the likes of Mike Hawthorn, Tony Rolt and Bernie Ecclestone (yes, the same one!) racing in the 30 June meeting but the season had opened on 17 May when Mike Hawthorn had lapped at 92.02mph in his Cooper-Bristol after Don Parker had managed 84.25mph in his Formula III Kieft. On 21 June 25,000 people squeezed into Boreham to see Reg Parnell make amends for his earlier misdemeanour and take victory in the Formula Two race aboard a Cooper-Bristol.

A crowd of 50,000 attended the *Daily Mail*-sponsored International Festival of Motorsport from 30 July to 4 August 1952 which was a mixed motorcycle and car meeting. The entry list read like a 'Who's Who' of contemporary motor racing with entries from ERA Ltd (Stirling Moss), Scuderia Ferrari (Luigi Villoresi), Ecurie Rosier (Louis Rosier, Eugene Chaboud and Yves Giraud-Cabantous), a Ferrari and two Lago-Talbots (all displacing 4.5-litres), Philippe Étançelin, also driving a Lago-Talbot while Tony Lago himself had entered one of his cars for Alberto Crespo. There were two V16 BRMs entered for Froilan Gonzales and Ken Wharton and no less that even Cooper-Bristols for Hawthorn, Alan Brown, David Murray (of Ecurie Ecosse fame), Eric Brandon, John Barber, Andre Loens and A. H. M. Bryde. Spencer King had entered a Rover to be driven by C. G. H. Dunham; this is the car campaigned in the 1990s by Frank Lockhart in historic events which confounds the rumour that they were built together!

Overall victory (and the *Daily Mail* International Trophy) went to Villoresi from Landi (Ferrari), Étançelin, Rosier and Giraud-Cabantous. The Formula Two section was taken by Hawthorn (his driving described as 'magnificent' by *Motor*) from Brown, Moss, Baird (Ferrari 1,980cc), Brandon and Peter Whitehead (Ferrari). The respective fastest laps were set by Villoresi at 90.15mph and Brandon at 86.81mph; the winner's

average speed was 82.85mph and Hawthorn was third overall — a not inconsiderable feat since his car had less than the half the capacity of the winner.

The meeting included a 100-mile sports car race divided into five classes: up to 1,100cc, 1,101-1,500cc, 1,501-2,000cc, 2,001-3,000cc and over 3 litres. Overall victory went to Moss from Hamilton and Dobson, all driving C-Type Jaguars, with Parnell (Aston Martin) taking the next class from the Ferraris of Salvadori and Cole. It would appear that there were two sports car races, one for the two larger classes and one for the smaller, for Salvadori also finished second behind Ken Wharton in the 1,501-2,000cc Class which was a Frazer-Nash benefit.

However, financial losses were crippling at what had become known as 'Britain's fastest circuit' and the International Festival meeting was the last major event held at Boreham. On 20 February 1953 *Autosport* reported that there would be no motor racing at Boreham in 1953 and there never was again. All the motor racing at the Essex circuit had been organised by the West Essex Car Club. The site was acquired by the Ford Motor Company in 1955 who moved Ford Motorsport there in 1963. Since the Ice Age the area had been rich in gravel deposits and in 1996 the circuit was being lifted in order to reclaim the aggregate for sale, there being very little prospect of it ever again being used for competitive motorsport.

However, a Formula One engine was again heard across the Essex countryside early in 1997 when Rubens Barrichello gave the new Stewart Grand Prix car its initial shakedown.

Above left: The map of Boreham reveals it as a typical airfield circuit laid out on the perimeter track with long straights broken by sweeping curves.

Left: This is the start of the 10-lap, 30-mile Formula III race at Boreham on 2 August 1952: it was won by Alan Brown driving a Cooper at 83.66mph from Don Parker in his trusty Kieft and Stirling Moss in another Cooper. Fourth was the Cooper of Eric Bandon from Webb's Kieft and Les Leston's Cooper. Fastest lap (and a new Formula III record) was set by the winner in 1min 59.6sec at 99.3mph. *Jaguar Daimler Heritage Trust*

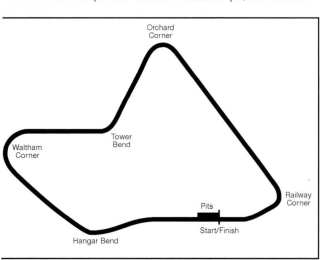

Orchard Corner

Tower Bend

Waltham Corner

Railway Corner

Pits

Start/Finish

Hangar Bend

BRANDS HATCH
BICYCLES TO CARS

Down in deepest Kent there lay a natural amphitheatre — a grassy bowl amongst the mushroom fields — known as Brands Hatch ('hatch' being the old English word for 'wattle gate') whence had gravitated in the 1920s cyclists with a bent upon racing. Those cyclists first raced at Brands Hatch in 1926 and were followed two years later by motorcyclists who also saw the advantage of competing in a natural arena just a few hundred yards off the A20, and with the passage of time, a kidney-shaped circuit came into use. The first motorcycle races were 'very informal' with much of the organisation being done on the spot. Initially the racing was on a straight strip approximately where Bottom Straight came to be when the circuit was tarmacked.

Following World War 2, cinders were laid on the track of what was by then known as Brands Hatch Stadium and motorcycle racing continued. That was until 1950 when the 500cc motor racing fraternity managed to persuade the managing director, Joe Francis, that the future for his stadium lay in car racing and motorcycle road racing. The organisation behind the 500cc racing cars was the 500 Club and it, together with the owners, invested the sum of £17,000 on a tarmac surface — not an inconsiderable figure in 1950.

The front cover of the programme of the very first motor racing event ever held at Brands Hatch (or Brands Hatch Estate as it was then called) on Sunday, 16 April 1950. The meeting was run by the 500 Club (later to become the British Racing & Sports Car Club) which had been formed specifically to organise races for the new 500cc motorcycle-engined racing cars which were later adopted as the International FIII. This was the first time that Great Britain had produced a motor racing formula which was adopted as an international one.

Thus Brands Hatch as a motor racing venue was born and Sunday, 16 April 1950 was scheduled for the opening meeting at the first purpose-built postwar racing circuit in England, approval having been given by the RAC following a demonstration by a handful of 500s in February. Amongst those giving the demonstration was a very young Stirling Moss. On the day, 7,000 spectators came to see the Formula III cars compete in 10 races.

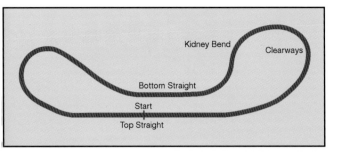

The first Brands Hatch victory went to a man who was to become a legend in Formula III, Don Parker. In the opening year, five more meetings were held in June, July, August, September and October with the programmes run to a similar format. The June meeting was a Moss benefit for he won all five races he entered in the Works Cooper and set a new lap record. The August Bank Holiday meeting saw the involvement of the national press for the first time with the *Daily Telegraph* sponsoring the main event of the day. The cinder track had been three-quarters of a mile in length but the tarmac circuit was lengthened to one mile and was run anticlockwise. The Maidstone & Mid-Kent Motor Club invited a number of sports car drivers to 'test' the circuit on 5 November, this being the first time that any car other than a 500cc had used it, and they ran clockwise.

The 1951 season comprised seven meetings, all for Formula III and they were organised by the Half-Litre Car Club to which the 500 Club had changed its name since becoming a Limited Company. In February, the Aston Martin Owners Club tested some 1.5-litre sports cars at Brands Hatch preparatory to the full International season commencing.

The *Daily Telegraph* sponsored three International meetings during the year. Some reckless driving had become evident in 500cc racing and in an endeavour to curtail the practice the organisers introduced a 'no spin' rule which meant that any driver who spun through more 180° or left the track was automatically disqualified. One of the earliest to suffer this fate was Bernie Ecclestone. The rule could be happily applied to a number of formulae today.

The 1952 season saw the emergence of Stuart Lewis-Evans who was to go on to greater things. Les Leston (who was to race at the Kentish circuit for 20 years) raised the lap record to 71.15mph in 50.6sec — the first time that 70mph had been exceeded. The *Daily Telegraph* was again involved, the highlight of the year being the newspaper's trophy at the August Bank Holiday meeting.

For 1953 the circuit was surrounded by raised spectator protection banks. This was Don Parker's year for he won the *Autosport* Formula III Championship taking seven races at Brands on the way to the title. Some 50,000 people packed into the *Daily Telegraph*-sponsored International and as the season

came to an end Parker raised the lap record to 74.38mph in 48.4sec. Thus the first era of Brands Hatch came to an end.

While Formula III racing was unquestionably close and exciting, it did have its limitations and spectators now wanted some variety and more powerful cars to watch, although despite the safety improvements of 1953, the circuit was still only RAC-approved for that formula. More money was spent at Brands Hatch during the winter of 1953/4 in order to accommodate larger capacity cars. First of all the direction was changed to clockwise and in so doing one of the most challenging corners in the world of motor racing was created — Paddock Hill Bend which was a fast sweeping downhill right-hander which became the stuff of which legends are made. At the bottom of Paddock Hill a quarter-mile extension to the circuit was added which took competitors up the other side of the valley to a right-hand hairpin which was called Druids Hill Bend. The new section of the track rejoined the old at another tricky corner, Bottom Bend, and the result was a circuit lengthened to 1.24 miles. The first race winner on the new track was Stuart Lewis-Evans at the wheel of a Mk 8 Cooper-Norton and a new name at the inaugural meeting on the new circuit was one N. G. Hill who was a 'graduate' of the racing school which had been established at Brands Hatch. Not only was the newcomer driving a Mk 4 Cooper-JA having his first race, he was also *seeing* his first race; he shot off the line to lead his junior heat, eventually finishing second. He went on to be World Champion in 1962 and 1968.

As the season progressed larger engined machines began to appear starting with small and medium capacity sports cars, then Formule Libre machines, and at the August Bank Holiday meeting a piece of history was written when a race was started by a cleric. The Rochester Cup was a Formule Libre event at which the Bishop of Rochester acted as honorary starter; victory went to Bill Whitehouse driving an A-Type Connaught. However, most races were still run for Formula III and 1954 saw the first of what was to become the traditional Boxing Day meeting down in Kent. The idea was put together by a press and public relations consultant named John Webb who had just become Brands Hatch's first press officer, and Christopher Jenning, the editor of *Motor*. Colleagues laughed at the idea but Webb put it to Brands Hatch circuit's managing director John Hall who passed the suggestion to the British Racing & Sports Car Club (which the Half-Litre Club had now become). A total of 15,000 spectators arrived at the Christmas meeting to watch a programme of seven races with the added attraction of

The carnage at the start of the 1976 British Grand Prix. Clear of the field is Niki Lauda in the Ferrari 312T2/028, followed by Patrick Depailler in the six-wheeled Tyrrell P34/2, with Carlos Reutemann in the Brabham-Alfa Romeo BT45/3 in third position - he had started from 15th place on the grid! Behind Reutemann is the second Tyrrell (P34/3) of Jody Scheckter whilst Regazzoni in the second Ferrari (312T2/027) is facing the wrong way in the middle of the top of the picture and to the left an unidentified car is departing to undertake some agriculture. As a result of this fracas the race was stopped and restarted.
National Motor Museum Photographic Library

ox-roasting and Stirling Moss as Father Christmas. As the year closed, John Hall revealed embryonic plans to extend Brands Hatch to a 2¹/₂-mile circuit.

It was Jim Russell's year in 1955, for he dominated Formula III, winning the *Autosport* National Championship as well as four of the Brands Hatch meetings. Cooper T39s and Lotus Mark 9s dominated sports car racing while Archie Scott Brown had a stranglehold on the over-1,900cc Class, driving either the works Lister-Bristol or Louis Manduca's C-Type Jaguar.

At the August Bank Holiday meeting spectators could avail themselves of the only permanent grandstand at a British motor racing circuit; it had been purchased second-hand from the defunct Northolt pony-trotting stadium and for the 1956 season, a telephone system was installed linking race control, the grandstand and the marshals' posts, while a modern hospital was opened at the circuit, complete with operating facilities.

As larger-capacity cars became more common 500cc racing

began to decline, but the formula still gave close, exciting racing. The first year that public race meetings were organised by other than the BRSCC was 1956 — in June the 750 Motor Club (one of the oldest in the country) joined forces with Club Lotus to offer a mixture of races including, for the first time, saloon cars. This was also the year that Brands Hatch grew up, running Formula One cars for the first time on 14 October. By now, British cars were at last beginning to challenge the might of Italy. Initially, a long-distance race was planned but in the end a 15-lap race was run which attracted four works entries from Connaught (B-Types for Archie Scott Brown, Les Leston, Jack Fairman and Stuart Lewis-Evans) opposed by privately entered Maserati 250Fs driven by Roy Salvadori and Bruce Halford and a selection of independents. Archie won from Lewis-Evans, with Salvadori setting a new lap record in the process in exactly 59sec at a speed of 75.66mph. Politics caused the cancellation of the Boxing Day meeting that year due to the Suez Crisis.

As a result of the Suez affair, forecasts for racing were gloomy for 1957 but the programme ran as planned, the two feature meetings of the year being run for the new Formula Two on Whit Sunday and August Bank Holiday Monday. The year saw a continued diversification at BRSCC meetings with fewer 500cc events and more for sports-racing machinery. The Kentish 100 was the biggest event yet run at the circuit for Formula Two with two 42-lap heats and attracted a truly International field. Formula Two featured at other meetings but at the August Bank Holiday meeting Formula III (later referred to as Formula Three) proved that it was not yet dead as it was run as the feature event for the *Daily Telegraph* Trophy.

The great Jim Clark made his Brands Hatch debut at the Boxing Day meeting when he drove the Border Reivers-entered Lotus Elite into second place behind Colin Chapman. At the August Bank Holiday Monday meeting in 1958, an 1,100cc sports car became the first to lap Brands Hatch in under a minute. Its creator had been unable to afford to purchase a Lotus so had designed his own car; the car was called a Lola and its creator was Eric Broadley.

The highlight of the 1959 season was again the Kentish 100, with no less than 40 drivers (including 10 Grand Prix names) fighting for just 16 grid positions. Brabham won both 42-lap heats driving the works Cooper-Climax. The feature race at the Boxing Day meeting was for Formula Junior, a new International Formula for single-seater racing cars using production engines up to 1,100cc; works entries were received from Elva, Gemini, Lola, Cooper and Lotus. This new formula was to prove the death-knell of 500cc racing.

In January 1960, a dream came true when Kent County Council gave planning permission for the extension of Brands Hatch — an extension which would double the length of the track thus offering a choice of long or short circuits. The new 2.65-mile track used all of the existing one with the exception of Kidney Bend; South Bank became a long, uphill 160° sweep out into the country and making the approach to Clearways very much faster. From South Bank Bend there followed a long straight dipping into and out of the next valley to the right-hand Hawthorn Bend followed by Portobello Straight to Westfield Bend leading to the dip to Dingle Dell, Dingle Dell Corner and the difficult left-hand Stirling's Bend. A short straight then brought the circuit back to Clearways at much higher speed than hitherto. To quote John Hall, 'For the first time ever, Britain will have a Grand Prix track within 20 miles of London'.

The new track was planned to be completed in time for the popular August Bank Holiday meeting and was ready for testing in June. July 1960 was to see the start of an association which was to last for well over a quarter of a century when the Lords Taverners benefited from a giant charity meeting jointly

A year later
than the first motor racing event at Brands Hatchand the programme had acquired an illustrated colour cover and Brands Hatch Estate had become Brands Hatch Stadium; racing was still exclusively for 500cc single-seater racing cars.

organised by the BRSC and the British Racing Drivers Club. The debut of the new track came in August as planned, with works entries from BRM, Cooper, Ferrari and Lotus together with independents such as Yeoman Credit, Scuderia Eugenio Castellotti and Scuderia Centro Sud. Record traffic jams were recorded on the A20 and the resultant huge crowd saw Jack Brabham in the works Cooper-Climax win by just 4.4sec from Graham Hill in the P48 BRM after the gearbox of Jim Clark's Lotus expired after leading for 22 laps of the 50-lap race. The fastest lap (and therefore of course the lap record) was set jointly by Clark and Brabham in 1min 40.6sec at a speed of 94.82mph.

Clark had his revenge a few weeks later on 27 August when the Grand Prix circuit saw Formula Two cars performing in the Kentish 100 with a hard-fought win over Dan Gurney; both were driving Lotus-Climaxes, Clark's was a works car and Gurney's a private entry. As the year drew to a close the management could look back on a successful 11 years and the birth of a new Grand Prix circuit.

It is said that success breeds success and so it was to prove with Brands Hatch, for in April 1961 it was announced that the property development company Grovewood Securities Ltd had acquired a controlling interest in Brands Hatch Circuit Ltd. This

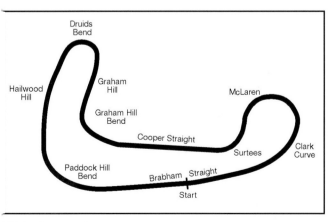

This is the second version of Brands Hatch, with the 1953/4 extension up the side of the valley to Druids Bend raising the circuit length to 1.24 miles. The names of the corners shown here were added some years after the extension was opened.

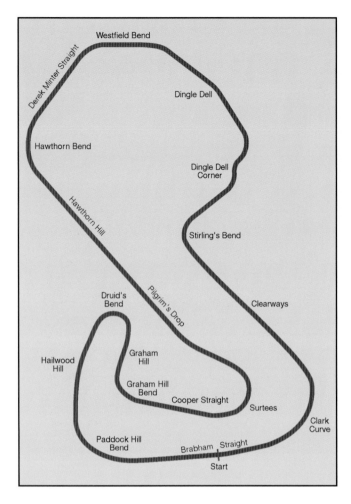

Westfield Bend
Derek Minter Straight
Dingle Dell
Hawthorn Bend
Dingle Dell Corner
Hawthorn Hill
Stirling's Bend
Druid's Bend
Pilgrim's Drop
Clearways
Graham Hill
Hailwood Hill
Graham Hill Bend
Cooper Straight
Surtees
Clark Curve
Paddock Hill Bend
Brabham Straight
Start

piece of intelligence caused much fluttering of feathers for immediately rumours were set in motion to the effect that the circuit would be lost as there were plans to develop it for

housing. The chairman and managing director of Grovewood Securities, John Danny, was quick to dispel these rumours, giving assurances that the new owners would 'continue to develop the track for racing in conjunction with the BRSCC'.

This was the year of the new 1.5-litre Formula One and on 3 June 1961 the Silver City Trophy was contested over 76 laps of the GP circuit by Grand Prix cars. Entries were received from Cooper Car Company Ltd, Team Lotus, BRM, UDT-Laystall and Yeoman Credit. Victory went to Stirling Moss driving the pale green UDT-Laystall Formula One Lotus 18/21 Climax from Jim Clark aboard the works Lotus 21 Climax and Tony Brooks driving the BRM P57 — this car was also Coventry-Climax powered as the new BRM unit was not yet ready. The 7 August meeting saw a name arrive in the sport — Carreras-Rothmans; the liaison with Brands Hatch was to last until 1974, the company's first commitment being to sponsor the Guards International Trophy for Intercontinental Formula cars. In effect, these were the 'left-over' 2.5-litre Formula One cars which had just been made redundant but which were still plentiful in number and needed to be raced. The race was a 76-lap affair over the GP circuit; Jack Brabham won in the works Cooper T53-Climax from Jim Clark (works Lotus 18-Climax) and Graham Hill (BRM P57).

The following year, 1962, did not see any major meetings at Brands Hatch but on 1 October the longest race staged so far at the Kent circuit took place. This was the *Motor*-sponsored Six-Hour saloon car race. The field of 35 entries included some foreign entrants and victory went to Mike Parkes and Jimmy Blumer driving a 3.8-litre Jaguar; the German pairing of Peter Lindner and Peter Nocker in another Jaguar from (quite incredibly) a Mini-Cooper driven by John Aley and one Denny Hulme a New Zealander who was employed by Jack Brabham as a mechanic. Sadly the new venture was poorly supported by spectators but was an experiment worth repeating. The Club Circuit (as the original was now known) had six meetings during the year and the coming of Formula Junior saw the lap record tumble to 55.6sec and the first-ever 80mph lap by John Fenning at the Easter Monday meeting, the actual speed being 80.29mph; the car was a Lotus 20 with Ford power. The 'Trio' meeting in July saw the end of an era when a 500 took the chequered flag for the last time with Mike Ledbrook at the wheel of a Mark 8 Cooper-Norton in the 500 and 250cc race. From here on the 'one lungers' would only be seen in races with larger-capacity cars where they would be totally outclassed. It was ironic that this piece of history should be written at the only non-BRSCC meeting of the year. At the Boxing

Above: And this is the 1960 full Brands Hatch Grand Prix circuit in all its glory, climbing and winding through the woods and measuring a full 2.65 miles.

Left: An aerial view of Brands Hatch on a Grand Prix day in the 1950s. *Brands Hatch Leisure*

Day meeting, Hulme, that shy young New Zealander, won the Formula Junior race driving the prototype Brabham BT6-Ford, setting a new outright lap record at 82.06mph in 54.8sec.

The winter of 1962/3 was severe, causing the cancellation of many football matches which would have resulted in empty television screens on occasions and it is, as they say, an ill-wind . . . The lack of sport to show on television on Saturday afternoons virtually created rallycross for on 9 February a rallycross-type event was staged on the slushy car parks of Brands Hatch in front of the TV cameras. This new event had been quickly organised by Raymond Baxter of the BBC and the London Motor Club and saw Timo Makinen win easily in the works Austin-Healey 3000. But we digress . . .

The second *Motor*-sponsored Six-Hour saloon car race was run in appalling conditions on 6 July. The crowd was larger but the favourite, a 7-litre Ford Galaxie driven by Dan Gurney and Jack Brabham floundered in the wet and the Jaguars dominated the race. Victory went to Roy Salvadori and Denny Hulme from Peter Lindner and Peter Nocker after the winners on the road, Mike Salmon and Pete Sutcliffe, were disqualified for engine irregularities in post-race scrutineering. The Guards Trophy was run for sports cars and went to Roger Penske driving his Zerex Special which was based on a Cooper Formula One chassis.

The British Grand Prix came to Kent in 1964 and was to be shared with Silverstone in alternate years until 1986. The race was given the courtesy title European Grand Prix and the management of Brands Hatch rose to the occasion. The date was 11 July, a cool but dry day which saw Jim Clark at his best in the Lotus 25 winning by 2.8sec from Graham Hill in the BRM P261 who was followed home by John Surtees in the V8 Ferrari; fourth and one lap down was Jack Brabham driving a car bearing his own name. A further lap down in fifth place was Lorenzo Bandini in the V6 Ferrari with Phil Hill taking the final Championship point in a Cooper. The race average was 94.14mph and Clark set the fastest lap at 96.5mph in 1min 38.8sec. The *Motor* Six-Hours had its third and final running on 6 June with victory going to the Alan Mann-entered Lotus-Cortinas of Sir John Whitmore/Peter Proctor and Henry Taylor/Peter Harper. It was not Jaguar's year!

The 1964 season saw 14 car race meetings, which made it the busiest ever at Brands Hatch; the British Automobile Racing Club organised its first meeting in Kent while the London Motor Club organised one in June. The year's Guards Trophy went to Bruce McLaren driving for Cooper in a 3.9-litre Oldsmobile-powered sports car.

With no Grand Prix in 1965, Brands Hatch promoted a non-championship Formula One race to be known as the Race of Champions sponsored by the *Daily Mail*. The race was run in two 40-lap heats with victory in the first going to Jim Clark in the works Lotus 33 while his team-mate, Mike Spence, won the second. The first 100mph lap was set by Clark in 1min 35.4sec. The longest race ever run at the Kentish circuit took place on 22/23 May, this being the Guards 1000 comprising two 500-mile races for production sports cars. One race was run on the Saturday and the other on the Sunday. The overall winner was the works MG MGB driven by John Rhodes and Warwick Banks who were first on Saturday and fourth on Sunday.

By 1964 the programme for the RAC British Grand Prix had grown to A4 size and the race carried the honorary title of European Grand Prix. *Authors Collection*

The British Grand Prix returned to Brands Hatch in 1966, the inaugural year of the new 3-litre Formula One and surely the first time that a circuit had run its first two Grands Prix for different Formula Ones. The works Brabham-Repcos were first and second in the hands of Jack Brabham and Denny Hulme; Brabham completed the 212-mile race in 2hr 13min 13.4sec at a speed of 95.49mph, lapping all runners except his team-mate in the process. Third was Graham Hill in the BRM from Jimmy Clark in the number one Lotus with Jochen Rindt fifth in the Cooper-Maserati and in sixth position, a further lap adrift, was Bruce McLaren in the McLaren-Serenissima. The event was notable for the only racing appearance of the Shannon in the hands of Trevor Taylor which, sadly, lasted only one lap. This was also the year that the FIA decided the end had come for Group 7 sports cars with their massive motors; John Surtees won the Guards Trophy on August Bank Holiday Monday driving the 6-litre Lola T70. The Motor Show 200 for Formula Two cars in October saw a young Austrian named Jochen Rindt win in the Roy Winkelmann-entered Brabham BT18.

The 1967 Race of Champions (still with *Daily Mail* sponsorship) saw the first of two victories by American cars at Brands Hatch when Dan Gurney brought his beautiful Eagle-Weslake over the line first by 0.8sec from Lorenzo Bandini's Ferrari 312/67. So good was the public's response to the race (run in two 10-lap heats and a 40-lap final) that John Webb decided to make the race an annual event. The other great American victory was to come later in the year when the be-winged 7-litre Chaparral 2F-Chevrolet driven by Phil Hill and Mike Spence won the BOAC 500 run over 211 laps of the Grand Prix circuit at an average speed of 93.08mph, from the Ferrari 330-4 of Chris Amon and Jackie Stewart. These two had lapped the rest of the field twice, third place going to the Jo Siffert/Bruce McLaren Porsche 910. Few had expected the automatic transmission Chaparral to last six hours at Brands Hatch for it had not survived earlier races during the year. The BOAC 500 was the final round of the FIA International Manufacturers' Championship and the entrants came to England with the Championship poised between Ferrari and Porsche — the victory of the Chaparral meant that the Championship would be decided by lower placings. Porsche had come to Brands just leading on points but the results referred to above allowed Ferrari to take the title by two points. Few of those who were present at Brand Hatch that day will forget the sight of the wing of the Chaparral above the banking. The year saw Brands Hatch with a number of 'firsts'; in July Tetsu Ikuzawa became the first Japanese ever to win a race in Britain, the first Mini Festival was run at Whitsun and the Mini-Seven Club ran the first ever all-saloon car meeting in February. But the biggest 'first' was the arrival of Formula Ford which was to become the proving ground and starting place of so many drivers who were to go on to greater things. The first Formula Ford race was run on 7 July and was won by Ray Allen in a Lotus 51.

It was a particularly busy season in 1968 with no less than five International meetings; the first was the Race of Champions followed by the BOAC 500, the British Grand Prix, the Guards Trophy and the Motor Show 200. The former race gave the McLaren marque its first Formula One victory when Bruce, driving his own car, led home the field ahead of Pedro Rodriguez in the BRM P133 and his new team-mate Denny Hulme. Sponsorship on racing cars was just beginning and a television executive was much distressed by the 'sailor man' on the side of the Gold Leaf Team Lotus cars and

On the programme cover for the 1968 BOAC International 500 sports car race, Jack Brabham adjusts his goggles prior to the start of a race. *Author's collection*

Top: The undoubted star of the 1963 Racing Car Show at Olympia had been Eric Broadley's beautiful Lola GT which was the centrepiece of the Lola stand: in the fullness of time was it was destined to spawn the Ford GT40. Here the Lola GT owned and entered by John Mecom competes in the Guards Trophy at Brands Hatch on 4 August 1963, driven by American Augie Pabst. *Steve Wyatt/Quilter House*

Above: Another picture from the same meeting: the late, great Innes Ireland at the wheel of works Aston Martin DB4GT Project 214, chassis number DB4GT 194R. The car finished the Guards Trophy sixth overall and second in class. Innes was one of the gentlemen of the track who never failed to acknowledge a flag signal — even if he was in the middle of an enormous spin! *Steve Wyatt/Quilter House*

threatened to withdraw television coverage if the offending item was not obscured, so Graham Hill was black-flagged to have the decal covered! This attitude smacked of double standards as advertising at other sporting events (principally horse racing) had been perfectly acceptable until that time but now the appearance of an advertisement upon a racing car resulted in near apoplexy in the powers that be in television stations.

The Manufacturers' World Championship came early to Kent in 1968, the BOAC 500 being run on 7 April. The winner was the Ford GT40 of Jacky Ickx and Brian Redman from the Porsche 907 of Mitter and Scarfiotti, these two being the only cars to complete the full race distance of 218 laps, the winner's average being 95.96mph in 6hr 1min 13sec. Two laps down in third place was another 907 driven by Vic Elford and Jochen Neerpasch and fourth place went to another GT40 driven by Paul Hawkins and David Hobbs which completed 210 laps.

Three months later came the British Grand Prix on 20 July when Jo 'Seppi' Siffert became the first Swiss driver to win a *Grande Epreuve* since 'Toulo' de Graffenried at Silverstone way back in 1949. Siffert's victory was noteworthy in that he won in a Lotus 49B which was delivered new to the circuit on the first morning of the meeting. It was completed in the paddock and was entered by the Walker-Durlacher team — a private entrant winning a Grand Prix. His winning speed for the 212-mile race was 104.824mph in 2hr 1min 20.3sec; in second place just 4.4sec behind was Chris Amon in the Ferrari, with his team-mate Jacky Ickx third, a lap down. Fourth was Denny Hulme in the McLaren also on 79 laps, from Surtees in the Honda on 78 laps, and Stewart a further lap down in the Matra-Ford. Ninth and the last finisher was another Swiss, Silvio Moser, in the Brabham-Repco.

Reference to the Formula Ford 'Star of Tomorrow' race in the programme for the 1969 Race of Champions Meeting makes interesting reading, for amongst the entries were James Hunt (Merlyn), Tony Trimmer (Titan), Tom Walkinshaw (Hawke) and Colin Vandervell (Lotus). The main event for Formula One cars had attracted 16 entries, including two works entries each from Gold Leaf Team Lotus for Graham Hill and Jochen Rindt; Bruce McLaren Motor Racing Ltd for the owner and Denny Hulme; Repco Brabhams from Motor Racing Developments for Jack Brabham and an un-nominated driver, and BRMs from the Owen Racing Organization for John Surtees and Jackie Oliver. There were single works entries from Ferrari for Chris Amon, and a Matra for Jackie Stewart. Amongst the private entries (those halcyon days, when it was still possible!) came from Rob Walker who entered Jo Siffert in his Lotus, Frank Williams (Racing Cars) Ltd who entered a Brabham for Piers Courage, and Reg Parnell who had a BRM for Pedro Rodriguez. The field was completed by another BRM for Peter Gethin, Pete Lovely's Lotus and a Brabham entered by J. R. Smith. It is interesting to speculate whether we would today have Williams Grand Prix Engineering competing in Formula One World Championships if le patron had not been allowed to run his private entries in the 1960s.

Easter Monday 1969 saw another brainchild of John Webb and the BRSCC's Competitions Director Nick Syreett come to fruition. This was Formula 5000 which was based upon the American Formula A, the cars being single-seater chassis powered by American V8 and V6 stock-block engines of up to 5 litres capacity. The idea was not entirely new for Robin Darlington had campaigned the Kincraft which was a Ford-powered device for some years and Chris Summers had dabbled with big-engined cars in Formule Libre but this was the first time that a specific formula had been devised for big-engined cars on this side of the Atlantic. The need for the new Formula was caused by the escalating costs of Formula Three, Formula Two and the decreasing number of non-championship Formula One events as more and more countries demanded a Grand Prix. The winner of the first Formula 5000 race was Peter Gethin driving a McLaren M10A with Chevrolet power.

Indianapolis-style single-car qualifying was introduced for the Race of Champions but it simply did not catch on — perhaps it did not have the glamour of the Indiana circuit; Jackie Stewart won the race in the Matra MS80 owned by Ken Tyrrell and went on to win his first World Championship with it.

The BOAC 500 was once again the British round of the Manufacturers' World Championship and was a Porsche benefit, 908s taking the first three places, the winners being Siffert and Redman who completed the 227 laps in 6hr 0min

From 1969 comes this programme for the Guards-sponsored International European Championship Six-Hour Saloon Car Race. The photograph shows cars approaching Russell bend at Snetterton! *Author's collection*

0.08sec; the second placed car of Elford and Attwood was two laps down and Mitter and Schutz completed 223 laps. The first Ferrari home was the 312P of Amon and Rodriguez. March made its Formula One-winning debut at the Race of Champions in 1970 when Jackie Stewart won driving Ken Tyrrell's March 701.

The British Grand Prix returned to Brands Hatch on 19 July and saw victory going to Jochen Rindt by less than 33sec from Jack Brabham who had run out of fuel. The Lotus driver was then disqualified following a protest over an aerofoil but was reinstated before the evening was out. Third place went to Hulme in the McLaren from the Ferrari of Clay Regazzoni; a lap down in fifth spot was the March of Chris Amon with Graham Hill sixth for Lotus. Rindt's winning speed was 108.69mph.

The World Championship sports car race was now the BOAC 1000, but measured in kilometres rather than miles, and was another benefit for Porsche, the fearsome 917s taking the first three places from a 908; first home was the Rodriguez/ Kinnunen car from Elford/Hulme and Attwood/Herrmann. The 908 was driven by van Lennepp and Laine and another came home sixth in the hands of Larrousse and Koch from the Ferrari 512M of Amon and Merzario. The race was run over 235 laps in 6hr 45min 29.6sec at a speed of 92.15mph.

Following the Mexican Grand Prix in November 'Black Jack' Brabham announced his retirement from motor racing and

Brands Hatch honoured him with a 'Salute to Jack Brabham' meeting later in the month. To date, Jack Brabham and Stirling Moss are the only racing drivers to have been knighted for their services to the sport.

Fog had caused the cancellation of the 1969 Boxing Day meeting — in 1970 it was snow. In the 21-year history of the Boxing Day event it was cancelled on only five occasions: for the reasons mentioned above, the Suez Crisis in 1957, snow in 1964 and the fuel crisis in 1973.

By now the ownership of Brands Hatch was in the hands of Motor Circuit Developments and 1971 saw the arrival of another, MCD-inspired, single-seater formula in the shape of Formula Atlantic. The BOAC 1000 saw Alfa Romeo take their first major success in 20 years with the chequered flag being

taken by the T33TT/3 of Andrea de Adamich and Henri Pescarolo who completed the 235 laps in 6hr 24min 32.2sec at a speed of 97.17mph. They were followed home three laps down by the Ferrari 312 of Ickx and Clay Regazzoni, with the Porsche 917 of Siffert and Bell a further three laps down in third place; Ferrari 512Ms were fourth and fifth piloted by Muller/Herzog and Juncadella/Hobbs with Kauhsen and Joest bringing their 917 into sixth place.

Motor racing is a dangerous game and there had been some fatalities at Brands Hatch over the years but in October 1971 the season drew to its close with the death of a major driver at the Kent circuit. Jo Siffert died in an accident in the Rothmans World Championship Victory Race. This was a race for Formula One and Formula 5000 arranged to mark Jackie

Stewart and Ken Tyrrell's joint World Championships. The race
was 40 laps in length; 'Seppi' lost control of his BRM P160 on
lap 15 after making a terrible start, hit the bank at Hawthorn
Hill, the car was engulfed in flame and the driver was
asphyxiated before he could be extricated. The circuit came in
for a great deal of criticism and there was talk of a drivers'
boycott but eventually it was agreed that a three-year
programme of safety improvements would be commenced
before the start of the 1972 season.

Twenty-one years down the line and the wattle-fenced
farmers' fields of 1949 had been transformed into the busiest
motor racing circuit in the world with something going on
practically every weekend, as is still the case today. However,
this was not just at weekends, for during the week Motor

Racing Stables (the racing school) was in operation, with the
British School of Motoring's High Performance in operation on
Wednesdays and Fridays, as well as film and television work.

The 1972 season was a particularly busy one with Formula
One cars visiting twice for the Race of Champions, on
19 March sponsored by the *Daily Mail* and the John Player-
sponsored British Grand Prix on 15 July (bearing the title
European Grand Prix) while the BOAC 1000 was the British
round of the World Championship of Makes, and Formula
5000 went from strength to strength. On 16 April what was to
be the last BOAC 1000 resulted in a complete Italian benefit
race with Ferrari and Alfa Romeo filling the first six places. The
235-lap race was won by Mario Andretti and Jacky Ickx in a
Ferrari 312PB in 5hr 55min 27.5sec at 105.12mph from Tim

Schenken and Ronnie Peterson, a lap down in a similar car. A further lap down in third place was the Alfa Romeo T33-3 of Rolf Stommelen and Peter Revson with another T33-3 fourth another lap down driven by Vic Elford and Andrea de Adamich. Fifth and sixth on 220 laps were the 312PB of Regazzoni and Redman from the T33-3 of Marko and Galli. And so to July and the Grand Prix carrying the courtesy title of European Grand Prix with 26 starters of whom just half finished. Seventy-six laps of the Grand Prix circuit adds up to just a few hundred yards over 200 miles which Emerson Fittipaldi completed in 1hr 47min 50.2sec at 108.67mph driving the John Player Special Lotus, from Jackie Stewart in the Tyrrell, Peter Revson in the McLaren, Chris Amon in the Matra-Simca, Denny Hulme (McLaren) and Arturo Merzario in the Ferrari.

The following year, 1973, was less hectic; the BOAC 1000 was cancelled when the FIA offered a date which was much too close to Easter and the sky fell in at the Race of Champions. Peter Gethin driving a Formula 5000 Chevron-Chevrolet beat the Formula One cars and James Hunt made his Formula One debut in Lord Hesketh's March while huge crowds were attracted to meetings hosted by pop stars and disc jockeys. Before the commencement of the 25th motor racing season £50,000 was spent upon a new grandstand adjoining the Grovewood Suite, while open seating and new pits were built to comply with FIA requirements. There were also safety improvements made between Westfield and Stirling's.

It rained again for the Race of Champions in 1974 and the more nimble Formula One cars showed their heels to the Formula 5000 contingent; the winner was Jacky Ickx driving a Lotus 72. The Grand Prix was held on 20 July and the RAC (who organised the race) came in for some censure from the governing body for allowing the pit lane to become blocked during the race thus preventing Jochen Rindt from rejoining at the end to claim fifth place which he was awarded on appeal.

The winner was Jody Scheckter in a Tyrrell who covered the 199.75-mile race in 1hr 43min 2.2sec at 115.73mph from Emerson Fittipaldi (McLaren), Jackie Ickx (JPR Lotus), Clay Regazzoni and Niki Lauda (Ferrari) with Carlos Reutemann (Brabham) sixth.

The BOAC 1000 had become the British Airways 1000 and was dominated by the works Matra-Simca 670Cs which finished first and second; first home were the Jean-Pierres — Jarier and Beltoise — with Henri Pescarolo and Gèrard Larrousse second. Third, no less that 11 laps down, was the Gulf-Ford GR 7 of Bell and Hobbs ahead of the Chevron B26 driven by Gethin and Redman. Fifth and sixth places were taken by Porsches — the Carrera Turbo of Muller and van Lennep and a 908/3 driven by Barth and Haldi. The race was poorly attended and future prospects were bleak for sports car racing; it was not included in the following year's programme.

The winter of 1974/5 was mild which was fortunate as for the first time in a quarter of a century the tar layers and road rollers moved in to resurface both circuits in their entirety, the work being completed in time for the opening meetings in March.

Thomas Maldwyn Pryce had made a name for himself in Formula Ford and Formula F100 at Brands Hatch. He came to the British Airways/*Daily Mail* Race of Champions on 16 March to continue his career as a works driver with Universal Oil Products Shadow. His mount was the DN5; Tom carved his way through the field closing relentlessly upon Scheckter until the engine of the Tyrrell blew and that was that.

It was the first win for Shadow and, sadly, it was to be the Welshman's only Formula One win for he died a little over two years later in a totally stupid accident in the South African Grand Prix. His was a truly great talent wasted, for he was a natural, one of the few who could really power slide a 3-litre rear-engine Formula One car and hold it on opposite lock.

It was again Grand Prix year in 1976 and notwithstanding the money already spent, another £100,000 was expended on track and safety work; the major change was a realignment of Paddock Bend which resulted in a slight shortening of the circuit, with the apex moved in to lessen the possibility of cars hitting the outside bank and with the old track left in situ as a run-off area. Bottom Straight was also realigned making it straighter and the marshals' posts were resited and more Armco inserted. It was at this time that the name changes occurred; Pilgrims became Hailwood Hill, Bottom Bend became Graham

Right: In 1986, the British Grand Prix was sponsored by Shell Oils, the front cover featuring World Champion Alain Prost's McLaren-TAG (Porsche) MP4/2c which also enjoyed sponsorship from Shell. The public was not allowed to forget that the RAF Aerobatic Team, 'The Red Arrows', would be appearing, as became a tradition at the British Grand Prix at both Brands Hatch and Silverstone. *Brands Hatch Leisure*

Below: This is a sight which may never be repeated — a factory-entered Aston Martin in combat — for this is the AMR1 at Brands Hatch on 23 July 1989 being driven into fourth place by David Leslie and Brian Redman in the Brands Hatch Trophy race. The government of the day having allowed Ford to buy Jaguar and Aston Martin, it was inevitable that both would not be allowed to continue to compete in International Sports Car Racing and it was the Newport Pagnell programme which suffered: that was a great pity for the AMR1 had shown considerable promise. *Mike Dixon*

Hill Bend, and Bottom Straight became Cooper Straight. The Grand Prix took place on 18 July and was somewhat controversial. Following a first-lap accident the race was stopped. National hero James Hunt was involved so he took over the spare car for the race, which he won, but was later disqualified by the FIA as it was deemed that he had not completed the first lap. Niki Lauda was declared the winner for Ferrari from the Tyrrell of Scheckter and John Watson's Penske. Tom Pryce brought the Shadow home fourth with Alan Jones fifth in the Surtees and Emerson Fittipaldi sixth in the Copersucar; the race distance was a fraction over 198 miles which Lauda covered in 1hr 43min 2.2sec at 114.073mph.

On 25 September the second British round of the World Championship of Makes arrived at Brands Hatch for the Six-Hours; it was run in a deluge which caused the race to be stopped for an hour and it was eventually run over 103 laps — 269 miles — which Ickx and Mass won at 97.696mph driving a Porsche 935/2 Turbo. The race was totally dominated by the Germans, the first five places going to Porsche 935 Turbos — a 934 Turbo was sixth with a Carrera seventh. A little relief came with the eighth-placed BMW 320i, ninth a Carrera Group 5 and another 934 Turbo tenth. In November, the Formula Ford Festival arrived at Brands Hatch and was won by Irishman Derek Daly in a Hawke DL17. While Brands Hatch always liked to think of the Formula Ford Festival as its own, the event had been instigated and run for many years by the East Anglian Centre of the BRSCC at Snetterton from whence it was moved.

August 1977 saw a memorable win when Tony Dron took the works Triumph Dolomite Sprint to head the Ford Capris to the line in the Bank Holiday round of the Tricentrol British Saloon Car Championship. During the year MCD came up with yet another formula — this time clothing Formula 2000 racing cars in sports car bodies and calling them Sports 2000. The following year, 1978, was one to remember for not only was it again Grand Prix year it was also Indy year. Controversy again loomed at the Grand Prix but trouble was averted; Niki Lauda had won the Swedish Grand Prix driving the Brabham 'fan-car' but before it arrived in Kent it was banned by the governing body. But Lauda made his point by finishing second in the conventional Brabham Alfa-Romeo BT46 behind Carlos Reutemann in the Ferrari, with John Watson third in the other Brabham. The race was a little over 198 miles in length which Lauda won at 116.608mph in 1hr 42min 12.39sec. Fourth place went to Patrick Depailler in a Tyrrell, with Hans-Joachim Stuck fifth in a Shadow and Patrick Tambay sixth for McLaren.

Important though the Grand Prix is, the high-spot of the 1978 season at Brands and Silverstone was the coming of the Indycars. In 1977, Angela and John Webb had gone to America to witness the organisation of Indy racing at first hand and as a result of that visit two rounds of the United States Automobile Club's Championship were run in England. The Silverstone race was wet and the one at Brands was dry. The costs were £0.5 million but, unfortunately, the races did not capture the imagination of British enthusiasts despite the appearance of such names as the legendary A. J. Foyt, Rick Mears, Tom Sneva and Danny Ongais. The Brands Hatch race was run on the Club circuit which was then renamed the Indy circuit in honour of the guests and was won by Mears, from Sneva with the fastest lap going to Ongais at 104.66mph in 41.4sec — a new outright lap record. The reaction of the British enthusiasts to the importation of Indycars was mirrored by the apathy with which Grand Prix racing was greeted in the United States of America at that time.

A saloon car championship was introduced in 1979, running on alcohol fuel — once common in motorsport but since fallen

Below: The late, great Tom Pryce on his way to victory in the 1976 Race of Champions at Brands Hatch driving his Shadow DN5-2A when he ran away and hid from the opposition. Sadly, this was his only Formula One win: had fate been a little kinder it would have undoubtedly been the first of many which could have led to him becoming the first Welsh World Champion. His was a truly towering talent wasted in a stupid accident which should never have been. *A. K. Porteous/Motor Racing Archive*

from favour. The idea did not have a long life which was a great shame for it was environmentally friendly at a time when the sport needed friends in places outside those who know and understand.

The circuit did not see a Race of Champions in 1980 — the Grand Prix calendar was now so full that the teams could not afford a week to run in a non-Championship race and henceforward British fans would have only one opportunity to see current Formula One cars in action per year. A little piece of motor racing history was written when Desiré Wilson became the first woman to win an Formula One race when she won a round of the British National Aurora Formula One Championship over 40 laps of the GP circuit.

On 16 March the Brands Hatch Six-Hours was run and saw a healthy invasion of Italian cars; Lancia Beta Monte Carlo's in the hands of Patrese and Rohrl with Alboreto and Cheever taking the first two places, the winning car being the only one to complete the full race distance of 147 laps, at 99.384mph. In third spot a further lap down was the De Cadenet LM of Alain de Cadenet and Wilson ahead of another Beta Monte Carlo driven by Facetti and Finotto. This was Alan Jones's World Championship year and on the way to his crown he won the Marlborough British Grand Prix at Brands Hatch on 13 July from Nelson Piquet and Carlos Reutemann. Piquet's Brabham split the two Williams, Derek Daly and Jean-Pierre Jarier in the Tyrrells filling the next two spots, with sixth going to Alain Prost in the McLaren. With the exception of the Ferrari and Renault entries the entire field was Cosworth-powered. The race was fractionally short of 199 miles in length and was won at 125.692mph in 1hr 34min 49.2sec. Mrs Wilson was not so fortunate on this occasion, failing to qualify. There was a slimmed down season in 1981 with but one International, the emphasis being on top-class national racing.

By contrast, 1982 was extremely busy. Brands Hatch Racing Club had been formed over the winter to organise race meetings in addition to the clubs who were already doing so; the new club's first meeting was run on 25 April. The highlight of the year was the Marlborough British Grand Prix and it was voted the best of the year by the members of the Formula One Constructors Association. To make the year complete, the Brands Press Service received the Prix Orange which is presented by the International Racing Press Association for the best press service at any Grand Prix. Once again the Grand Prix was run over 199 miles (76 laps), the winner being Niki Lauda in the McLaren from the Ferraris of Pironi and Tambay; fourth was the Lotus of Elio de Angelis, fifth the Williams of Derek Daly, with Alain Prost in the Renault in sixth position. The winner took 1hr 35min 33.8sec at a speed of 124.650mph.

It was a non-Grand Prix year at Brands in 1983 but the Marlborough *Daily Mail* Race of Champions was successfully staged on 10 April notwithstanding the fact that it was only a week before the French Grand Prix and clashed with a Michelin tyre test at Paul Ricard. To bring some real excitement, noise and spectacle back into British motor racing, the BRSCC invented Thundersports. The new formula had its debut on Easter Monday and the country's first major sports car race since the mid-1970s was a resounding success. Then, the year turned into a Grand Prix one after all; following the

cancellation of the New York Grand Prix, John Webb lobbied FISA in company with the RAC MSA and was granted the opportunity to run the Grand Prix d'Europe on 25 September thus giving Britain one of those rare-as-hens'-teeth years when it saw two Grands Prix.

The full circus arrived in Kent and Elio de Angelis placed his Lotus on pole position; the race was 76 laps/199 miles long which Nelson Piquet in the number one Brabham-BMW won in 1hr 36min 46sec at 124.411mph. Alain Prost followed him home 6sec later in the Renault with Nigel Mansell third for Lotus; in fourth place was the Alfa Romeo of Andrea de Cesaris and the last two point-scoring places were taken by the Tolemans of Derek Warwick and Bruno Giacomelli — five different chassis and four different engines in the top six was a very healthy situation.

In 1984, Brands Hatch become the first British circuit to hold Grands Prix in three consecutive years since the 1950s. This was officially the year for Kent to host the British Grand Prix but it was fraught with politics as Tyrrell was adjudged by the sport's international governing body to have infringed the rules at the Canadian Grand Prix and was excluded for the remainder of the season. A court injunction ensured that the cars started in their home Grand Prix but Stefan Belloff and Stefan Johansson qualified the cars on the back row of the grid, the former finishing 11th but Johansson being eliminated in a first-lap accident. The result repeated history with five makes and four engines featuring in the results; the winner was Niki Lauda for McLaren from Derek Warwick in the Renault and Ayrton Senna driving the Toleman. Fourth came Elio de Angelis in the Lotus with the Ferrari-mounted Michele Alboreto and René Arnoux being the final point scorers. The race distance was a mere 185 miles (71 laps) which Lauda covered at 124.382mph in 1hr 29min 28sec.

On 22 September 1985, Brands Hatch hosted the second British round of the Endurance World Championship for Teams (another euphemism for sports car racing) in the form of the Brands Hatch 1000 (Silverstone having run a round in May). It was Porsche's year, the marque scoring 107 points to Martini-Lancia's 58 and so it was at Brands Hatch that the Stuttgart team took three of the first six places; first was the 962C of Derek Bell and Hans Stuck (who took the drivers' title) with the identical car of Jacky Ickx and Jochen Mass second — these two were the only contestants to cover the full race distance of 238 laps. Five laps down in third spot was the Lancia-Martini of Wolleck/Baldi/de Cesaris, with the similar car of Riccardo Patrese and Alessandro Nannini fourth from the Holbert/Schuppan Porsche 956. British honour was upheld by Ray Mallock and Mike Wilds who brought the C2 Ecosse-Ford home in sixth place — the highest-placed C2 car.

In 1985, for the second time in three years, Great Britain staged two Grands Prix counting for the World Championship in one year: in July, the British Grand Prix was staged at Silverstone, but the loss of a race elsewhere in the world made a date available in Europe towards the end of the season. The management of the Kent circuit made a bid for it; Brands Hatch was granted the race which was run under the courtesy title of Grand Prix d'Europe on 6 October.

It was fitting that Nigel Mansell should score his first Grand

Prix win on this occasion, at the wheel of a Williams, completing the 75 laps of the Grand Prix circuit in 1hr 32min 58.1sec at 125.795mph from Ayrton Senna's Lotus and team-mate Keke Rosberg in the other Williams. Alain Prost brought his McLaren home fourth with Elio de Angelis a lap down in fifth spot in the second Lotus and Thierry Boutsen taking the final point in an Arrows. Jacques Laffite set a new lap record in 1min 11.526sec at 130.805mph in his Ligier. There were 26 starters and one non-qualifier.

In October that year, rumours started to circulate regarding the future of Motor Circuit Developments: at the time the Company was the property of Eagle Star Holdings which had been sold to British American Tobacco. This caused some alarm as to the future of the circuits. Thanks to the efforts of John Webb, enter John Foulston! He was Chairman of Atlantic Computers plc and a staunch enthusiast and Historic and Thundersports racer. His bid of £5.25 million secured the future of Brands Hatch, Oulton Park and Snetterton for 'the foreseeable future'. Early in 1987 he added Cadwell Park to his fold which was now known as the Brands Hatch Leisure Group.

The Kentish circuit was to host the Grand Prix only once more and that was on 13 July 1986 (making five years in a row), after which it was to be run continually at Silverstone. Sadly, the race was to see the premature departure from the Formula One scene of a highly respected and well-liked driver; at the end of the first lap an accident occurred on the approach to Paddock Bend which trapped the Frenchman Jacques Laffite in his Ligier — his legs were badly injured, as a result of which he was to race no more in Formula One. It was his 176th Grand Prix, equalling Graham Hill's record. It is, however, an ill wind . . . Nigel Mansell's Williams had rolled to a stop shortly after the start but as a result of the race stoppage his car was rectified and he took the restart, eventually winning from his team-mate Nelson Piquet. The race distance was 196 miles which Mansell completed in 1hr 30min 30sec at 129.007mph. Third was Alain Prost for McLaren with fourth going to René Arnoux in the other Ligier, with the Tyrrells of Martin Brundle and Philippe Streiff taking fifth and sixth. Thus ended the Grand Prix era at Brands Hatch.

Whether the Grand Prix will ever return south of the Thames is open to question; one of the great beauties of Brands Hatch is that the Grand Prix circuit was built through the woods which still stand and it must be wondered whether the international governing body will envisage returning to a track which could be construed as dangerous. A week after the 1986 Grand Prix the World Sports Car Championship contingent arrived in Kent for the Brands Hatch 1000, the second British round. The first three places were taken by Porsche 956s, the winning car of Wolleck and Baldi being the only one to complete the full distance of 238 laps, at 104.608mph. Second were Bell, Stuck and Ludwig with Boutsen and Jelinski third, four and five laps down respectively. Jaguar XJR6s came in fourth and sixth piloted by Warwick/Schlesser and Cheever/Brancatelli split by the Porsche 956 of Ludwig, Barilla and 'John Winter'.

Almost exactly a year later Brands Hatch again echoed to the howl of the sports cars but the championship had now become the World Sports-Prototype Championship for Teams and the race was the Shell Gemini 1000 run on 26 July 1987. This was the year of the Silk Cut Jaguar team and the XJR8 of Rouel

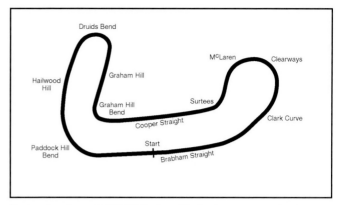

During the winter of 1998/9 Graham Hill Bend was realigned to become a sharp left-hander instead of the sweeping curve it used to be. The length of the Indy Circuit, shown here, is now 1.2262 miles.

Boesel and John Nielsen who won at Brands at an average of 111.80mph with the Porsche 962C of Baldi and Dumfries second, these two being the only cars to run the full distance. Third, no less than nine laps adrift, was Lammers and Watson's XJR8 followed by three more Porsche 962Cs piloted by Stuck and Bell, Mass and Laurrauri (both on 228 laps) and Weidler and Nissen on 225 laps.

If the Grand Prix was lost to Brands Hatch, large-capacity single-seater racing cars were not entirely so and on 23 August the seventh round of the Intercontinental F3000 Championship was run there and as in the previous year, the cars were all Cosworth-powered Lolas, Marches and Ralts. The race was over 45 laps, making a race distance of 117 miles, which Julian Bailey won at 119.30mph in a Lola. In second place was Mauricio Gugelmin followed by Roberto Moreno, both Ralt-mounted, with Stefano Modena and Yannick Dalmas fourth and fifth in March 87Bs, and in sixth place was the Lola T87/50 driven by Mark Blundell.

The big sports cars arrived in Kent again on 24 July 1988 for the seventh round of the World Sports-Prototype Championship and the second in Britain. It was the year of the Jaguar XJR9 and the Martin Brundle/John Nielsen/Andy Wallace team was the only starter to cover the full race distance of the Brands Hatch 1000, taking 5hr 33min 23sec at a speed of 112.31mph. In second place came the Bob Wollek/Klaus Ludwig Porsche 962C on 239 laps, with the Sauber-Mercedes driven by Mauro Baldi and Jo Schlesser third, a further four laps adrift. The next three places were all occupied by class C2 Spice SE 88C-Cosworths driven by Spice/Bell, Coppelli/Thyrring and Los/Taylor.

A little under a month later the F3000 brigade arrived to contest the seventh round of the International F3000 Championship. Practice was marred by a series of worrying accidents but Johnny Herbert took pole position with his new team-mate Martin Donnelly alongside in the Q8 Team Ford Reynards. In the race they were in a class of their own with Herbert taking up a commanding lead but this was short-lived as the race was stopped following an accident at Paddock Bend. At the restart Donnelly moved into the lead from Pierluigi Martini but Gregor Foitek and Herbert touched, resulting in a bad accident and a second race stoppage. Herbert was seriously injured, suffering major leg fractures. At the third start Donnelly went away to score a debut win in the Formula at 120.8mph for the 109-mile race from Martini in a March and Mark Blundell in a Lola T88. Fourth to sixth places were filled by Reynard 88Ds in the hands of Barilla, Euser and Weidler. Bernard was fifth on the road but was disqualified.

On 23 July 1989 the World Sports-Prototype Championship contenders arrived in Kent for the first of two British rounds of the Championship. The race was the Brands Hatch Trophy run over 115 laps of the Grand Prix circuit making a race distance of 299 miles, which was won by the Sauber C9 Mercedes of Mauro Baldi and Kenny Acheson in 2hr 41min 37sec at an average speed of 111.15mph. Into second place came a Porsche 962C contested by Wollek and Jelinski from the second Sauber of Schlesser and Mass which was a lap adrift. A further two laps down in fourth place was the Aston Martin AMR1 of David Leslie and Brian Redman ahead of the first Jaguar XJR11 home, that of Lammers and Tambay on 111 laps, with another Porsche 962C piloted by Brun and Pareja sixth.

A month later, on 20 August, the sixth round of the International F3000 Championship (the second in Britain) was run over 48 laps of the Grand Prix circuit making a race distance of 125 miles, which Martin Donnelly won for the second successive year in a Reynard 89D with Mugen power at 120.66mph in 1hr 2min 3.7sec. Second was his team-mate Jean Alesi 13sec behind, followed by Eric Comas and Eric Bernard in Lola T89/50-Mugens. Fifth and sixth were Brabham and Langes respectively driving a March 89D-Judd and a Lola T89/50-Cosworth.

Exactly a year later on 19 August 1990, they were back to contest the eighth round of the Championship and the second in England. The point-scoring positions were shared between Lola and Reynard with a preponderance of Cosworth engines. Alan McNish won the 125-mile race at 108.26mph in 1hr 9min 9.6sec in a Lola T90/50 with a Mugen engine, followed by Damon Hill in an identical car with a Cosworth power plant. Reynard 90Ds with Mugen engines filled the next four places driven by Apicella, Irvine, Chaves and Chiesa. The Sports-Prototypes did not come to Kent in 1990.

The seventh round of the 1991 International F3000 Championship took place at Brands on 18 August to run over 48 laps, a shade under 125 miles. Reynards filled the first three places, first home being Emanuele Naspetti driving a Cosworth-powered 91D in 1hr 26min 28sec at 123.9mph from Alessandro Zanardi in a similar car. Third was Christian Fittipaldi (famous nephew of a famous uncle) in the Pacific Racing Mugen-engined Reynard from Marco Apicella in a Lola T91/50 Mugen, with Antonio Tamburini in a Reynard-Cosworth and Damon Hill taking the final point in a Lola-Cosworth.

International motor racing returned to Brands Hatch in 1996 when a round of the International BPR Series for GT1 and GT2 sports cars was staged there on 8 September. The Porsche 911 GT1 of Hans Stuck and Thierry Boutsen led home three McLaren Formula One GTRs driven by Andy Wallace/Olivier Grouillard, Owen Jones/Raphanel and Nielsen/Bscher. Fifth was the Ferrari F40 GTE of Olofsson/della Noce with a 911 GGT driven by Konrad/Wollek/Ortelli sixth.

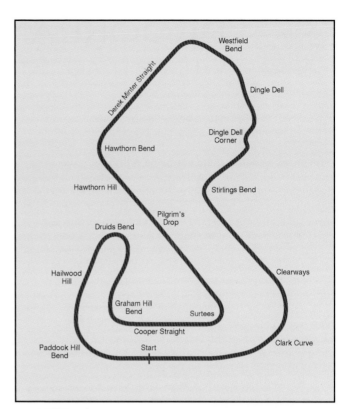

The 1998/9 realignment of Graham Hill Bend had this effect upon the Grand Prix circuit, lengthening it to 2.6228 miles.

In October 1999 Octagon commenced negotiations for the purchase of Brands Hatch Leisure Group: in December agreement was reached, control of Brands Hatch, Cadwell Park, Oulton Park and Snetterton passing to the new owners. Octagon obtained the right from the FIA to run the British Grand Prix from 2002 and announced the intention of rebuilding the Grand Prix circuit in Kent whilst at the same time negotiating with the British Racing Drivers Club to run the Grand Prix at Silverstone. Agreement was reached which will ensure the British Grand Prix will be run at Silverstone for 15 years. This in turn means that the gloriously challenging Grand Prix circuit at Brands Hatch will not be altered.

At the close of the 2000 season the outright lap record on the original Grand Prix circuit stood to the credit of Emanuele Naspetti in 1min 13.86sec at a speed of 126.73 mph at the wheel of a Reynard 91D on 18 August 1991. On the original Indy Circuit the record was set five years later on 26 August 1996 by Luiz Garcia driving a Reynard 95D at 111.78 mph in 38.76sec. With the change wrought upon Graham Hill Bend between the end of the 1998 season and the commencement of the 1999, these records will now stand in perpetuity. The outright lap record on the new 2.6228 mile Grand Prix circuit stands to the credit of Antonio Pizzonia driving a Dallara F399-Mugen Honda in 1min 18.822sec at 119.79 mph; the record was set on 4 June 2000. On 5 April 1999 Nigel Greensall set the record on the new 1.2262-mile Indy Circuit in 39.41sec at 112.01mph driving his Tyrrell-Judd 023.

BROOKLANDS
WHERE IT ALL STARTED

Above: The programme cover from the Whit Monday meeting at Brooklands in 1928; promoted by the Brooklands Automobile Racing Club, the early influence of horse racing is apparent in the title of the programme: Official Race Card.

Left: The Official Race Card front cover from the Brooklands Race Meeting held on 17 May 1937; this design was used extensively through the 1930s.

H ugh Fortescue Locke-King was a wealthy industrialist and patriot; when he witnessed the Sicilian Targa Florio race in 1906 he was outraged to find that there were no British cars competing and wished to know why this was so. It was explained to him that the principal reason was that there was nowhere on the British side of the Channel where cars could be tested at high speed and, as the speed limit was still 20mph, there was no possibility of testing on the public highway. He resolved to do something to amend this sad state of affairs and at a luncheon hosted by Lord Northcliffe and attended by Lord Montagu of Beaulieu, he proposed the construction of a circuit where British cars could be tested.

This suggestion was heartily endorsed by those present and plans were put in hand. In order to achieve his aim, Locke-King invested some £150,000 of his own money in the construction of a massive oval some three miles in length on part of his estate near Weybridge in Surrey; that sum would

BROOKLANDS
WEYBRIDGE

OFFICIAL RACE CARD

WHIT-MONDAY,
MAY 17th, 1937

1st Race: 1-30 p.m.

Price - One Shilling

COPYRIGHT.

All literary matter in this Programme, including the Lists of Competitors, is Copyright, and any person found making illegal use thereof will be prosecuted.

THE RIGHT CROWD AND NO CROWDING

equate to about £9 million today. A marshy part of the estate was chosen on the opposite side of the main London & South Western Railway line from his home, Brooklands House. Six miles of railway lines were laid from the LSWR line and some 2,000 Irish navvies moved in and laid 200,000 tons of cement in order to make the 30ft high bankings and track which was to be 100ft wide. The work started in October 1906 and the Brooklands track was ready for use by June 1907. It is interesting that, despite the nature of the work in progress, very few motor lorries were used in the construction, with the bulk of the movement of materials carried out by horse-drawn wagons.

Brooklands was the first purpose-built motor racing course in the world — although some people residing in Indiana, USA, would like to dispute that fact! On 28/29 June S. F. Edge (who had been instrumental in persuading Locke-King to build a race-track as opposed to a pure test track) drove a 20hp Napier the 'stupendous distance' of 1,581.75 miles in 24 hours at a speed of 65.9mph. It should be remembered that Edge had *averaged* three times the legal speed limit for a day and a night and the public must have been mesmerised by such a feat.

In order to run the races at Brooklands, the Brooklands Automobile Racing Club had been formed but this new body had nothing upon which to draw for guidance so decided to

base its operations on horse racing which resulted in the drivers wearing coloured silks as jockeys did. The first race meeting was held on 6 July 1907 but it appears the public were somewhat disappointed because the place was so vast that the cars were difficult to see in the distance and the drivers in their silks were hard to identify.

Two years later in 1909, salvation came in the shape of A. V. Ebblewhite who persuaded the powers that be of the Brooklands Automobile Racing Club to adopt numbers for the competing cars instead of the silks. 'Ebby' was the starter and handicapper and became part of Brooklands lore.

The British Broadcasting Corporation held its first motor racing outside radio broadcast from Brooklands but as its charter forbade any form of advertising the commentator was unable to name the cars which he saw on the track so he had to describe them only by colour!

The circuit suffered its first accident at the second meeting on 20 July 1907 when a Darracq crashed and the first fatal accident occurred at the September meeting when Vincent

Left: A publicity poster for one of the Brooklands 500-mile races.

Below: This scene from the second British Grand Prix held at Brooklands in 1927 shows three Bugattis negotiating the final section of one of the two artificial chicanes inserted before the pits to give the course a 'Continental' feel. The first is driven by George Eyston, who shared the car with Sammy Davis, and is followed by the Count Carlos Conelli/'Williams' car in the hands of the former. The third car is the mount of E. Materassi: none of them was classified as a finisher in a race which was run under dull conditions with an unpleasant drizzle falling at the start. *National Motor Museum Photographic Library*

Above: In England motor racing art commenced at Brooklands; this relatively early poster for the International Trophy organised by the Junior Car Club features a stylised Maserati. *Author's collection*

Left: The famous Henry Birkin supercharged 4½-litre single-seater Bentley is seen here airborne over the famous hump in the Members' Banking where the track crossed the River Wey. The Brooklands Society has plans to preserve a piece of the banking within the 40-acre site and the section chosen stretches from the approximate position of the lower car back round and under the Members Bridge which is to be replaced. *National Motor Museum Photographic Library*

Hermon driving a Minerva entered by J. T. C. Moore-Brabazon (later Lord Brabazon) overturned coming off the Finishing Straight on to the Members' Banking: he was trapped under the car and died of his injuries that night.

Retaining straps on the bonnets of racing cars were first used as a result of an incident when the bonnet of a competing car blew off, nearly decapitating its driver and riding mechanic. Following that frightening moment it was decided to restrain the bonnet with a strap in future, and the habit spread. The first car to attain 100mph at Brooklands was Lambert's Talbot in 1913 and the all-time lap record stands to John Cobb's mighty 24-litre Napier-Railton in 1935 at 143mph; he also recorded the fastest absolute speed at 151.97mph.

The very last motor race meeting at Brooklands before the Great War was held on the day before hostilities broke out, although two motor cycle races were held during the War — 'All Khaki' on 7 August 1915 and 'United Services' on 4 September 1915. But it was to be six long years before another motor race was held at Brooklands.

On 7 August 1926 Grand Prix motor racing finally came to England when the Royal Automobile Club staged the first British Grand Prix at Brooklands and attracted what was, for the time, an outstanding entry of 13 cars. Given the nature of Brooklands the RAC decided it was necessary to make the course a little more like Continental tracks and so inserted two chicanes constructed of sandbanks along the pit straight. Of that outstanding entry just nine cars came to the line to start under 'Ebby' Ebblewhite's *red* starting flag. In the week

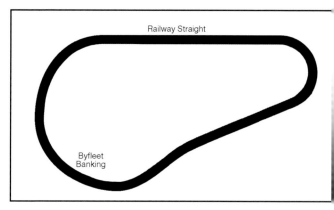

Above right: Brooklands had four circuits within its confines. When the famous and familiar oval of the Outer Circuit was opened it was unique, in that it was the only place where motor vehicles could be driven flat-out for hours on end without interruption. The Outer Circuit measured 2³⁄₄ miles; the track was steeply banked to a maximum height of 29ft at the Weybridge end and 22ft at the Byfleet end. It was run anticlockwise.

Right: In 1926 the first ever British Grand Prix was run at Brooklands and the event was repeated in 1927. In order to give the track a 'Continental' feel, two chicanes were inserted in the Finishing Straight and are here represented by the white marks.

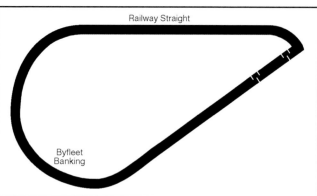

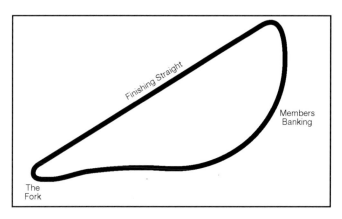

Left: With the retirement of Col Lindsay Lloyd as Clerk of the Course in 1930, the position passed to A. Percy Bradley, one of whose innovations was the Mountain Circuit illustrated here. This fast and furious circuit measured a mile and a quarter and was run clockwise and consisted of the start on the Finishing Straight, a right-hander round the Members' Banking, then right again at The Fork and back on to the straight. During the year of the new circuit's inauguration each of the Brooklands Automobile Racing Club's events contained one Mountain Handicap race: the Mountain lap record was established by Raymond Mays in an ERA in 1936 at 84.31mph. The last ever race on the Mountain Circuit was won by the well-known band leader Billy Cotton.

Below left: Until 1937 Brooklands was unchallenged as the only motor racing circuit on the British mainland but in that year Donington Park and Crystal Palace were opened. The Brooklands Automobile Racing Club faced up to this new challenge and decided to construct a new circuit which would provide the maximum road racing track possible without intruding upon the sewage farm or the Outer and Mountain Circuits. The result was the Campbell Circuit which was designed by and named after Sir Malcolm Campbell who was a national hero at the time. The new circuit was run anticlockwise and the lap record was set by Raymond Mays in 1939 driving a blown 2-litre ERA at 77.79mph.

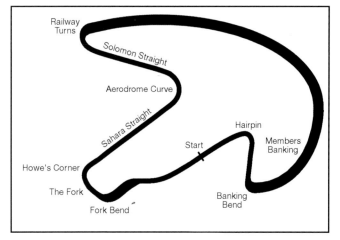

preceding the race three brand-new Talbots arrived from the Suresnes factory of Sunbeam-Talbot-Darracq and Louis Delage sent three of his cars freshly rebuilt at Courbevoie. The remaining three starters were Captain Malcolm Campbell in a Bugatti 39A, Captain George Eyston's Aston Martin Anzani and Major Frank Halford's Halford Special which consisted of his own engine mounted in an Aston Martin chassis.

The race was run over 110 laps of the circuit, a distance of just under 288 miles, and was won in 4hr 56sec by the Delage of

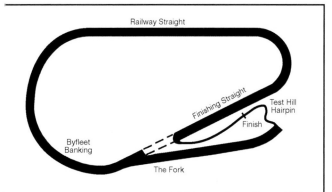

Above: This 3.369-mile circuit was used for the first 'International Trophy' which was probably the first race to have a rolling start in England. The pilot car was driven by John Cobb with Capt George Eyston acting as starter: the competitors were lined up on the Old Finishing Straight and at three o'clock the pilot car moved off, leading the field straight across the Fork on to Byfleet Banking and Railway Straight, where they would have been doing approximately 100mph. When the pilot was roughly halfway along the straight the starting signal was given. Once the race was under way, cars took a right on to the Old Finishing Straight then left it by taking a sharp left hairpin on to the Campbell Circuit Straight, followed by the Test Hill Hairpin and a tricky right at the junction of the road circuit and the outer track.

Right: This poster assures potential spectators that no race will be longer than six laps. This was an attraction? *Author's collection*

Robert Senechal and Louis Wagner at 71.61mph. Second (almost 10 *minutes* behind) was Campbell from the Delage of Robert Benoist (who was executed in Buchenwald concentration camp in 1944) and André Dubonnet. The fastest lap was set by Sir Henry O'Neil de Hane Segrave at 85.99mph in a Talbot. All the Talbots had been painted green for the occasion.

Encouraged by the success of 1926 the RAC accepted 2 October the following year as the date to run the second British Grand Prix. On this occasion it was to be run over 125 laps of the circuit making a race distance of 327 miles. Sixteen entries were received; there were three works entries from Automobiles Delage, six Bugattis (including three works entries from Molsheim), three Fiats, two of Parry Thomas's Specials (which had been scratched the year before), a front-wheel-drive Alvis and the Indianapolis-winning single-seater Duesenberg driven by George Souders. Sadly, this splendid entry was depleted when the Fiats did not come over and the Alvis and Duesenberg scratched.

The start of the Grand Prix was scheduled for noon and the competitors left the start line on the Railway Straight at the drop of the red flag in drizzle under a grey sky on a wet track. It did not turn out to be much of a race; in fact it was a Delage benefit with the cars finishing in race number sequence, Benoist (No 2) winning in 3hr 49min 14.6sec at 85.59mph from Edmond Bourlier (No 3) and Albert Divo (No 4). Fourth was Louis Chiron in a Bugatti; thus ended the two-year 1.5-litre Grand Prix Formula on a very low note

and England was not to see another Grand Prix for eight years when the Donington Grand Prix was run in 1935.

If that was the end of Grand Prix racing at Brooklands it was most certainly not the end of the circuit for mighty feats were enacted thereon. Not surprisingly English Racing Automobiles were a part of the Brooklands scene from 1935 to 1939 but the only man ever to take one of them into one of the Outer Circuit races was St John Horsfall. While the Surrey track might have remained the home of British motor racing throughout the 1930s it had to share the limelight with Donington Park and Crystal Palace.

The winds of war sounded its death-knell and shortly after the commencement of hostilities Brooklands was taken over as an aircraft establishment. From the earliest days Brooklands had been an important aviation centre, flying taking place from inside the circuit since 1910, and by 1939 Vickers and Hawker were churning out Wellington bombers and Hurricane fighters, both of which were so important to Britain during the war. The track was fatally mutilated by the Byfleet Banking being cut in two to allow traffic in from Oyster Lane.

ROAD RACING AT BROOKLANDS

WEYBRIDGE

SATURDAY, JULY 10

START 3 P.M.
Admission - 3/6
Children - - 2/-

Cars to Enclosure 5/-
Cars to Car Park 2/6

Combined Rail and Admission
Tickets at all main S.R. Stations

Programme includes **GRAND 'NATIONAL' RACE** for Prizes value £350
Also
Long & Short Handicaps
No Race longer than 6 laps

old banked track and the one in four Test Hill. Many of the original buildings have been restored and the Motoring Village includes Malcolm Campbell's workshop which now displays historic Brooklands racing cars and motor cycles. The Museum also has a collection of over 30 aircraft. It is open from Tuesday to Sunday and Bank Holidays and regularly hosts events sponsored by motor clubs.

The following track records will be held in perpetuity: Outer Circuit, 2.767 miles; John Cobb — Napier-Railton at 143.44mph set on 7 October 1935 in a car designed by Reid Railton in 1933 and built within the circuit at the premises of Thomson & Taylor. Mountain Circuit, 1.17 miles; Raymond Mays — ERA at 84.3mph. Campbell Circuit, 2.267 miles; Raymond Mays — ERA at 77.79mph.

Left: A poster by the great Gordon Crosby publicising the first long-distance race in Britain, the Double Twelve, the breaking of the race into two 12-hour parts necessitated by the restriction on night racing at Brooklands.

Below: Roy Nockolds' work, showing two cars on the banking giving a good impression of speed.
  Author's collection

Upon the cessation of hostilities it was found that the ravages of time had had a serious effect on the 40-plus-year-old concrete on which there had been precious little maintenance and the bill for repairs in 1946 was considered insuperable. A bid was accepted from Vickers Armstrong and Brooklands was lost to the sport for ever.

That was not, however, the end of the Brooklands story. In 1967 a rally was held to celebrate the Diamond Jubilee of the circuit which attracted several hundred historic vehicles and as a result the Brooklands Society was formed to perpetuate the history of the first motor course in the world. In 1991 Brooklands Museum opened on 30 acres of the original 1907 circuit. It features the most historic and steepest section of the

BROUGH
STIRLING'S FIRST WIN?

Brough lies in what used to be known as the East Riding of Yorkshire on the north bank of the Humber, the main straight running parallel to the river some 10 miles west of Kingston Upon Hull. The racing was organised by Blackburn Welfare Motor Club and the Northern Centre of the British Racing and Sports Car Club, competition taking place from 1949 to 1957. The first meeting was a combined car and motor cycle event on Sunday, 10 April 1949. The Formula III lap record was 64mph in 1956 and 65.81mph in 1957. The circuit length was 1.17 miles and managed to cram in no less than 10 bends and corners of considerable variety and a half-mile straight.

Brough's main claim to fame is probably that Stirling Moss recorded his first circuit win there and it also saw the debut of his Kieft; Don Parker was also a regular competitor.

Right: This is the programme cover from the first combined car and motorcycle race meeting at Brough aerodrome. It is interesting to note that the races for the 500cc cars were organised by the '500 Club'.

Below right: This is the original Brough circuit. As no map has been found with the start/finish line marked, it has been assumed that it was in the same position as on the later circuit, approximately one-third of the way along The Runway Straight, so named because it occupied a large amount of the main runway. The Club Bend was the first corner, being two 90° rights separated by a short straight leading on to the Perimeter Straight. This was followed by the second longest straight on the track, which led to a 90° right followed by The Hairpin, a 180° left and another 90° right on to a short straight; this led to Paddock and Shrubbery Bends. There then followed a sharp right and a short straight followed by Welton Bend and thus back to the start and finish line.

Bottom right: This is the second and more familiar circuit at Brough aerodrome. The Runway Straight was somewhat longer than on the first circuit and ended in the Runway Harpin, a 180° right on to a straight which returned parallel to the Runway Straight then to the left-hand Brough Bend and a short straight leading to the right-hand Perimeter Bend, thus eliminating the Hairpin of the earlier circuit. The remainder of the circuit was as the original.

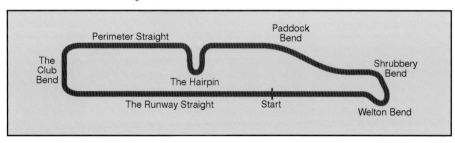

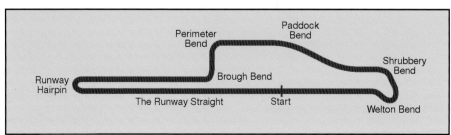

OFFICIAL PROGRAMME

BLACKBURN WELFARE
MOTOR CLUB

(OPEN TO CENTRE)

ROAD RACE MEETING
FOR
MOTOR CYCLES & CARS

BROUGH AERODROME
Sunday, 10th April, 1949

R.A.C. Permit No. B. 44   A.C.U. Permit No. D. 19

The Races for 500cc Cars are organised in co-operation with the "500" Club.

WARNING

Motor Racing is dangerous. You are present at this meeting entirely at your own risk, and admission is subject to the condition that all persons having any connection with the promotion or conduct of the meeting, including the owners of the land, are absolved from all liability in respect of personal injury to you or damage to your property, howsoever caused.

CADWELL PARK
THE WORLD'S MOST PICTURESQUE RACING CIRCUIT

The story of this Lincolnshire circuit, situated near Louth, has its roots back in 1926 when Mr Mansfield Wilkinson bought the land on which it stands with a view to using it for a very different sport — shooting. However, his son Charles was a little more 'modern' in his outlook, taking a healthy interest in the technology of motorcycling, and he formed the Louth & District Motorcycle Club. From this, Charles persuaded his father to let him run the first motorcycle racing in 1934 but it was not until the circuit was lengthened to 1¼ miles in 1952, with the extension to Mansfield Corner, that Formula III cars were sometimes included in motorcycle race meetings. This extension was later to become the stock car circuit. In August 1961 the circuit was increased by another mile to 2¼ miles after Charles Wilkinson had purchased some adjoining land, and it fell to the British Racing & Sports Car Club to run the first proper car race meeting at Cadwell Park in May 1962.

The new track was officially opened by Tony Brooks who conducted his father around it in a 1958 Ferrari Testa Rossa. The first day's competition consisted of seven 10-lap races, the lap record at the end of the day standing at 1min 44sec at a speed of 77.88mph to the credit of Brian Hart in a Formula Junior Lotus-Ford who won that race by 16sec.

Cadwell Park eventually passed into the ownership of Grovewood Securities and over the years the circuit has hosted race meetings for all forms of motor racing seen on British circuits, with the exception of Formula One. As the 20th century drew to a close, ownership of the circuit passed to the Octagon Group upon its purchase of Brands Hatch Leisure.

Cadwell Park is still in regular use for Club Racing, with all of the major Clubs promoting meetings there throughout the season, but it does seem unlikely that it will again host a major meeting. The longevity of the lap record bears witness to this! At the close of the 2000 season the outright lap record stands to the credit of Formula 3 driver Enrique Mansilla in 1min 23.4sec at a speed of 93.57mph. It was set on 20 June 1982!

Ronnie Peterson was ever spectacular and here he gives the March 693 an outing in the International Formula 3 race at Cadwell Park on 28 September 1969 apparently oblivious to the fact the right rear tyre has acquired a puncture. This was the first ever race for a March car. *Mike Dixon*

Top: Formula Three has undoubtedly been the breeding ground of some great drivers over the years; on 23 June 1978 Nelson Piquet passes The Cottage at the wheel of a Ralt RT1 in the Formula Three Championship at Cadwell Park. The Cottage is now consigned to history, having been demolished some time ago. *Mike Dixon*

Above: Nigel Mansell takes his Unipart-sponsored March 793 around Cadwell's Hairpin on 17 June 1979 in a round of the Vandervell Formula Three Championship. *Mike Dixon*

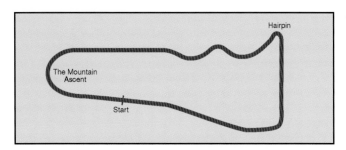

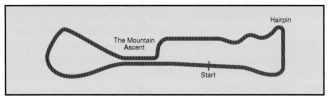

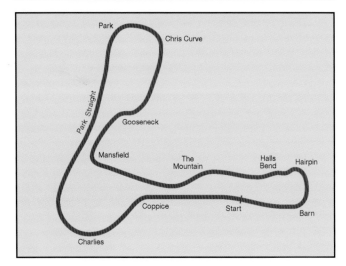

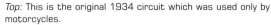

Top: This is the original 1934 circuit which was used only by motorcycles.

Centre: In 1953 the circuit was extended and Formula III cars occasionally competed in motorcycle meetings.

Above: 1961 saw the circuit extended further to 2.17 miles and cars then regularly competed at the Lincolnshire circuit. At the time of writing Cadwell Park encompasses three circuits within its confines — the Full Circuit, the Club Circuit and the Woodlands Circuit. From the start line the track sweeps left uphill at Coppice and continues to climb through Charlies, a long right-hander which almost takes competitors through 180°. There then follows Park Straight, which has a gentle left-hand bend in it, followed by Park and Chris Curves which combine to make another 180° right turn; a short 'almost straight' leads to the right and left of the Gooseneck followed by a sharp drop and Mansfield with a more than a 90° left. Two short straights with a left flick between them take the circuit to The Mountain which is another steep climb followed by the right, left, right Hall Bends and the right-hand Hairpin. The final corner is Barn, which leads downhill to the start and finish line. Cadwell Park is demanding, narrow and beloved of drivers. It also has the, probably unique, distinction of making drivers car-sick — it's not unknown for a competitor to pull off and be physically ill!

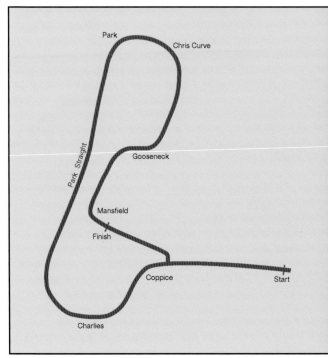

Left: The Club Circuit measures 1.476 miles and excludes the Mountain section but retains the start line of the Full Circuit. The Finish line is situated just after Mansfield and the circuit then takes a 90° right at Coppice. The Club Circuit is the only one currently in use in England which has the start and finish lines situated in different places. The Woodlands Circuit consists of the Mountain section and is used by motorcycles and occasionally karts so does not feature in this book.

Above: The picturesque nature of Cadwell Park is well illustrated in this view from the Vintage Sports Car Club's meeting on 28 August 1988. A. Pugh's 1928 Frazer-Nash Super Sports is leading the field past the start and finish line in the five-lap Handicap race for Frazer-Nash and GN chain-driven cars. It goes without saying that all of these venerable cars are still being campaigned regularly as the new century dawns. *Mike Dixon*

Right: What could possibly be nicer than having racing cars passing your front door on a regular basis? Taken from the garden of The Cottage on 15 May 1988, at the Historic Sports Car Club Meeting held at Cadwell Park on that day, this picture shows James Conyers' 1950 Bond Formula III (a great rarity, being a front-engined 500cc car) leading Chris Alford's 1100cc Formula Junior Lotus 22 which dates from 1962. They were competing in the Lenham Storage Formula Junior Championship. *Mike Dixon*

CASTLE COMBE
NEARLY 50 YEARS UNCHANGED

astle Combe nestles in Wiltshire and is a very picturesque English village — it is also home to another circuit which owes its origins to the RAF as it too started life as World War 2 airfield. Castle Combe is unique in that it is the only circuit in the country which retained its original configuration for 48 years, although the position of the start/finish line has moved on more than one occasion.

The life of Castle Combe as an airfield was seven years and four months; it opened in May 1941 and was decommissioned in September 1948. The tarmac for the perimeter track (which now forms the circuit) was laid in April 1943 and from

4 November that year it was a satellite for Babdown Farm which was a grass runway airfield. Castle Combe was a training airfield and Airspeed Oxfords were used. At an unconfirmed date a Stirling bomber carrying five magnetic mines crash-landed on the airfield; two of the mines exploded causing extensive damage to the ground installations and halting training for three days. Strangely it was not until March 1945 that the airfield became fully serviceable, just two months before VE Day, and the last plane was flown out in July 1945 by Sqn Ldr Ted Cowling. The station was then unoccupied for a year until July 1946 when it was used by Polish refugees who occupied huts in what is now the Paddock until June 1948. It

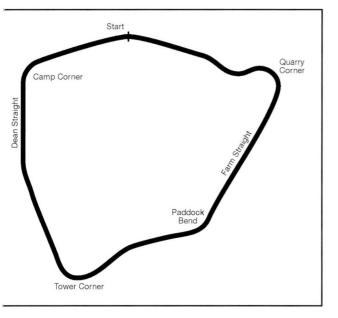

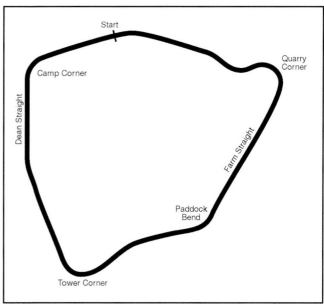

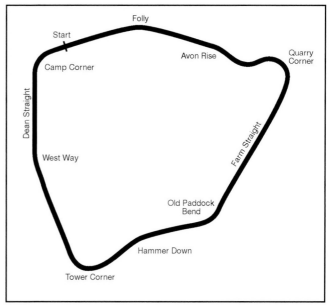

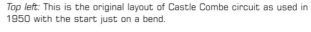

Top left: This is the original layout of Castle Combe circuit as used in 1950 with the start just on a bend.

Top: For 1951 the start/finish line had been moved back to allow a short straight before competitors had to negotiate the first bend.

Above: This is Castle Combe as it has been from 1975, until 1998, with the start/finish line moved back a considerable distance. From these three circuit maps it can be seen that the Wiltshire circuit has indeed not changed its outline at all for 48 years. Paddock Bend has become Old Paddock Bend acknowledging the fact that the site of the Paddock was relocated.

Left: A grid of nine Formula III 500cc racing cars ready to start at Castle Combe at the Easter meeting in 1950. More than 50 years on, the advertising on the start/finish banner makes interesting reading; there is a marked lack of protection for the considerable number of spectators and it is quite obvious that this was an airfield.
G. Millington collection

Moss drove an HWM and Ken Wharton an ERA. The day saw the birth of a new marque which was to do much for British prestige in International motor racing, for Kenneth McAlpine drove the very first of the A-series Connaughts (A1) into second place behind Moss. The meeting was rounded off with two sports car races and a Formule Libre event which attracted the aforementioned drivers. Brian Shawe-Taylor driving a supercharged ERA won the main race at 81.23mph and established the lap record at 1min 20.2sec at 82.6mph. The next meeting did not take place until a year later, on 6 October 1951, when Bob Gerard, also at the wheel of a 1,488cc supercharged ERA, reduced the lap record time to 1min 19.2sec at 86.25mph and won the Hastings Trophy at 81.27mph.

When the Town and Country Planning Act was introduced in 1952 the family applied for and was granted temporary planning permission to decide various levels and conditions of usage. Badly advised, this was allowed to run on for 10 years when, in fact, a Certificate of Established Usage could have been obtained for 5s — just 25p in decimal coinage! Through all of this, usage somehow became restricted to just five days a year.

In October 1952, on the fourth of the month, that man Gerard was back with a 1980cc supercharged ERA, to take nearly 3sec off the lap record leaving it at 1min 16.8sec at 86.25mph: his race average was 85.13mph.

A further year on and the scream of the V16 BRM was heard in Wiltshire as Ken Wharton won the Hastings Trophy in a Mark II car at 87.49mph and took exactly 3sec off the lap record, leaving at 1min 13.8sec, 89.77mph. Although the lap record was inexorably falling, it would be 15 years after the opening of the circuit before it exceeded 100mph and no less than 20 years before the minute was broken.

On 23 August 1954 Horace Gould and Bob Gerard, driving Cooper Bristols, respectively won the Formula One Fry Memorial Trophy at 83.56mph and the Formule Libre Hastings Trophy

was from their occupation of the site that the name of Camp Corner originates. With the departure of the Poles the site became inactive and it was disposed of in September 1948.

The land was part of the Castle Combe Estate which was owned by the Gorst family, much confusion over the ownership being caused by the fact that Katherine Gorst married three times, being originally Mrs K. R. Lysley, then Mrs K. R. Maurice and finally Mrs K. R. Thomas when she met and married the Chief Designer of Frazer-Nash and the Chief Engine Development man at Bristol Cars.

The circuit which opened in 1950 was originally administered by the family and the first meeting took place on Saturday, 8 July, the Bristol Motorcycle & Light Car Club running a 'closed to Club' event which was a joint motor cycle and car race affair. Whilst exact records of the first meeting do not survive, it is reasonably certain that the fastest race of the day was won by Tony Crook at the wheel of a 1,971cc Frazer-Nash Le Mans at a little over 75mph. The next meeting was held on 7 October when the RAC Steward was none other than Dean Delamont; drivers were 'recommended' to wear crash helmets but vizors or goggles were compulsory! It was a National meeting with races for Formula III (two heats and a final), 500cc to 1,100cc racing cars, 1,100 to 1,500cc racing cars and 1,500 to 2,500cc racing cars; in the last of these Stirling

t 86.25mph, but the lap record remained to Ken Wharton's credit.

1 October 1955 saw the first International Meeting at Castle Combe. Harry Schell drove the pre-Chapman/Costin chassis Vanwall to victory in the Formula One Avon Trophy race and the Formule Libre Empire News Trophy at 86.07mph and 86.77mph respectively. He left the lap record at exactly 90mph in 1min 13.6sec.

The Bristol & District Motor Cycle and Light Car Club had organised all of these meetings with Formula One, Two and Libre races drawing record attendances but in 1955 (following the Le Mans disaster) the RAC decreed that safety banking all around the circuit was required which the Club decided could not be afforded and racing ceased. Shortly before this the entire estate had been broken up, resulting in a major auction which included very property, house, pub, inns and shops in the village including the Manor House which is now the famous Manor House Hotel. Somewhere about the mid- to late 1950s the circuit was leased to AFN (the old Frazer Nash Cars Company) who ran the circuit as AFN Castle Combe Ltd. From 1956 to 1961 Castle Combe Circuit was used only for motorcycle races, sprints and speed trials although testing still continued.

Following negotiations by Nick Syrett, the Chief Executive of the British Racing and Sports Car Club, the Club funded the safety banking around the circuit and car racing recommenced on 9 September 1962 when Chris Summers, driving a 4.6-litre Chevrolet-engined Cooper won the Formule Libre event at 89.20mph, whilst John Taylor, driving his 1,498cc Cooper Ford, took the lap record to 92mph in exactly 1min 12sec. Summers lowered the lap record twice during the year to 1min 11.2sec at 93.03mph on 7 July and 1min 9.2sec at 95.72mph on 8 September.

The increased usage brought about the necessity of resurfacing the entire track. The first meeting on the newly resurfaced track took place on 27 July 1964 and saw the lap record fall to a sports car when Hugh Dibley (a BOAC pilot) took a 2½-litre Brabham BT8-Climax round the Combe in 1 min 6.4sec at 99.76mph. The 100mph lap was very close!

It came on 9 October 1965 when Chris Summers returned with a 5.4-litre Chevrolet V8-engined Lotus 24 (this was long before Formula 5000 was invented!) which he took round in 1 min 5.2sec at 101.59mph. 21 May 1966 saw Tony Lanfranchi driving Sid Taylor's 6-litre Chevrolet engined Lola T70 reduce the lap record to 1min 4.6sec at 102.54mph.

The Hagley & District Light Car Club ran a meeting on 20 August 1966 when Max Wilson won the Hagley 100 at 93.19mph in a 2-litre Climax-engined Brabham BT8.

AFN Castle Combe Ltd applied for 21 years planning permission (still instead of permanent) but the story was leaked and some local residents grouped together as objectors and the application before Calne & Chippenham Rural District Council was refused. AFN Castle Combe Ltd went to appeal which was heard by the Planning Inspector S. R. H. King at Corsham Town Hall from 21 to 24 May 1968. The Inspector recommended the continuation of usage limited to 19 meetings per annum between March and October but excluding International Meetings. Unfortunately, the Minister, Mr Anthony Greenwood, did not accept his Inspector's report and decided against

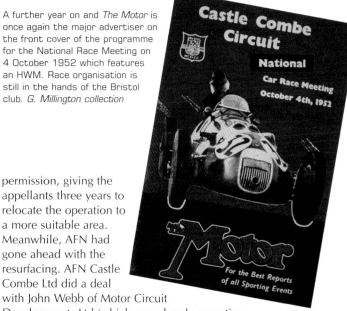

A further year on and *The Motor* is once again the major advertiser on the front cover of the programme for the National Race Meeting on 4 October 1952 which features an HWM. Race organisation is still in the hands of the Bristol club. *G. Millington collection*

permission, giving the appellants three years to relocate the operation to a more suitable area. Meanwhile, AFN had gone ahead with the resurfacing. AFN Castle Combe Ltd did a deal with John Webb of Motor Circuit Developments Ltd (which was already operating Brands Hatch, Mallory Park, Oulton Park and Snetterton) to sub-let Castle Combe for the remaining three years of the lease: this arrangement did not please Mrs Thomas who was told that the new lessee had agreed to attempt to settle the planning problems. In the event, nothing was done and when the three years were over Castle Combe looked destined to close.

In the meantime AFN had become a subsidiary of Porsche GmbH and the Porsche importers and the company was looking for much larger premises in the United Kingdom to use as the importation centre. Plans were hatched to site this facility in the circuit paddock area with the bonus of a test track on site: the fact that the site could be used for 14 days' motor racing a year had not gone unnoticed. By implementing an Article 4 Direction Order limiting the number of racing days to five per year, it was hoped to get the deal recommended to Wiltshire County Council. Whilst the Council recommended the proposal, it also ensured that permission was not granted. John Aldington was furious and Mrs Thomas outraged and it proved to be the beginning of the end between the latter and AFN.

While all of this was going on the important matter of motor racing continued and Jim Moore reduced the lap record to 1min 4.4sec one minute four point four seconds at 102.86mph, driving the Kincraft Ford (where is that glorious car now?) This record was equalled by Ron Fry's Ford GT40 on 13 July.

Two years later, on 9 May 1970, Castle Combe could claim to be the second fastest circuit in the country when Peter Gethin and Howden Ganley driving 5-litre Chevrolet-powered McLaren M10Bs finally broke the magic minute to circulate in 56.6 sec at one 117mph — a staggering increase of nearly 15mph! This was in a Formula 5000 race run as a round of the European Championship which Gethin won at 113.19mph. Within two years the race average was higher than the lap record had been. Early in 1972 AFN applied for permission to run only five days' racing a year and received a three-year permission; the company also attempted to increase the package by building up the scope of other activities, especially Dealer Demonstration days, but none was accepted.

Above: Gerry Millington negotiates Camp Corner at the Easter 1951 meeting in his works Norton-engined self-built Milliunion; such cars as this were the very epitome of early 500cc racing.
G. Millington collection

Right: In practice for the above event Gerry Millington drives without a crash helmet. *G. Millington collection*

Below: As the 1998 season drew to its close there came news that Castle Combe circuit was finally to change its outline in order to reduce the speed of competing cars. There had, sadly, been a fatality during the 1998 season when a wheel from a competing car struck a spectator so the decision was taken to make some changes. It was decided to insert two chicanes into the circuit, one a little over halfway along Farm Straight between Quarry Corner and old Paddock Bend, to be known as The Esses, and the other between Tower Corner and Westway, to be called Bobbies. Nothing stays the same for ever but Castle Combe had done well to retain its original configuration for 48 years.

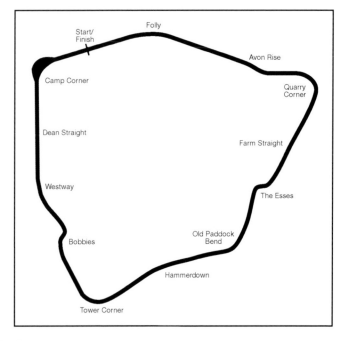

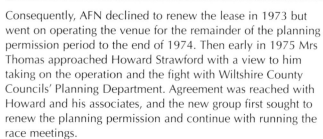

Consequently, AFN declined to renew the lease in 1973 but went on operating the venue for the remainder of the planning permission period to the end of 1974. Then early in 1975 Mrs Thomas approached Howard Strawford with a view to him taking on the operation and the fight with Wiltshire County Councils' Planning Department. Agreement was reached with Howard and his associates, and the new group first sought to renew the planning permission and continue with running the race meetings.

Under the guidance of accountant Bob Davies, AFN Castle Combe Ltd was acquired from Porsche GmbH and the company name changed to Castle Combe Circuit Ltd; a new lease was arranged with Mrs Thomas and when this was all in place the takeover was announced in mid-1975. Over a 20-year period a slowly, slowly policy of expansion of usage was followed under the guidance of Martin Chick who had joined the consortium following employment by the Wiltshire County Council and in 1979 permission was sought to establish a racing school at Castle Combe for École de Pilotage Winfield, as Mike Knight (who ran the school), wished to relocate from Goodwood. The application was refused and although an appeal was lodged which was successful, delays resulted leaving only eight months of the two years asked for, which was too little for Knight to establish an operation. As a result, the Castle Combe Racing School was instead started by Strawford, Knight and Davies.

An appeal (at which James Hunt and Howard Strawford were

(tar witnesses) in February 1981 saw the number of racing days increased to 12 from five a year and some time later, in an attempt to attract the Touring Car package to the Wiltshire circuit, an application was made to run two two-day meetings a year. As was now customary the matter went to Appeal and was won with costs; having started at just five, the total number of days usage now stands at 250!

The first 120mph lap was set on 7 July 1984 by Tony Trimmer, driving his 5.7-litre Lola T330 Chevrolet, when he circulated in 55.2sec sec and it was extended to 122.21mph in 54.2sec by Alo Lawler at the wheel of a 3-litre McLaren M30 Ford a year later on 6 July 1985.

The circuit has been considerably refurbished, massively landscaped and totally resurfaced in 1995, the company having been successful in buying the freehold from the Trustees of Castle Combe Estate. Whilst the usage is high, the circuit is well-known for its noise control. The British Racing & Sports Car Club organises all 11 days of the car racing each year, the 12th day being given over to motorcycle racing which is held in order to retain links with the sport, and the all-important track licence.

Castle Combe Circuit is still run by the Strawford family, Howard and his wife Pat having been joined by daughters Karen (and husband Graham) and Emma and Bob Davies. In 1995 Rodney Gooch joined the team as Marketing and Promotions Manager.

Castle Combe lives and thrives in spite of a Ministry of Housing and Local Government closure order! However, as 1998 drew to its close there came news that two chicanes were to be inserted in order to reduce the speed of competitors so Castle Combe lost its proud claim to never have changed.

At the end of the 2000 season the outright lap record stands to the credit of Nigel Greensall at 130.93mph; he set the record on 25 August 1997 driving his 3½-litre-engined Tyrrell 022.

Right: On 9 April 1953 Gillie Tyrer corners his C-Type Jaguar RAV450 at Castle Combe. The car is road-equipped and has the windscreen of an XK120, giving the car an unfamiliar appearance for we are more used to seeing this particular model with a low perspex racing screen.
Ferret Fotographics

Below: The start of the seventh event on Saturday, 3 April 1954 found Roy Salvadori aboard a Maserati A6GCM chatting to Jimmy Stewart who is driving a C-Type Jaguar at the time referred to as an XK120C) prior to doing battle with him. On the second row the nose of another C-Type can just be seen beside an unidentified car driven by A. P. O. Rogers, with B. Baxter's XK120 on the third row.
National Motor Museum Photographic Library

CATTERICK
RACING WHERE THE ROMANS TROD

atterick must be the only motor racing circuit in the world to be situated on a site once occupied by the Roman Legions: nearly 2,000 years ago the Catterick area was the site of the Roman army station of Cataractonium, which was on an important routeway from York to Hadrian's Wall.

Catterick was opened in 1914 as a Royal Flying Corps airfield to train pilots and to assist in the defence of northeast England. Upon the formation of the Royal Air Force on 1 April, the airfield became Royal Air Force Catterick and is thus one of the oldest military airfields in the world.

Catterick was 'discovered' as a motor racing circuit by the Darlington & District Motor Club whose first interest was in Catterick Hill within Catterick Garrison. This circuit is adjacent to the A1, just south of the village, and uses the perimeter track/airstrip-cum-training fields. The first event was a hill climb held in 1955 but racing took place on four wheels from 1958 to 1963, the first race meeting for cars taking place on 4 October 1958. There was a further meeting in 1959 on 9 September, followed by two meetings in 1960 on 3 July and 11 September, one in 1961 on 3 September, one in 1962 on 2 September and three in 1963 on 12 May, 16 June and 1 September — a grand total of eight. On each occasion permission had to be sought from the Air Ministry to use the airfield. A three-hour team race was run on one occasion but it is likely that no single-seaters competed at Catterick. The main event at Catterick was the 'Battle of Britain Trophy Meeting' which was won on 3 September 1961 by Jimmy Blumer in his Cooper Monaco; he won the second heat and final and just to make it a good day won the 15-lap race for Sports Racing Cars

Racing came to an end on 1 September 1963 when a Lotus Seven spun on a corner adjacent to the main road, passed through the hedge and ended up on the southbound carriageway of the A1.

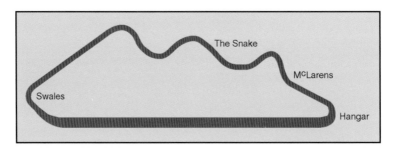

It has not proved possible to obtain a map of the circuit at Catterick and this outline has been reconstructed from an aerial photograph of the airfield and descriptions of the circuit gleaned from contemporary magazine reports. It was 1.6 miles in length and, unlike most airfield tracks, climbed and fell. The exact location of the start and finish line is not known but it must be assumed to have been on the main straight which was on the main runaway and ran at almost 90° to the main A1 Great North Road. From the hairpin at Swales, the circuit made a winding climb to The Snake to descend via swinging left- and right-handers to a wide bend at McLarens which was followed by a short straight and Hangar Straight before returning to the main straight.

The motorcycle circuit at Catterick was a very different animal.

CROFT
THE ONE THAT CAME BACK

R AF Croft near Darlington in North Yorkshire was one of the most northerly airfields of World War 2. The site was chosen because of its unique vantage point in terms of air travel — follow the River Tees and turn left! Built for Bomber Command, construction work commenced in 1940 following the compulsory purchase by the government of 160 acres of farmland, the airfield being developed into a standard bomber example with three concrete runways. It opened in October 1941 as a satellite station for nearby RAF Middleton St George with several RAF squadrons based there flying a variety of different bomber aircraft, including Wellington, Whitley and Stirling bombers. On 1 October 1942 they were joined by No 419 Squadron Royal Canadian Air Force which then moved on to Middleton St George on 9 November. No 419 Squadron was replaced by No 427 (Lion) Squadron RCAF which formed on 7 November 1942. Croft was then transferred to No 6 Group (RCAF) on 1 January 1943 and thereafter was active throughout the war, being home to No 431 (Iroquois) and No 434 (Bluenose) Squadrons RCAF who flew Halifax and Lancaster bombers. After VE Day the Canadians returned home and Croft saw very little activity until being brought back into use in the autumn of 1945, finally closing for flying in the summer of 1946 when it became a redundant satellite airfield and was abandoned by the RAF.

Some form of motorsport had taken place at Croft since 1927, interrupted by the matters referred to above. In 1947 a lease was taken on the airfield by a local businessman, John Neashem, who set about rallying support for what was to become the Darlington & District Aero Club and the inaugural meeting was held on 2 August but after only five years the club began to lose momentum, the members choosing to use other nearby airfields.

The Darlington & District Motor Club (DDMC) had been reformed in 1946 and ran some small Club motor and motorcycle races in 1948 but it was in 1950 that 'proper' racing arrived: the Royal Automobile Club having approved the circuit in the March (according to a report in the *Northern Echo* on the 25th), the first meeting took place on Saturday, 6 May but with the proviso that on Sundays practice could not commence until noon so as not to interfere with the local church services. It would appear that the first meeting was devoted entirely to sports cars. In 1958 the circuit was used for a Special Stage of the RAC Rally of Great Britain.

With some evidence of contact on the near-side front of the car, former Formula One star Gabrielle Tarquini in Honda No 10 leads the field past the new race administration building at Croft whilst contesting a round of the British Touring Car Championship on 29 June 1997. *Tony Todd*

The lease expired in the early 1960s and in 1962 half of the airfield was bought at public auction by a consortium, led by Bruce Ropner and a shipping company based in Darlington, who appointed a residential manager. He was L. R. Dixon Cade who had charge of a clubroom, bar and other social facilities, the Darlington & District Motor Club meeting there every Friday. Some 18 months after acquiring the site, planning permission was granted to build a circuit which was completed in July 1964 (the original racing 'control tower' was a converted lorry) and Bruce Ropner had the pleasure of driving his Jaguar XK150 around his own circuit.

The main attraction each year was the Battle of Britain Meeting which was organised by the DDMC in conjunction with the local Royal Air Force Association Branch. In 1978 the meeting was officially opened by Patrick Tambay.

Being the only racing circuit in the northeast, Croft enjoyed a great deal of success, operating under the title Croft Autodrome, with the racing being organised by the British Racing & Sports Car Club, the British Automobile Racing Club, Batley & District Motor Club, the Yorkshire Sports Car Club and the Nottingham Sports Car Club. During that time the circuit was host to complete novices and to World Champions in the persons of Denny Hulme and James Hunt. Niki Lauda has raced at Croft and, in latter days, Damon Hill.

By 1970 the Guards International Trophy was run for Formula Three cars with victory going to Carlos Pace who went to become a Grand Prix star with Brabham, but as the decade wore on Croft faced increasingly strong competition from the southern circuits and as Brands Hatch and Silverstone strengthened their grasp on the International events the Tees-side circuit began to stagnate.

In the early 1980s ownership changed, the major shareholder being a local farmer Mr George Shields, but in 1981 tarmac racing ceased. Croft turning its attention to Rallycross, at which it was brilliantly successful.

From 1994 media attention at Croft was higher than ever and the owner, Kate Chaytor-Norris, decided to return her circuit to tarmac racing. The Renaissance Season was 1995 when a number of Club meetings were run and the Darlington & District Motor Club was given the reins to run a race meeting for the first time in 14 years.

Kate then set her sights on hosting rounds of the Auto Trader RAC Touring Car Championship. This needed some major improvements and in a little under six months there was a major transformation, the circuit being extended to 2.127 miles, 60% of the new circuit being built on old runways, with a completely new control tower, at a cost of a £1½ million. And the touring cars came in June 1997. The circuit is currently operated by Croft Classic & Historic Motorsport Ltd.

As the 20th century closed, the outright lap record stands to the credit of Luciano Burti at the wheel of a Formula Three Dallara F399 in 1min 14.551sec at a speed of 102.71mph. The record was set on 6 June 1999.

Left: On 11 July 1971 Terry Croker, driving a Lola T210, leads Peter Hanson (Taydec FVC M42), followed by Brian Martin in his Martin BM8-FVA. The entrant of the leading car is Brian Hart who is well-known in today as the builder of Formula One engines. *National Motor Museum Photographic Library*

Below: This the first circuit at Croft, measuring 1.64 miles. The start and finish line were located on a straight leading to a sharp right named Tower Bend; a straight then led to The Esses and the right flick of Barcroft and the 90° right of Sunny Corner. Railway Straight was the longest straight on the circuit, which ended in the left-hand Spa Bend; a short straight brought competitors to Oxo Bend, a long right, followed by a short straight and a right flick before the chicane and the end of the lap.

Right: The 1970s saw some changes at Croft: The Esses were renamed the Jim Clark Esses in honour of the great Scottish World Champion and Hangar Complex was inserted along Railway Straight. Oxo Bend had gone completely, as had Spa Bend, which was renamed Hawthorn Bend after the first English World Champion, Mike Hawthorn; it was still a left-hand corner but turned right much short of what had been Oxo Bend before heading for the chicane. This circuit measured 1.8 miles.

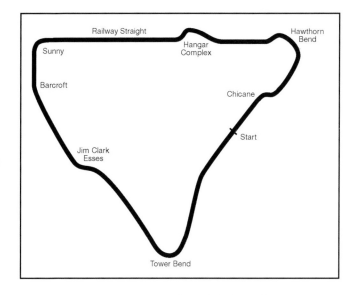

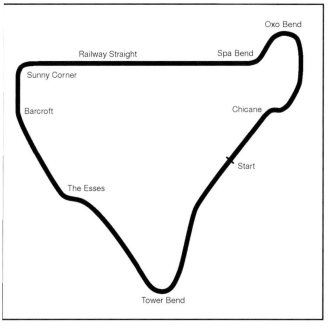

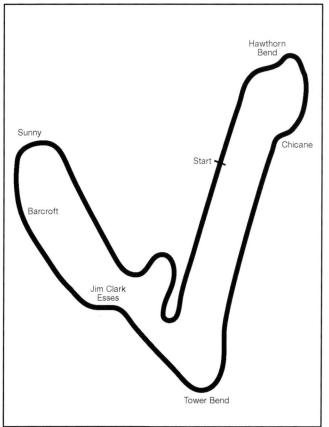

Right: 1997 saw a dramatic change in the layout of Croft: the track between Sunny and Hawthorn Bend has gone completely to be replaced by a new and exciting section which has taken the circuit length out to 2.1 miles. Sunny is now two right-handers leading on to a straight, followed by sharp left and right corners and a very tight left hairpin leading on to the pit straight, which has the start and finish line a little over halfway along it and which ends in the new corner Clervaux close to where Spa Bend was on the original circuit. It is best described by the great Derek Bell who says of the new circuit: 'A flying start down the pit lane straight getting up to top gear at around 120mph, then down to third at Clervaux doing about 70mph, third through Hawthorn Bend and fourth through the chicane and back up to top gear down the back straight; you do about 140mph down here. It's quite bumpy under braking and relatively tricky to control down the gears down to second at Tower Bend. You need a good exit here to build momentum up towards the Jim Clark Esses, flat in fifth, then sixth up to Barcroft, flat through there in sixth for the courageous, then down to third for the tricky two right-handers in and out of Sunny. You make the first one in third and second in fourth, you need to keep your speed flowing in this difficult

section, then fourth down to the tricky left-hander, brake mid-corner, take third, second and then turn into the tight right-hander: it's tricky as you have to change direction from left to right and you need a good exit for traction. Into third out of the corner and down to first for the hairpin. You then need a good exit to build up speed for the straight.

'The best overtaking places are into the first corner, but watch you don't take the corner too fast; then under braking down the back straight for Tower Bend and at the hairpin of course, you keep with someone through the fast sections, there are plenty of chances to dive past him at the slow corners.'

CRYSTAL PALACE
LONDON'S OWN CIRCUIT

An early programme from the Crystal Palace road circuit dated June 1938 featuring the London Grand Prix: in a simple two-colour layout the cover features both cars and motorcycles and includes one of the towers which were a feature of the circuit before World War 2. The towers were demolished shortly after the outbreak of hostilities as it was feared that they were too distinctive a landmark for enemy bombers. *Author's collection*

A motor racing venue within the confines of a major city is something of a rarity, but London's own circuit at Crystal Palace can claim that distinction and is probably unique in that it has seen all forms of motorised competition on two, three and four wheels. First there were motorcycles and combinations, then came speedway racing, followed by cars and motorcycles on a tarmac service and eventually karts.

Racing first took place there in 1902 when the Motor Cycling Club held an event which was reported in *The Autocar* of 1 March. Competition in some form then took place at Crystal Palace from 1927 until 1972. Brooklands was well established when London Motor Sports Ltd was formed with the ambition of seeing motorcycle road racing on a closed circuit within the capital. This was the dream of Fred Mockford and Cecil Smith and some fellow enthusiasts who had a one-mile course laid out over the paths of the park. It was well planned for racing as all potholes were filled, the bends tarred and a concrete abutment added but the remainder of the track was still loose-surfaced although it was hard-packed.

A Sunday morning early in 1927 was set aside for riders to practise and evaluate the new circuit. They emerged full of enthusiasm and 21 May was set as the date for the inaugural Crystal Palace Road Racing Meeting when 10 races were run before a crowd of 10,000 Londoners who paid their admission fee of one shilling plus tuppence in tax — about 6p in decimal coinage. The track was widened for the second meeting which was staged on 6 August, entrants paying an entry fee of 5s (25p) for all events except the Crystal Palace Solo Championship the entry fee for which was one guinea (£1.05). Public attendance on this occasion was 16,000 who saw only racing as practice had taken place on two evenings and an afternoon preceding the event. By the end of the year attendances had risen to 17,000, a figure which many circuits would be happy to contemplate today. Remembering that it was a loose surface it is remarkable, judging from the photographs published at the time, how few of the riders wore goggles. Perhaps they were bred tougher in those days!

Path racing continued in 1928 and 1929 and at a meeting in July cars made their first racing appearance at Crystal Palace when two Austin Sevens driven by the Steward and Judge of the meeting ran a light-hearted race, victory going to F. Pike at a speed of 22.08mph. Both cars carried passengers to assist with the cornering. At the August meeting an event was run for six cars which consisted of a Singer, four Austins and an MG Midget but just how cars managed to pass on a track which was but 12ft wide in places does not really bear thinking about.

Cars did not appear in competition again at Crystal Palace until the tarmac-surfaced circuit was opened. The final motorcycle path race took place on 2 July 1934 although it had not been planned that way. Overlapping the path races was another form of two-wheeled racing which was imported from Australia and which soon attracted a large following throughout the country — speedway. At Christmas 1927 Lionel Wills of the W. D. & H. O. Wills tobacco company returned home from the Antipodes full of enthusiasm for the new sport and sold the idea to Mockford and Smith. These entrepreneurs obtained the agreement of the Trustees of Crystal Palace to install a 440yd oval around the outside of the already extant football pitch which had the necessary grandstands in place. The cinder track was laid by Richard Crittall Ltd. The first speedway meeting at Crystal Palace was held on a very wet 28 May 1928 which did not deter 20,000 people from turning out to pay their admission fees of 5s (25p) for adults and 6d (2½p) for children. It soon became the vogue to give the teams nicknames and the Crystal Palace team became known (not too surprisingly) as the Glaziers.

The first proper motor race meeting took place here in 1937, and the last in September 1973. The first car race meeting organised by the Road Racing Club was on 24 April 1937, the main event being for the Coronation Trophy for which 20 cars had been entered. These were six ERAs including the works cars of Pat Fairfield and Raymond Mays, three Maseratis, Altas, MGs, Rileys and a Bugatti. The organisers decided to follow Continental practice and run the event as two 20-lap heats and a 30-lap (60-mile) final. The ERAs had set fastest times in practice and victory in the first heat went to Fairfield at 52.63mph from Charlie Brackenbury in his 4CM Maserati and the Honourable Peter Aitken's Frazer-Nash. ERAs took the first three places in the second heat, Mays winning from Austin Dobson and Peter Whitehead. Pat Fairfield won the final in 1hr 7min 8.8sec from Dobson and Robin Hanson's Maserati 6CM. Fairfield set the fastest laps and the first lap record at 54.59mph in 2min 12sec.

The London Grand Prix, run on 17 July, was the first appearance at the circuit of Prince 'B. Bira' and the event was again run as two heats and a final, the meeting being augmented with a sidecar race. After Major Goldie Gardner

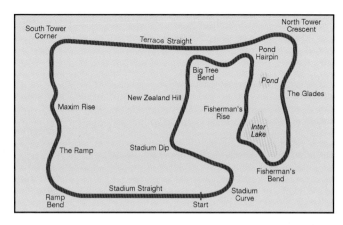

Above: Crystal Palace had three different circuits during its lifetime: this is the original, measuring 2 miles, which was used from its opening until after World War 2.

Below: The second heat of the Coronation Trophy on 24 April 1937: Raymond Mays leads Arthur Dobson (both ERA mounted, in works cars) through Stadium Dip on his way to victory. Mays won the 20-lap, 40-mile race in 45min 40.9sec at 52.63mph but lasted only seven laps in the Final. Note the twin rear wheels on both cars, used to improve traction. *National Motor Museum Photographic Library*

had given a demonstration in one of his record-breaking cars the first heat was won by Raymond Mays from Ian Connell (ERA) and Percy Maclure's Riley. Bira won the second heat driving ERA R2B *Romulus* from Dobson and Reg Parnell driving an MG and set a new lap record at 56.47mph. The final over 15 laps was won by Bira in 33min 3.7sec, finishing just over a minute ahead of Connell with Maclure third.

On 14 August a Grand Composite Meeting was held with races for bicycles, cars and motorcycles. The 30-lap car race rounded off the day's racing in slippery conditions; victory went to Bert Hadley driving one of the works supercharged Austin 750s from Bira's Maserati (after he had had an 'off') with Reg Parnell third in his MG.

9 October saw Crystal Palace host its biggest event to date in the shape of the International Imperial Trophy Race. History was written on that day for it was the occasion of the very first outside television broadcast of a motor race, the BBC devoting much of Saturday afternoon to it at a time when television was very much the prerogative of the wealthy and broadcasting was little more than four hours per day. It was, of course, a live transmission and there were four visits.

While the Silver Arrows never actually raced at Crystal Palace, it was on this occasion that Richard Seaman demonstrated the mighty 645hp Mercedes-Benz W125. There was a truly impressive entry of 21 cars for the Imperial Trophy and it was undoubtedly of an International flavour having attracted entries from Scuderia Ambrosiana who had sent three Maseratis for Count Trossi, Count 'Johnny' Lurani and Luigi Villoresi. There were three more Maseratis for Hanson, Aitken and Hyde and six ERAs to be driven by Mays, Dobson, Bira, Connell, Whitehead and Martin. Sadly, Pat Fairfield was missing; he had been killed at Le Mans. The race followed the now-established Crystal Palace format of two heats and a final but on this occasion the race was divided into three handicap classes with the works Austins, the MGs and Raymond Mays' ERA in Class A but the last-named became a non-starter when his 1,100cc engine expired in practice. Class B consisted of the rest of the entry except for Hyde's eight-cylinder 3-litre Maserati which was alone on scratch in Class C. Class A received a 50sec start and Class B 10sec.

The first heat went to Percy Maclure in his Riley from Dobson's ERA by just one second, with Lurani third. The second heat saw Trossi win from Martin and Bira, with Charlie Goodacre's little Austin fourth. Twenty cars came to the grid — by far the largest number yet to start at the Palace. The race was over 15 laps and saw Bira and Dobson fighting for the lead throughout. Dobson finally won by 0.6sec and Goodacre was third, with Villoresi fourth. So ended the first motor racing season at Crystal Palace. This was a time when car ownership was very small and motor racing very much a rich man's pastime, and the London circuit had brought the sport to the man in the street — and he had taken it to his heart.

Despite the gathering war clouds over Europe in 1938, the Road Racing Club announced there would be five combined car and motorcycle events and one solely for motorcycles, with bicycles being abandoned for the time being. The season began on 2 April with two heats and a final for the Coronation Trophy; Bira won the final in his ERA from Johnny Wakefield

driving a Maserati, with Dobson's ERA third by a second. The race was covered by radio commentary on the BBC World Service. At the 21 May meeting the cars competed for the Sydenham Trophy; George Abecassis seemed certain of victory in his Alta until a spin nearly put him in the lake and the lead was inherited by John Smith who went on to win from Bira and Maclure. In the process of his chase for the lead, Bira set the fastest lap at 56.6mph. The next meeting on the 1938 calendar was the London Grand Prix on 25 June which attracted entries from across the Channel in the shape of two blue Simca-Fiats to be driven by Anne Itier and no less than Amédée Gordini who was later to become famous as a constructor of racing cars bearing his name.

Bira and Dobson won their respective heats and Bira took the final from Dobson by 14sec, with Duddon-Fletcher's MG third and the Alta of George Abecassis fourth. The day was rounded off by another Palace 'first', a five-lap Ladies' Race which was won by Mrs Lace in an Alta from Kay Petre's Riley and Mrs Thomas in a Delahaye. On balance, the cars were more popular than the motorcycles at Crystal Palace; the Road Racing Club was ever-watchful of attendance figures and decided to drop the sidecar event from the car programmes and replace it with a sports car race with a Le Mans-type start.

The next meeting was on 13 August when there were 21 entries, 19 of which ran on alcohol fuel. Arthur Dobson won in his Riley from the Alta of Abecassis. In the following Crystal Palace Cup Abecassis won, leading home the ERAs of Tony Rolt, Wakefield and Dobson. The final meeting of the year was the second running of the Imperial Trophy which the BBC again televised on 8 October but the events in Munich cast a shadow over the meeting. Despite these problems the organisers had attracted a good International entry and the prospect of a Match Race between the arch-rivals Bira and Dobson promised much for the crowd. The Match Race started the proceedings at 2.30pm; the two opponents both held the lap record and were driving identical 1.5-litre ERAs but *Romulus* punctured a rear tyre on the third lap and Bira was out of contention. However, in the main race, the Siamese Prince was unstoppable, winning the first heat from Abecassis, Wakefield and Connell. Dobson took the second heat from the MG of Cuddon-Fletcher, the ERA of Tony Rolt and the Scuderia Ambrosiana Maserati driven by Eugenio Minetti. It rained for the final, so some of the competitors fitted twin rear wheels; this ruse accompanied by its independent rear suspension gave the Alta of George Abecassis the edge over the beam-axled ERAs for he just beat Bira, with Minetti third and Rolt fourth. Another season had come to an end and the organisers looked forward to the next. They were less than popular when they announced the abandonment of motorcycle racing entirely to concentrate upon cars.

The new season began on 15 April 1939 with the eighth running of the Stanley Cup. This event had previously been contested at Brooklands and Donington Park; on this occasion the racing was not run by the Road Racing Club but by a consortium of Frazer-Nash, the BMW Car Club and the Vintage Sports Car Club. For the first time the Link Circuit was to be used for a car race. The entries ranged form a 747cc Austin Seven to a 2-litre Benz with a wide selection in between

The 1939 Link Circuit cut out the section running to North Tower Curve and Fisherman's Bend: it measured 1.193 miles.

including John Bolster driving *Bloody Mary* which was delicately listed in the programme as a 'Bolster Special'. All the competitors were clubmen out for a good day's sport. The event was run as a team race with victory going to the United Hospitals & University of London Motor Club team which included Bob Gerard. Driving in the Cambridge University Automobile Club team was one R. R. C. Walker at the wheel of a Delahaye; he was later to become very well known as an entrant in major formulae, including Formula One — Rob Walker.

The Sydenham Trophy meeting was next on the agenda on 20 May with the Road Racing Club in charge of proceedings and the BBC again present with the television cameras — what a pity they did not have videotape in those days! Heat One went to Dobson and Heat Two to Hans Ruesch in his Alfa Romeo who had to fend off Bira to the last. The final saw two ERAs home in the hands of Bira from Dobson with Ruesch third. Bira then won the sports car race in his Delahaye. The penultimate meeting of the year (although it had not been planned that way) was on 1 July and a shadow was cast over the meeting for Richard Seaman had died as a result of a crash at Spa — it is said that at his funeral there was a wreath from Adolf Hitler. On a brighter note, Raymond Mays returned having not been seen at Crystal Palace in 1938. Bira won Heat One of the Crystal Palace Cup from Mays, with Heat Two going to Bert Hadley from Percy Maclure's Riley. The final saw Mays and Bira in a three-cornered tussle with Hadley's Austin which Mays won with Hadley 2/10 sec ahead of Bira. In the struggle Mays broke the two-minute/60mph barrier for the first time, setting a lap record of 60.92mph in 1min 58.1sec which was to stand for all time as the outright lap record on the two-mile Crystal Palace circuit. In two years and two months the lap record had risen from 54.59 to 60.97mph.

As the season rolled on the Road Racing Club decided to bring the Imperial Trophy meeting forward from October to August and let the London Grand Prix revert to its autumn date;

as a result of this decision the London Grand Prix was never to be run again. Saturday, 26 August 1939 saw the third running of the Imperial Trophy just eight days before the winds of war engulfed Great Britain and later most of the civilised world.

Bira did not appear for the first heat which allowed Bert Hadley a fairly comfortable win in his Austin from the MG of Stuart-Wilson. Heat Two saw Mays win from Dobson. Abecassis took the sports car honours in his Alta and the vintage race went to Hampton's Bugatti. The honour of winning the last race on the south London circuit for the time being went to Hadley who won the final of the Imperial Trophy by two minutes from Dobson who set fastest lap. And so the curtain came down on the two-mile circuit at Crystal Palace which was to be taken over by the military during hostilities. In company with Donington Park, Crystal Palace was destined to rise, phoenix-like, from the ashes (unlike Brooklands) but it would be nearly 14 years before internal combustion engines would be heard again racing in London.

With the cessation of hostilities in 1945, the Crystal Palace circuit was in a state of decay and the Ministry of Defence was none too swift in removing its tanks and guns, not to mention one or two unexploded bombs. London County Council was now in charge of the site and had decided by 1951 that the time had come for motor racing to return to London, so the Crystal Palace Motor Sports Committee was formed to organise it on their behalf. Things did not go as smoothly as was hoped for the NIMBY contingent was not as compliant as in prewar days and the local populace did not regard with equanimity the prospect of their weekends being shattered by the roar of racing engines, and obtained a court injunction restricting the number days for racing to *five per year*. This limitation lasted right through to the end of the 1960s.

The new committee was not overawed with this decision and pressed ahead but decided that the original circuit was too slow and revised the two-mile track, inserting the New Link which reduced the circuit length to 1.39 miles. The first cars to use the circuit for practice and testing since before the war appeared in early May 1953 and were watched by the workmen putting the final touches to the circuit crash barriers.

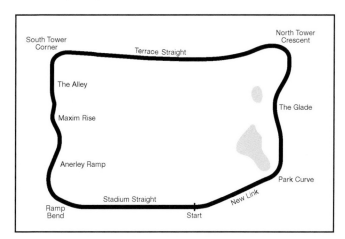

The final Crystal Palace circuit which was used from the time of the reopening in 1953 until final closure in 1972: the circuit length was 1.39 miles.

Racing returned to Crystal Palace in Coronation year on Whit Monday, 23 May, the venue now being advertised as 'London's Own Circuit' with organisation in the capable hands of the British Automobile Racing Club. It was billed as an International with the main event for Formula Two cars (up to 2 litres normally aspirated or 500cc forced induction). The meeting attracted over 42,000 spectators who saw Tony Rolt win the first heat of the main event in Rob Walker's Connaught and setting the first lap record on the new circuit at 72.73mph. Second was Ken Wharton in his Cooper-Bristol from Lance Macklin driving an HWM and Stirling Moss in the Cooper-Alta. The second heat went to Peter Whitehead in another Cooper-Alta from Peter Collins' HWM and Graham Whitehead's Cooper-Bristol. Before the final there was a 500cc race which Moss won in a Cooper from Reg Bicknell (Erskine Staride), Stuart Lewis-Evans, George Wicken, Don Parker and Jimmy Brown of later Silverstone fame. The final of the Coronation Trophy was won by Wharton from Rolt — the new Crystal Palace had been well and truly christened.

The postwar history of Crystal Palace can be divided into three eras: 1953-9, 1960-9 and 1970 to closure. To further commemorate the Coronation the Elizabethan Trophy on

11 July 1953 attracted 60 500cc entries for four 10-lap heats and a final, with victory going to Stuart Lewis-Evans from Les Leston and John Brown, Dennis Taylor and Ivor Bueb. In addition to the Trophy Lewis-Evans went home with £35. The meeting had been organised by the Half-Litre Car Club.

The final meeting of the 1953 season was on 19 September when the same club ran an International meeting for Formula Two, Formula III and a couple of sports car races. Stirling Moss won the Formula Two race in his Cooper-Alta from Tony Rolt's Connaught and Bob Gerard in his Cooper-Bristol — Bernie Ecclestone was sixth in his Cooper-Bristol. Moss's winning speed was 70.68mph. Driving in the sports car race was someone described in the programme as 'a rather unusual young man' who built and raced his own fragile-looking 1,172cc engined cars. His name was Colin Chapman. The season had established Crystal Palace as being well and truly back on the motor racing map after a gap of 14 years and a further 19 seasons were to pass before it was to fall silent, most of these seeing two motorcycle meetings and three for car events.

The 1954 car season opened with the BARC running a meeting on Saturday, 18 June when Ken Tyrrell made his Palace debut in the Formula III race. August Bank Holiday Monday was attended by 32,000 spectators who saw Reg Parnell win the main race of the day in his Ferrari from Roy Salvadori in a Maserati 250F entered by Gilby Engineering. At the end of the 1954 season the Half-Litre Car Club ran the meeting in September with the Redex Trophy for Formula III cars which was run as three heats and a final, which went to Ivor Bueb who also collected £40. Bueb was driving a Cooper and led home Bicknell in his self-built Revis and Stuart Lewis-Evans. The London Trophy for Formule Libre was in

Old racing cars never die — they just go on racing. This is one of the Ecurie Ecosse D-Type Jaguars which covered themselves with glory at Le Mans, having started life as the 1955 Jaguar Team cars. MWS 302 is chassis number XKD 502 and is seen performing with her usual aplomb at Crystal Palace on 26 May 1969 during the Greater London Trophy Meeting organised by the British Racing and Sports Car Club. Fred Scatley

two parts, each of which produced the same result, Bob Gerard winning in his Cooper-Bristol from Don Beauman's Connaught and Alan Brown driving another Cooper-Bristol. Colin Chapman won the Anerley Trophy for sports cars from Archie Scott Brown driving a Lister-MG.

The 1955 car racing season at Crystal Palace opened on Whit Monday, 30 May with a meeting organised by the British Racing and Sports Car Club which had evolved form the Half-Litre Car Club. Over 90 entries entertained the 32,000 spectators and the club was still to promote Formula III for many years to come. The main event was the London Trophy for Formula One cars, run as two 12-lap races with the result to be decided on aggregate. The first race saw two Maserati 250Fs home in the hands of Peter Collins and Roy Salvadori, with Bob Gerard's Cooper-Bristol third. The second part saw Peter Collins win from Gerard after Salvadori's Gilby Engineering 250F expired. Bob Gerard had announced his retirement at the end of the 1953 season but the retirement had been very short-lived! The Redex Trophy for Formula III was again run as three heats and a final in order to accommodate the number of entries. The JAP engine was now showing its age and the fastest Coopers were Norton powered, all three heats going to these cars driven by Ivor Bueb, Dennis Taylor and Cliff Allison. Victory in the final went to Bueb from George Wicken, Allison and Don Parker driving his faithful Kieft.

Before the BARC ran the next meeting at the Palace on 30 July new grandstands were erected, such was the popularity of the sport in London. Some 15,000 spectators arrived and saw Mike Hawthorn make his debut there driving Stirling Moss's Maserati 250F. He won his heat from the acknowledged master of the Palace, Roy Salvadori. The second heat went to Harry Schell in the Vanwall, with the final going to Hawthorn who had a flag-to-flag victory from Horace Gould, Schell and Salvadori. Hawthorn also established a new lap record at 78.93mph. The supporting Formula III race saw Jim Russell win a nail-biting race from Ivor Bueb. The meeting closed a short season which had been overshadowed by the tragedy at Le Mans.

Whit Monday, 21 May saw the BRSCC open the 1956 season when it attracted nearly 35,000 spectators. The London Trophy was a two-part Formula One event both of which Stirling Moss won from Paul Emery in his Emeryson-Alta. Bob Gerard was third in the first part, still not having retired, while Moss set a new lap record at 79.94mph. Third overall was George Wicken in his Cooper-Alta. The British Automobile Racing Club was in charge of the August Bank Holiday meeting on the sixth of the month when 10,000 spectators arrived despite the inclement weather of the morning. The main event was the August Trophy for sports cars. Keith Hall started from the back of the grid and won the first heat, with victory in the second going to W. Ellis from Mark Zervudachi, both driving Lotus Elevens. The final was a Lotus Eleven benefit, Hall again winning from Cliff Allison — a repeat of the first heat. Colin Chapman had stuck with

During the 1950s the Crystal Palace programmes took on this format, still featuring one of the long-gone towers and using a picture of a car commensurate with the class of racing performing on the day in question. In this instance, from Whit Monday, 25 May 1953, the International meeting was organised by the British Automobile Racing Club and the featured car was an 'A' Type Connaught. As was so often the case in the 1950s, *The Motor* is much in evidence. *Author's collection*

front engines and sophisticated chassis design.

The BRSCC kicked off the 1957 season with the meeting on Whit Monday, 10 June; Formula Two was the main attraction, supported by Formula Three — as Formula III was now universally designated. The Formula Two entry consisted of 14 cars, 11 of which were Coventry-Climax-powered Coopers opposed by just three Lotuses which were also Climax powered. These three consisted of two works cars in the hands of Cliff Allison and Hugh Mackay-Fraser, with Graham Hill in control of Tommy Atkins' car. These Formula Two cars were competing for the London Trophy and produced a battle between the works Coopers of Roy Salvadori and a newcomer from Australia named Jack Brabham, and they finished in that order ahead of George Wicken and Les Leston. The Australian finished first in the second heat, winning the London Trophy on aggregate and setting a new lap record in the process. Second was Wicken from Salvadori and Leston, all of whom were driving Coopers. The Redex Trophy was once again run for Formula Three cars in four heats and a final, which went to Stuart Lewis-Evans from Jim Russell, Don Parker, Tommy Bridger, Trevor Taylor and David Boshier-Jones, all of whom were Cooper-Norton-mounted.

The next car meeting at the Palace was a long time a-coming for it was not until Whit Monday, 26 May 1958 that cars returned, the meeting on this occasion being organised by the BARC. London was in the grip of a bus strike which probably contributed to the low attendance figure of a little over 13,000. Formula Two was the feature of the meeting, with the heats being won by Ivor Bueb in a Lotus-Climax and Ken Tyrrell in the first of Alan Brown's Cooper-Climaxes, the other one being driven by Carroll Shelby. A close-fought final went to Ian Burgess (Cooper) by 0.8sec from Tommy Bridger and Bruce McLaren also Cooper-mounted, with Ivor Bueb's ailing Lotus-Climax in fourth spot.

Formula Two was also the feature event at the BRSCC meeting in July when Syd Jensen won from Ivor Bueb and Jim Russell, all of whom drove Coopers. The meeting scheduled for 14 August was cancelled, so the July meeting was the last of the year at the Palace.

Whit Monday 1959 saw touring cars running at Crystal Palace for the first time under the auspices of the BRSCC. The entry list included Graham Hill at the wheel of a Speedwell-converted Austin A35 opposed by Les Leston in a Riley 1.5, Bill Blydenstein in a Borgward Isabella and a collection of

Renault Dauphines, Morris Minors and Ford Prefects. The larger class consisted of Jaguars, Ford Zephyrs and MG Magnettes; this category of racing was to prove extremely popular with the Palace crowds. At the BARC-run meeting on 22 August the sports car race was to be dominated by the name of Lola: Eric Broadley's incredible little car had proved to be so successful that he had but recently given up his job as a building site manager to become a racing car manufacturer — the rest of that story is now history.

As 1959 drew to a close there came news of the intention to construct the National Youth and Sports Centre within Crystal Palace and concern was felt about the future of motorsport — fears which were to prove well-founded in future years. Early in 1960 work commenced on the new complex and £2.75 million was to be spent before His Royal Highness Prince Philip, the Duke of Edinburgh, officially opened it in 1964. The slogan for the project had been 'Sport For All' but it was dominated by athletics and the writing was on the wall; the opening of the Centre can, in retrospect, be seen as the beginning of the end for motor racing and motorcycle racing in the capital.

In the meantime there was still sport to be enjoyed on two, three and four wheels; as was now standard practice at the Palace, the season started with motorcycles and the cars made their first appearance of 1961 on Whit Monday, 6 July, the meeting being in the hands of the BARC when nearly 30,000 spectators arrived. The main attraction was the entry of a young Scot who was down to drive for Team Lotus in the Formula Two and Formula Junior races; his name was Jimmy Clark but in the event he was unable to attend and his place was taken by Trevor Taylor for whom it was a lucky break. He won the Formula Junior heat and the final but then the sunshine of the morning turned to rain and the main event of the day, over 36 laps of the circuit for the Crystal Palace Trophy, was run on a wet track. Trevor Taylor won this race as well, from George Wicken's Cooper-Climax. This proved to be the only car race meeting of the year, for the Bank Holiday Monday meeting was a motorcycle affair after which the contractors moved in to start building the new sports complex. It was the last meeting with the start/finish line on the bottom straight.

The 1961 season opened on Easter Monday, 3 April, with the ACU National Meeting but on Whit Monday, 22 May, the BRSCC gave the car racing fraternity its first taste of the new-look Crystal Palace. The improvements included a new five-acre paddock and the start/finish line was now at Terrace Straight which was widened by 5ft to 35ft to accommodate the grid. The main race was the 37-lap London Trophy for Formula One cars; Reg Parnell had retired as a driver but he was now the team manager for the Yeoman Credit Racing Team whose Cooper-Climax won the race in the capable hands of Roy Salvadori from Henry Taylor driving the UDT-Laystall Lotus-Climax. Salvadori had three other wins that day in John Coombs' E-Type Jaguar, the Yeoman Credit Cooper-Climax sports car and the saloon race in Coombs' 3.8-litre Jaguar. The Formula Junior race went to Alan Rees in a Lotus-Ford.

The final meeting of 1961 was on 2 September when the BARC had Formula Junior as the main event which attracted a disappointing crowd of barely more than 6,000. Dennis Taylor

won the first heat in his Lotus with the second going to Trevor Taylor in the works Lotus; he also won the 25-lap final by 3.5sec from Dennis Taylor.

Easter was late in 1962 which meant that the first appearance of cars was on 11 June, the earliest available date for the BARC to run its National meeting with Formula One as the main event. Coventry-Climax and BRM had built new 1.5-litre V8 engines for the new Formula One which had come into effect the previous year and the Palace crowds were keen to see the new cars. Innes Ireland started from the back of the grid in the UDT-Laystall Lotus-BRM but drove through the field to beat the favourite Roy Salvadori into second place in the Bowmaker Racing Lola-Climax V8. In the course of doing so Ireland took nearly $2^{1}/_{2}$sec off the lap record, leaving it at 57.2sec at a speed of 87.46mph. Bruce McLaren brought the works Cooper home third ahead of Tony Settember's Emeryson. During the course of the construction of the new facilities the season was restricted to two motorcycle and two car meetings per year, so an abbreviated season came to a close on 1 September when the BRSCC ran a meeting whose feature race was the 25-lap London Trophy for Formula Junior cars. Victory went to Alan Rees in a Lotus, with Mike Spence second in the Ian Walker-entered Lotus.

The 10th anniversary of the reopening of the Crystal Palace circuit occurred in 1963 and to mark the occasion the British Automobile Racing Club opened the car racing season on 3 June with a 50-mile sports car race for the Crystal Palace Trophy. Roy Salvadori led the first 25 laps in a Cooper Monaco until transmission trouble interfered which let the Normand-entered Lotus-Fords of Jim Clark and Mike Beckwith into the lead which they held to the end.

Around this time saloon car racing had been infiltrated by the mammoth 7-litre Ford Galaxies from across the pond and on this occasion victory went to the John Willment example driven by Gentleman Jack Sears from the tyre-smoking 3.8-litre Jaguars of Roy Salvadori and the reigning World Champion Graham Hill. Herein lies a graphic example of just how much the sport has changed (not necessarily for the better) for there is no question today of the current World Champion being seen racing a saloon nor yet a sports car unless it be at Le Mans.

The Anerley Trophy was run for Formula Junior cars in heats and a final, with the final going to Denny Hulme in the works Brabham from his team-mate Frank ('If you've never bent one you've never really tried') Gardner, with Alan Rees third in the Roy Winkelmann Racing Lola.

The final meeting of 1963 was run by the British Racing & Sports Car Club on 7 September. Alan Rees had won the last five Formula Junior races at the Palace so was starting as favourite, but on this occasion it was not to be. The winner was Roy Pike in the Gemini from Brian Hart in a Lotus; Brian is now well known as a builder and designer of Formula One engines.

With the advantage of hindsight, 1964 can be seen as the year when the storm clouds began to gather for motorsport at Crystal Palace; the National Sports Centre was open and the more far-sighted could see that there would be inevitable clashes and that officialdom would come down on the side of athletics. There was, however, one bright spot in the year for motor racing enthusiasts at the London circuit in the arrival on the scene of a young Austrian who was destined for great things — his name was Jochen Rindt. He had bought a new Formula Two Brabham at the 1964 Racing Car Show and brought it to Crystal Palace for the Whit Monday meeting which was organised by the British Automobile Racing Club. The race was run in two heats and a final, the first heat being for 'established' drivers and the second for 'novices'; victory in the first race went to Graham Hill driving John Coombs' Cooper from Jim Clark.

The start of the second race found the young Austrian in second place on the grid and he proceeded to win from Alan Rees, who had the consolation of setting fastest lap. The front row of the grid for the final was Graham Hill, Jochen Rindt and Alan Rees; Rindt won and set fastest lap and the crowd took him to their hearts.

The feature race at the Jaguar Drivers' Club meeting on 13 June was the Pontin Trophy for GT cars where a duel was expected between the Cobras of Jack Sears and Frank Gardner but many had come to see a new young Scottish talent named John Young Stewart driving John Coombs' Jaguar E-Type. The BRSCC closed the 1964 season in September.

Between the 1964 and 1965 seasons the government of the capital changed with the London County Council becoming the Greater London Council, the new authority being responsible for a greater area than its predecessor. The new authority agreed that motorsport should continue at Crystal Palace and the first car meeting of the year under the GLC fell to the British Racing & Sports Car Club who ran an International Meeting on Whit Monday, 7 June, the main race being the London Trophy for Formula Two cars. Early on the entry list was Jack Brabham in one of his own cars to be powered by a Honda engine, the Japanese company starting out on its long and successful journey to the top of motor racing which finished at the very pinnacle in Formula One. Jim Clark won in the Ron Harris Team Lotus car from Graham Hill driving the Cooper of John Coombs and Richard Attwood. The season saw two Saturday meetings run by the Jaguar Drivers' Club on 3 July and BARC on the 31st of the month.

Whit Monday, 2 May 1966 saw Formula Two back for the London Trophy, the race being a qualifying round of the *Autocar* Championship. Jack Brabham and Denny Hulme in the works Brabhams were first and second on the programme and on the road, with Alan Rees and Jochen Rindt third and fourth in the Roy Winkelmann Brabhams.

The 40th anniversary of racing at Crystal Palace occurred in 1967 and the main event of the year was the BRSCC's British United Airways-sponsored International Trophy meeting on Whit Monday, 27 May. It was run for Formula Two over two heats and a final and was won by the Belgian Jacky Ickx in Ken

Tyrrell's Matra, the works Matra of Jean-Pierre Beltoise and Bruce McLaren driving his own car. The Norbury Trophy for Group 4 sports cars had entries from no less than seven Ford GT40s and six Ferrari 250LMs; Paul Hawkins won in his GT40.

The 1968 car season opened on Whit Monday, 3 June, with the Spring International Holts Trophy Meeting organised by BARC for Formula Two cars; it was the fourth round of the European Formula Two Championship but an air of sadness hung over the meeting for the great Jim Clark had been killed shortly before Easter. The Championship was for ungraded drivers though graded drivers could compete, but not for Championship points, and amongst the entries from the former was one from Piers Courage who was to drive a Brabham entered by Frank Williams. The race was over two heats and a final, the fastest eight from each heat to contest the final which went to Jochen Rindt from Courage, Derek Bell, Jackie Oliver (later to be of Arrows fame), Jacky Ickx, Chris Lambert, Dickie Attwood and Frank Gardner. Rindt set the fastest lap at 96.6mph, the magic 'ton' still proving elusive, although it was to fall to him two years later. The second heat went to Kurt Ahrens from Brian Redman, Clay Regazzoni, Robin Widdows, Pedro Rodriguez, Johnny Servoz-Gavin, Jo Schlesser and Graham Hill. Rindt led the 90-lap final from flag to flag, leading Redman home by 30sec ahead of Regazzoni and Oliver.

The BRSCC ran the Anerley Trophy meeting on 3 August and the BARC closed the season proper on 14 September with the Holts Trophy Meeting but there was still one major event to come late in the year.

On 24 November the London-Sydney Marathon started from Crystal Palace, the circuit having been chosen as the starting point as the publicity machine could then promote the route being from Sydenham to Sydney. The event was jointly sponsored by the *Daily Express* and the *Sydney Telegraph* and attracted the largest crowd ever seen at the circuit on what was a lovely day for the time of year. Ninety-eight cars took the flag on the 10,000-mile, 10-day marathon to Australia. Fifty-six cars made it to Sydney, the unexpected winner being the Hillman Hunter of Andrew Cowan, Brian Coyle and Colin Malkin.

The 1969 car racing season began on Whit Monday, 26 May, with the BRSCC's International Greater London Trophy meeting; the traditional Formula Two feature event had given way to the Formula Three 1-litre 'screamers' which Tim Schenken won in

In the 1970s the programme cover changed quite significantly, the circuit being referred to simply as Crystal Palace with a stylised racing car and details of the meeting and the organising club. On the earlier cover racing is organised for the London County Council but now the Authority has changed to the Greater London Council. In 1953 the programme cost 1s (5p) and 18 years later the price had only trebled to 15p — inflation was not so rampant then as it soon was to become! *Author's collection*

CRYSTAL PALACE
Saturday 7 August 1971 2.15
Daily Express Trophy
with Petonyer Trophy F3 Race
Organised for GLC by BRSCC. Official programme 15p

It's the real thing. Coke.
Enjoy Coca-Cola

Rodney Bloor's Brabham-Ford. Formula Three was also the order of the day at the 3 August *Daily Express* Trophy Meeting organised by the British Automobile Racing Club when victory went to Reine Wissel driving the works Chevron.

The same club closed the season on 13 September with the British Road Services Trophy meeting when the feature event was run in two 20-lap races for GT cars with the winner decided on aggregate. Roger Nathan won in his Astra from Alistair Cowan's McLaren and Martin Konig's Nomad-BRM. There was a Formula Three race for the Reg Parnell Trophy which had previously been contested at Goodwood; the race saw Emerson Fittipaldi score his most important win to date.

As 1970 dawned the court injunction which had restricted Crystal Palace motor sport activity to five days per year expired and the Greater London Council decided to take advantage of this and announced that there would be 14 meetings during the coming year. Crystal Palace motor sport had almost always run at a loss despite extensive advertising in the press, on railway stations and on the Underground so there was logic in taking advantage of the new situation. With the new decade came a greater emphasis on safety, led by Jackie Stewart and the Grand Prix Drivers' Association who insisted on the removal of trees and earth banks where they were a potential hazard to drivers. After inspection of the circuit the GPDA announced that they wished to see the erection of an Armco barrier on the inside of North Tower Crescent but the council was not happy at the prospect of a metal barrier so near to the concert hall. A compromise was suggested in the shape of a demountable barrier — which was still going to cost a little short of £¼ million pounds.

The British Automobile Racing Club opened the 1970 car season on 25 May with the Alcoa Britain International Trophy for Formula Two cars. In 1970 it was still possible to see the reigning World Champion and his counterparts competing in something other than a Formula One car and so it proved on this occasion for the entry list included the 1969 Champion Jackie Stewart driving John Coombes' Brabham BT30, who won Heat One from Francois Cevert's works Tecno, with Carlos Reutemann in a Brabham third and Graham Hill fourth in a works Lotus. The Palace favourite Jochen Rindt won the second heat from Clay Regazzoni in the second works Tecno and Andrea de Adamich in a Brabham. Stewart won the final after Rindt retired from the lead, with Alan Rees in second place, 12sec behind, and Emerson Fittipaldi third for Lotus. Rindt had the consolation of setting the first ever 100mph lap at Crystal Palace and the Greater London Council had a silver plate

made to mark the achievement but Jochen was killed at Monza before he could receive it and it was presented to his widow Nina by the circuit manager, Alan Tyler.

The first club to take advantage of the GLC decision to increase the number of racing days was the Thames Estuary Automobile Club who ran a Clubman's meeting on 13 June for saloons and single-seaters and it was followed by the Aston Martin Owners' Club who celebrated the 50th anniversary of the marque with a Jubilee Festival on 11 July. 13 September saw the BARC run the Forward Trust Trophy for Formula Three cars which was televised by the BBC. It was not the most pleasant of days, being wet throughout. As was now the norm, the main event was run in two heats and a final, victory in the first heat going to Dave Walker driving the Gold Leaf Team Lotus car from Dave Morgan's March. Heat two was run in torrential rain and so bad was the carnage that it was stopped at the end of the fifth lap when Carlos Pace was declared the winner from Bev Bond and Chris Skeaping. Pace won the final on a drying track from Cyd Williams (Brabham) and Walker.

The 1970 car season closed on 3 October with the British Racing & Sports Car Club-run *Daily Express* Trophy meeting where the feature race was once again for Formula Three cars. The day was made memorable by James Hunt punching Dave Morgan and flooring him after they had had a coming together on the final lap of the race!

The 1971 season opened on 31 May with the Hilton Transport Trophy meeting for Formula Two organised by the British Automobile Racing Club. The final went to Emerson Fittipaldi from Tim Schenken and Ronnie Peterson. Rindt's lap record of 49.6sec/100.89mph had been equalled by Jackie Stewart on the same day and on this occasion no less than four drivers also equalled it — Schenken, Peterson, Fittipaldi and Jean-Pierre Jaussaud.

In an attempt to liven up matters, it was decided to run a night race meeting on 18 June but it was all rather abortive, the weather being so bad that many of the entrants decided not to risk their cars on a one-off event. 7 August saw the British Racing and Sports Car Club run the *Daily Express*-sponsored Peytoner Trophy for Formula Three cars: James Hunt won the first heat in a March whilst the second went to Alan McCully in his Lotus-Vegantune after a shunt on the grid eliminated the majority of the leading contenders. Winner of the final was Roger Williamson from Chris Skeaping's Chevron and the Brabham of Alan Jones.

The British Automobile Racing Club was back on 11 September to run the Iberia Airlines Trophy meeting, the main event being for Formula Three cars. Victory in the first heat went to the Gold Leaf Team Lotus entry of Dave Walker, from Colin Vandervell in his Brabham. Heat two saw James Hunt's March lead home the Merlyn of Jody Scheckter — two future World Champions. The final saw Roger Williamson win from David Purley. The final car meeting of the year on 25 September was he *Daily Express*-sponsored Historic Meeting organised by the Aston Martin Owners' Club. Whilst there had been historic races at Crystal Palace before, this was the first totally historic meeting to be held and was a resounding success.

The 1972 season opened under a cloud for shortly before its commencement the Greater London Council Arts & Recreation Committee announced that this would be the final season of motorised sport at the Palace.

But there was one more season to be enjoyed and it kicked off with a bike meeting on Easter Monday. The final International Motor Race meeting was run on Spring Bank Holiday, Monday, 29 May, and was the fifth round of the European Formula Two Championship. A clash with another meeting at Oulton Park kept some regulars away but there was a class entry including John Surtees (making his first appearance at the Palace since 1967) and Mike Hailwood made his four-wheel debut in a Surtees (not having been to the circuit since 1957). Other notable entries were Graham Hill, François Cevert, Henri Pescarolo and Jean-Pierre Beltoise. Carlos Reutemann won the first heat in the Rondel-entered March from Vic Elford's Chevron and Scott's Brabham. 'Mike the Bike' won the second heat by 4sec from Jody Scheckter's Impact McLaren and the Surtees of Andrea de Adamich. The first six from each heat plus the next four fastest were to contest the final which went to Scheckter from Hailwood, Reutemann and Elford. Mike Hailwood had the satisfaction of setting the fastest lap and a new lap record at 103.39mph in 48.4 seconds — it was destined to stand as the all-time lap record at Crystal Palace.

12 August saw the British Racing & Sports Car Club run the Peytoner Trophy for Formula Three cars for the last time and on 9 September the British Automobile Racing Club made its final appearance at the Palace to run the Hexagon Trophy Meeting for Formula Three. Heat One went to Mike Walker's Ensign from Russell Wood's March, which won the second heat. Walker won the final and thus became the final winner of a Formula Three race at Crystal Palace; second was Peter Hull.

And so the final sad day came on 23 September when the Aston Martin Owners' Club ran the *Daily Mirror* Historic Meeting. So great was the interest that 150 would-be entrants had to be turned away. It turned out to be a truly memorable day with most of the great names who had ever raced at Crystal Palace in attendance. The honour of winning the last-ever race at London's own circuit went to the last Lister-Jaguar ever built: it was entered by Hexagon of Highgate and driven by Gerry Marshal.

It remains only to record the movement of the respective lap records: on the 2-mile circuit the lap record was only ever held by an ERA (which must, in itself, be something of a record) and by four drivers. On 24 April 1937 Pat Fairfield set the first lap record at 54.59mph and over the course of two years it changed hands between Prince Birbongse and Arthur Dobson four times, finally resting for all time with Raymond May at 60.97mph on 4 July.

Postwar the first lap record on the 1.39-mile circuit was set by Tony Rolt in a Connaught on 25 May 1953 at 72.73mph; four years later the 80mph barrier was breached on 10 June 1957 by Jack Brabham in a Cooper-Climax at 80.19mph. 7 June 1965 saw Denny Hulme raise it to 87.79mph in a Brabham-Honda, then on 29 May 1967 Jacky Ickx and Jean-Pierre Beltoise jointly took it to 94.59mph in Matra-Fords. As has been recorded above, Jochen Rindt was the first through 100mph on 25 May 1970 and the outright lap record will stand for ever to 'Mike the Bike' on 24 May 1972 at 103.39mph.

7 August 1971 — James Hunt driving a March 713 leads Roger Williamson, also driving a March 713 (and using a modicum of opposite lock), and Steve Thompson (Ensign), contesting the Peytoner Trophy Race for Formula Three cars. *Mike Dixon*

DAVIDSTOW
FORMULA ONE IN CORNWALL

avidstow is one of those little-known circuits whose life was short but showed a promise later confounded by elements beyond the control of those who tried so hard to establish motor racing in the West Country. Its proudest boast is that before the untimely end came, the circuit saw true Formula One motor racing.

RAF Davidstow Moor, in North Cornwall, was established in 1942 and opened for operational use on 1 October that year; such a late establishment in World War 2 is explained by the fact that it was initially thought that all RAF bases should be situated in the east of the United Kingdom, closest to the enemy. The fall of France led to some rethinking on this score as there was now the distinct potential of an attack on the south coast and the West Country; RAF Davidstow Moor thus became a much-needed Coastal Command base on a small, boggy plateau high on Bodmin Moor. It would appear that the local populace was somewhat doubtful of the wisdom of building an airfield in such a locality, being well aware of the vagaries of the weather on the moor; their doubts held true when motor racing came there. The airfield consisted of three runways with the requisite taxiways and dispersal bays, and at 970ft above sea level, was the highest operational airfield in the United Kingdom. In such a situation it was frequently ravaged by gales coming straight off the Atlantic Ocean accompanied by heavy rainfall. Apparently the American GIs stationed at Davidstow were none too appreciative of the conditions!

Motor racing commenced on 9 August 1952 when three races were run over the 2.6-mile circuit; from 1953 to 1955 the shorter 1.85-mile circuit was used.

Sadly, the racing history of Davidstow can be counted in the number of races run — a grand total of 44. The first race meetings at Davidstow were organised by the Cornwall Vintage Car Club — itself only three years old when racing commenced — and by the Plymouth Motor Club which had been formed in 1908. Racing arrived at Davidstow on Saturday, 9 August 1952 — and so did the rain. The preceding Thursday and Friday had seen the members of the promoting clubs labouring in torrential rain to prepare the track and facilities and as race day dawned there was no let-up in the weather. A crowd of 800 had been expected, but 3,000 arrived. Practice commenced with 25 of the 28 entrants having materialised. The programme consisted of three 20-minute high-speed trials, a standing start half-mile sprint and ending with a team event relay race over nine laps of the circuit. It had

From the beginning, Cornwall Motor Racing Ltd managed a two-colour cover for the programmes for its Davidstow race meetings, as witness the red and blue on this cover from the race meeting held on Whit Monday in 1953.

Programme of the Whit Monday Meeting
MAY 25th 1953
AT Davidstow Circuit
Nr. LAUNCESTON, CORNWALL
Promoted by Cornwall Motor Racing Ltd. (A joint committee of the Cornwall V.C.C.) and The Plymouth Motor Club
Price One Shilling

been a truly appalling day weather-wise but everyone appears to have enjoyed themselves.

If Davidstow had one clear advantage over other circuits it was that there was a distinct absence of a complaining populace. Two meetings were planned for 1953, on the Whit Monday, 25 May and on 1 August. The Bank Holiday Monday dawned over Cornwall as a lovely summer's day and a crowd of 20,000 was hoped for at Davidstow which had boasted a prize fund of £500 in pre-event publicity. But Davidstow was always a law unto itself and it was blanketed in fog. Practice had been due to start at 10.30am but by well after midday not a wheel had been turned in anger. After the sheep had been cleared from the back straight(!) the weather had improved sufficiently to allow the competitors to have their statutory three laps of practice.

So at around 3.30pm Davidstow's first real motor race commenced (as opposed to speed trials and relay races) over five laps for the first heat of the sports car race up to 1,500cc. It was won by M. G. Llewellyn in a rather special MG TD at 61.27mph which probably reflects more upon the conditions than on the ability of the driver or his car. The second race was Heat One of the unlimited sports car event which was won by Carnegie in his Jaguar XK120 at 62.51mph. By now the fog was closing in again and matters had to come to a stop and the 12,000 spectators and some of the competitors started to leave. Then at 5.30pm the fog lifted completely and the programme was hastily rearranged and Davidstow witnessed its first race for real racing cars — Formula III over 20 laps. Contemporary illustrations show the grid as being six cars wide. Two Kiefts won from two Coopers, Paulson and Westcott leading home Nurse and Piers. The winner's average speed was 71.53mph with the fastest lap being shared by Westcott, Paulson and Ivor Bueb (Arnott) at 73.9mph.

The second heat for the sports cars was abandoned, the 10-lap final of the up to 1,500cc event going to W. A. Cleave's Morris Special and the unlimited event to Watkins' 5.5-litre Cadillac-engined Allard at 73.97mph.

Saturday, 1 August was a better day which was not, perhaps, best for Davidstow, people preferring to take to Cornwall's beautiful beaches rather than risk the vagaries of the moor. However, the sun shone for most of the day and the programme followed much the same format as the May meeting with two heats and a final for sports cars up to 1,500cc and the same for unlimited sports cars. The Formula III event was expanded on this occasion to be run as two heats and a final, and attracted some of the great names of the day.

Prior to race day an engineless ex-Plymouth City double-decker bus was manoeuvred into place to be used for the timekeepers and race control and a single-decker Dennis was in use as paddock control. The main interest focused upon the Formula III races; Don Parker won the first heat in his Kieft at 74.28mph from Stuart Lewis-Evans in a Cooper, with Les Leston third in his own Leston Special and Ken Tyrrell fourth in another Cooper. Parker set the fastest lap at 76.62mph. Both the Formula III heats were over 10 laps, with the second win going to Eric Brandon in a Cooper from Don Truman (of BRSCC fame) second in another Cooper, third was N. Berrow Johnson in a Martin Special and fourth, A. A. Butler also in a Cooper. The winner's speed was 76.31mph and he also set the fastest lap at 77.88mph which was a new lap record.

The final was over 20 laps, Brandon winning at 75.99mph and equalling his own lap record from his heat, with Parker second from Lewis-Evans and Leston. Sadly, the gate had been well down, influenced, no doubt, by the fact that many people still worked a half or full day on Saturday and the circuit had a weather reputation to live down. The season had ended on a high note and there were hopes of a better 1954.

In order to run the meetings at Davidstow the two organising clubs had formed Cornwall Motor Racing Ltd and in September 1953 the Plymouth Motor Club held an extraordinary general meeting specifically to report on the finances of the circuit. The treasurer was able to state that a profit had been made on the first two meetings but, paradoxically, the August event had virtually wiped this out. It was therefore decided that it would not be a good idea to run meetings on Saturdays in future and it was proposed to try to run on two Bank Holiday Mondays in 1954. Permits were duly received which were of National status, with the bonus that races would be run for Formula One, Formula Two and Formule Libre in addition to the usual format of heats and finals for sports cars and Formula III.

The first meeting of 1954 was scheduled for 7 June which dawned to high winds and driving rain, but 20,000 spectators arrived hoping for some good motor racing and an improvement in the weather. For the first time, practice had been held on the preceding day. As the cars came to the grid for the first sports car race at 11am there was no improvement in the weather but it was notable as being Bruce Halford's first race. The Formula III race produced 12 starters but none of the established names of the Formula figure in the results, the winner being A. Loens in an Erskine Staride at 66.66mph from D. Watts in a Cooper. Second on the road but demoted to third was F. Westcott in a Kieft, with A. Denley fourth in another Cooper; the race was over 20 laps.

The first big race of the day was the sixth on the programme and was for Formula Two cars which saw 11 starters come to

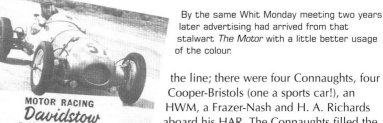

MOTOR RACING
Davidstow
Nr. LAUNCESTON, CORNWALL
Whit-Monday
MAY 30th, 1955
Held under R.A.C. NATIONAL PERMIT
Promoted by Cornwall Motor Racing Ltd.
A joint committee of the
Cornwall V.C.C. and the Plymouth Motor Club
OFFICIAL PROGRAMME 1/-

By the same Whit Monday meeting two years later advertising had arrived from that stalwart The Motor with a little better usage of the colour.

the line; there were four Connaughts, four Cooper-Bristols (one a sports car!), an HWM, a Frazer-Nash and H. A. Richards aboard his HAR. The Connaughts filled the first four places and were driven by Riseley-Prichard, Leslie Marr, C. D. Boulton and John Coombs who was deputising for Ken McAlpine. The winner's speed was 73.9mph but Horace Gould took fastest lap in the Cooper-Bristol at 78.25mph. The Formula One race was the eighth on the programme and, like the Formula Two race, was over 20 laps. There were seven starters although, truth to tell, there was not a true Formula One car amongst them, the majority of the entrants being runners in the Formula Two race; Riseley-Prichard won at 74.2mph in the Connaught from Walton's Cooper-Bristol and Brooks' HWM, with another Cooper-Bristol fourth in the hands of Tom Kyffin.

The programme was due to run over 12 races but the final two were abandoned due the bridge over the track collapsing, so the Formule Libre event was the last of the day. There were 23 entrants but only 12 came to the line and it resulted in an HWM one-two with G. Scali's HWM-Jaguar sports car winning from Brooks' Formula Two car while Riseley-Prichard was third in a Cooper-Connaught, with the very first ERA built (R1A) fourth, driven by A. W. Birrell. A notable entrant in the unlimited sports car race was Tommy Sopwith driving something called the *Sphinx*.

The second meeting of 1954 was scheduled for Bank Holiday Monday, 2 August, with practice on the preceding day. Once again the weather took a hand in the proceedings with the circuit blanketed in fog which later turned to a penetrating drizzle. This, at least, allowed racing to get under way and the first race was away at a little after 11am, the full programme of eight races being completed. The day's racing followed the now-familiar pattern of sports cars and single-seaters of varying formulae. First race of the day was for sports cars up to 2.5-litre and saw victory going to Walton's Cooper-Bristol from John Coombs' new Lotus Mk 8 from another Cooper-Bristol driven by Tom Kyffin. In poor visibility Walton averaged 71.58mph and set the fastest lap at 74.23mph.

Next was the first heat of the Unlimited Sports Car race. HWMs took the first two places in the hands of George Abecassis and G. Scali from three Jaguars (two C-Types and an XK120) driven respectively by G. Hogg, M. Connell and John Buncombe with H. Hay's 'Embiricos' Bentley. The race was run at 71.84mph, with the fastest lap at 1min 29.6sec at 74.23mph being set by Connell's C-Type. The second heat was run somewhat faster at 73.9mph, with Tommy Sopwith taking the honours in his Sphinx from the Lotus Mk 8 of John Coombs and Bruce Halford's Riley Sprite. Jack Walton set the fastest lap at 76.27mph before his premature departure from the day's proceedings, his propshaft coupling having broken. These two races had been run over 10 laps — the rest of the programme was over 20 laps. Next came

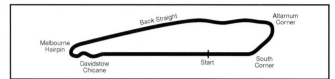

Top: This is the original circuit at Davidstow; measuring 2.6 miles in length, it proved to be very fast but both drivers and spectators alike found it to be uninteresting. None of the corners appear to have been given names and it was used only for the first meeting on 9 August 1952.

Above: From 25 May 1953 this shorter, 1.9-mile circuit was used; the start/finish line is in the same place but before the first corner a chicane has been inserted and the hairpin corner has received the same name as the one at Donington Park. Altarnun Corner is named after a nearby village, and the last corner on the track indicates its geographical location.

the Formula III brigade (all 10 of them) in the still miserable conditions; one did not complete a lap. Despite the conditions this was a great race, with victory going to Rodney Nuckey at 70.39mph from Ken Tyrrell and Eric Brandon all mounted on Cooper-Nortons. The winner also set fastest lap at 73.41mph.

The fifth race of the day was billed as being for Formula One and Formula Two cars but in truth no Formula One car was in sight and only seven cars came to the line and some of those were sports cars. The race was originally planned to be over 30 laps; John Coombs won in the Connaught-engined Lotus Mk 8 at 72.65mph and he shared the fastest lap with Nuckey at 74.73mph. The next three places were filled by Cooper-Bristols driven by Tom Kyffin, Gibson and G. Rolls. Eleven cars came to the line for the final of the Unlimited Sports Cars event: Abecassis won from Sopwith and Scali, with Connell and Hogg taking fourth and fifth places. The race was run at 76.21mph and George Abecassis also set the fastest lap at 77.69mph.

The penultimate race of the day was for sports cars up to 1,300cc and was run at 63.2mph, with W. A. Cleave taking the honours in his now-familiar Morris Special from Sid Broad's Mk 6 Lotus and the MG TC of Sir Thomas Beevor. Austen Nurse set the fastest lap in his Lotus at 66.64mph before retiring.

And so the last race of the day, a Formule Libre handicap event. Handicap events are never easy to follow and it is particularly difficult when conditions are so bad that the competitors can barely be seen, but the race appears to have attracted anything that could run, from Tyrrell's Cooper to the Bentley of Hays. G. Rolls won in his Cooper-Bristol at 67.19mph from Bruce Halford in the Riley Sprite and the Bentley. Fourth was the HWM of Scali from Clay's closed-bodied Healey and Ken Tyrrell. No one could have been sorry to see the close of the day's racing which had been run in continuous rain.

For the 1955 season the organisers decided to concentrate on just one race meeting and to hold it on Whit Monday, 30 May, abandoning the August Bank Holiday meeting as there were too

may counter-attractions. It was not their intention that the May 1955 race meeting would be the last at Davidstow but so it was to be. However, the circuit bowed out on a high note. At the very end *real* Formula One cars competed at Davidstow. There was much excitement when it became known that Peter Collins had entered a Maserati 250F (chassis number 2509) and an Aston Martin DB3R but with only three days to go it was learned that he had also entered a meeting at Crystal Palace.

Race One was for sports cars up to 1,300cc over 10 laps and was a run-away for Eric Brandon driving his self-designed and self-built Coventry Climax FWA-powered Halseylec at 75.49mph, setting the fastest lap at 78.25mph. Second was the Elva of McKenzie Low with C. D. Boulton's Lotus third. A bit of rule bending appears to have taken place in the 20-lap second race for sports cars of 1,301-2,750cc as Brandon appeared again in the Halseylec. The race boasted a grid of 16 cars which F. Rolls won in his Tojeiro-Bristol at 77.69mph from Brandon and Tom Kyffin in the Cooper-Bristol who also set fastest lap at 82.72mph.

Third on the programme was another sports car race, this time up to 1,500cc over 10 laps and Brandon had his second win of the day in his remarkable car at 75.51mph and again set fastest lap at 78.60mph. Second was McKenzie Low in his Elva from Evans driving an E. & C. Tojeiro. Race four was another 20-lapper for sports cars of unlimited capacity and while the Halseylec was again entered, it was outclassed. There were 20 starters, with the winner being F. Dalton in an Austin Healey 100R from M. Burn's RGR Atalanta. Third home was Gillie Tyrer in his Jaguar C-Type ahead of Bruce Halford in his HWM Jaguar and David Shale's Austin Healey 100S. Then came Eric Brandon, by no means shamed to come home sixth against cars with double and nearly three times his engine capacity. Four starts, two wins, a second and a sixth all in the same car; quite a satisfactory day's motoring with the Formula III race still to come. The winner's speed was 79.69mph with Burn setting the fastest lap at 86.15mph — it was creeping up but the best was yet to come.

The programme was now halfway through and the fifth race was for Formula III cars over 20 laps. There were 10 entrants, the only non-Cooper being Middlehurst who was Kieft-mounted in ninth place on the grid. And that fellow Brandon was out again to join the battle with Ken Tyrrell; Ken won from Eric at 78.19mph with W. Higham third, Tyrrell setting the fastest lap at 79.75mph.

Event Six was the big one! At last Davidstow was to see a pukka Formula One car performing. Three Connaughts and three Coopers formed up on the grid, the undoubted star being the B3 Connaught driven by Leslie Marr; B3 was the streamlined car which was, arguably, the prettiest car ever to run in the 2.5-litre Formula One and one of only two streamlined cars to compete under the Formula, the other one being the Mercedes-Benz, notwithstanding the one-off streamlining of the Maserati 250F. The car had set fastest lap and was joined on the grid by Tom Kyffin in the Equipe Devone Cooper-Bristol, Charles Boulton in Connaught A7 and Bob Harris in Connaught A4 which he had borrowed(!) from its owner Dick Gibson. Gibson himself was next driving Tony Crook's Cooper-Bristol running in single-seater trim and finally F. Sowery in a Cooper JAP-1100. There were three other nonstarters in addition to Peter Collins; Tony Rolt was down to drive Rob Walker's Connaught B4 but it was not ready, Ken Tyrrell decided not to run against the assembled company and G. H. Rolls' Tojeiro-Bristol which was present but did not come to the line. Leslie Marr was in his element, winning comfortably at 85.84mph from Boulton, Kyffin, Gibson and Lowery. Not surprisingly Marr set the fastest lap in 1min 15.4sec at 88.21mph. But the best was yet to come!

The penultimate race of the day was for production cars. The entry of 27 stretched the interpretation of the word 'production' somewhat, there being four early Lotuses and two Bucklers; there were also two Bentleys, three Aston Martin DB2s, three Austin Healeys, two Triumph TR2s, a Jaguar Mk VII plus a sprinkling of other makes but there was a limit of 20 starters. Gillie Tyrer won in his C-Type Jaguar from the Austin Healeys of Dalton and Shale and Wilson-Gunn. Fifth was the AC Ace of Standridge and H. H. Rowcliffe's DB2 finished sixth. Tyrer set the fastest lap at 81.3mph.

What was to be the final race at Davidstow was a 20-lap Formule Libre event run on handicap. The cars lined up Le Mans fashion with the drivers already seated awaiting the signal to start, although not all the drivers were happy with the handicapping system. It is fitting that the last race at Davidstow was won by a Cornishman: Sid Broad brought his Lotus Six home at 67.676mph from Gillie Tyrer in the C-Type and Charles Boulton's Connaught. Leslie Marr left the outright lap record at a fraction under 90mph in the B3 in 1min 14sec at 89.88mph.

So ended Davidstow as a motor racing circuit; it had been a short career but by no means an inglorious one.

Davidstow is one of those circuits of which it has proved particularly difficult to find illustrations but this picture of the Paddock gives some impression of the nature of the Cornish circuit. On one of those rare occasions when it did not rain upon RAF Davidstow Moor, two Formula cars, a Cooper No 20 and a Staride No 21 find repose upon the grass whilst the keepers of the former enjoy a cigarette not too far from the petrol cans! Note the primus stove and saucepan ready to make the requisite brew — a world away from the vast American motorhomes which inhabit the paddocks of even the most humble Club meetings of the last quarter of a century. *Ferret Fotographics*

DEBDEN
IN DEEPEST ESSEX

The construction of RAF Debden began in 1935 but it was still incomplete at the time of the official opening on 22 April 1937 when it became an operational unit with Fighter Command. Completion of the airfield took place after the commencement of hostilities. The first squadrons to operate from RAF Debden were Nos 87, 80, 73 and 29, who arrived in that order, flying such famous aircraft as the Gloster Gladiator and the Hawker Demon. The first Hurricanes arrived in July 1938, followed a few months later by Blenheims, and when war was declared the station was home to two squadrons of Hurricanes. RAF Debden received a considerable amount of attention from the Luftwaffe and can boast of having played a vital role in the Battle of Britain. The American volunteers in the RAF were known as the Eagle Squadron and they were posted to Debden, then in May 1943 the station became the first RAF fighter base to be handed over to the Americans, thus becoming a unit within the United States 8th Army Air Force, Mustangs and Thunderbolts being added to the list of aircraft which flew from the Essex airfield. September 1946 saw the end of the American occupation of RAF Debden and the station became a Technical Training Command Unit.

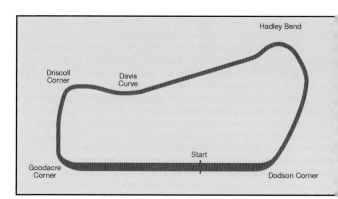

Above: The circuit at RAF Debden was a typical aerodrome track utilising part of one of the runways and the perimeter track. A mile and a half long, Debden was essentially a right-hand-biased circuit as can be seen from this circuit map, with the start/finish line situated approximately halfway along the main straight.

Below: A scene from the 750 Motor Club's race meeting at Debden on 22 September 1962: the cars are at the end of the main straight and turning into Goodacre Corner, the first on the track. They are a Ginetta G4 followed by a Mini, an Austin-Healey Sprite sandwiched between two Terriers, and an Elva Courier. *Steve Wyatt/Quilter House*

The official opening of the Debden circuit took place at a 750 Motor Club meeting on 9 June 1962, with the second meeting of the year taking place on 22 September. 1963 saw three meetings on 13 April, 1 June and 14 September, with another three in 1964 on 28 June, 19 July and 19 September.

1965 saw but one race meeting on 27 June when the Gala of Motor Sport & Motoring was held with the racing once more in the capable hands of the 750 Motor Club. From the programme for that day, it emerges that at an earlier meeting a competing car had contrived to reach the public highway through a fence when the driver lost control at the end of the straight. As a result of this incident, the Royal Automobile Club notified the 750 Motor Club that before another permit would be issued it would require a barrier to be erected along the boundary fence in an attempt to guarantee that no car would again reach the public highway. The organising club felt that it could not afford the cost involved and envisaged problems with the RAF as the station was still operational, and added to this the surface was breaking up. As a result the Board of the 750 Motor Club decided on 1 July 1965 that it would not apply for any further permits to use Debden for racing and the scheduled meeting for 18 September was abandoned.

The circuit measured a mile and a half and was roughly

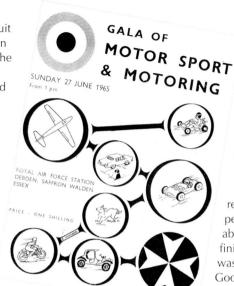

GALA OF MOTOR SPORT & MOTORING

SUNDAY 27 JUNE 1965
From 1 pm

ROYAL AIR FORCE STATION
DEBDEN, SAFFRON WALDEN
ESSEX

PRICE - ONE SHILLING

This is the programme cover from the very last race meeting held at RAF Debden: it had a glossy cover and considerable content but for details of the competitors in the race meeting spectators had to refer to a duplicated insert. The day's events consisted of go-karting for the Senior Service Trophy, motor racing organised by the 750 Motor Club, a vintage and veteran car display, driving tests for the public, an air display, motorcycle sprints and a display by RAF police dogs. *G. R. Heath Collection*

rectangular, using a runway and part of the perimeter track. The main straight was about half a mile long with the start and finish line halfway along it; the first corner was a fairly sharp right-hander called Goodacre, followed by a gradual curve leading to another right named Driscoll Corner, which screwed in on itself and had an adverse camber. From Driscoll the road meandered through Davis Curve and a couple more unnamed bends to Hadley Bend, another right-hander which continued as a gentle curve to the last corner (yet another right) named Dodson Corner, and thus back to the start. The Inaugural Meeting featured a number of excursions at Driscoll Corner with which the marshals coped, but they were somewhat miffed when one of the errant competitors ran over their sandwiches! Debden is still used for the occasional sprint and the M11 passes its doors.

DONINGTON PARK
THE WORLD'S ONLY PRIVATELY OWNED GRAND PRIX CIRCUIT

The history of Donington Park can be divided into two distinct eras, pre- and post-World War 2, and it was the vision of two men (one in each era) which made motor racing possible on this circuit and, as a result, it can claim to be the oldest and the youngest Grand Prix circuit in the United Kingdom. It was certainly the first licensed circuit in England and although located mainly in Leicestershire (the nearest town is Castle Donington) just a little bit of it protruded into Derbyshire which was to cause some problems in later years.

Fred Craner was a Derby garage owner who had raced motorcycles extensively in the Isle of Man TT until a crash ended his career. He then set about organising a team to compete on the island with training to take place on the gravel track at Syston Park. There appears to have been a major falling-out between Craner and the owners of Syston, with Craner vowing to establish a better venue; it was a very tall order.

There were three possible sites on which to establish a new circuit but the most favourable was Donington Park which, in the 1930s, was owned by the Shields family who (fortuitously) opened the grounds and the Hall to the public upon payment of the princely sum of 6d (2^1/2p).

The 1937 Donington Grand Prix was, arguably, the greatest motor race seen in Great Britain up to that time, attracting as it did the cream of the world's racing cars in the shape of the Daimler-Benz and Auto Union factory cars, the former sending four entries and the latter three. Not surprisingly, the German cars dominated the race and here we see Rudolf Caracciola and Manfred von Brauchitsch in the mighty 5.6-litre straight eight-cylinder supercharged Mercedes-Benz W125s numbers 1 and 3 which they took to second and third places ahead of the Auto Unions of Müller and Hasse. Von Brauchitsch had started from pole and Caracciola from the middle of the second row of the grid. The crowd is immense and the protection for them rudimentary. *Daimler-Benz Classic Archives*

Fred Craner paid his entry fee and set out to explore the undulating parkland, only to fall foul of the gamekeeper but he liked his story and took him to meet Mr Shields in the Hall. The owner of the estate greeted the proposals with not much enthusiasm but was soon won round and five weeks later the first dirt circuit had been laid out and the first motorcycle meeting was held on Whit Monday in May 1931 — Donington had arrived and the new circuit was 2 miles 327yd in length.

The start/finish line was on a short downhill straight between Red Gate Lodge and Holly Wood, then ran through a long right-hand bend followed by a left which led to the Hairpin Bend then under Starkey's Bridge, not for the faint-hearted as it was just wide enough to take one vehicle at a time. There followed two lefts separated by a short straight leading to McLean's Corner, a sharp right which led on to one of the longest straights on the track followed by Coppice Corner a very sharp right and was a no-overtaking area as the circuit passed between farm buildings. Some fairly gentle curves led through Coppice Lane and Starkey's Hill to the right-hand Red Gate Corner followed by a straight leading back to Red Gate Lodge and the start line and all through undulating parkland.

For 1932, improvements were made and sidecars were catered for, but the racing was still only for motorcycles. However, for the 1933 season the track was widened, corners were redrawn, the not inconsiderable sum of £12,000 was spent on tarmacking the circuit and the first car race meeting took place on Saturday, 25 March that year with a Le Mans start for the four participants. There were three further car meetings, culminating in October when run in inclement weather.

For the following year there was an extension of 650yd to the circuit and five car meetings were held. The new part of the circuit started at Red Gate Corner where it ran straight ahead instead of turning right to Starkey's Corner which was virtually

Above: The colossal power of the Silver Arrows is amply demonstrated in this view of Manfred von Brauchitsch in a power slide at the wheel of his W125. Donington was to be the last race for cars complying with the 750kg Formula and those who were fortunate to be present for the race will not have forgotten the spectacle. It is interesting to note that the only advertising in view is directly linked to the sport. *Daimler-Benz Classic Archives*

Right: This is the original 1931 Donington Park circuit, measuring just 2 miles 327yd.

Below right: By 1935 the circuit had been extended and now measured 2 miles 971yd. Where reference is made to wood in the identity of parts of the circuit it should be remembered that the circuit was at that point passing through woodland.

Bottom right: The second extension to the circuit with Starkey's Corner being extended to the Melbourne Hairpin took place in 1937; everything else is as in 1935 but the track length was now 3 miles 220yd.

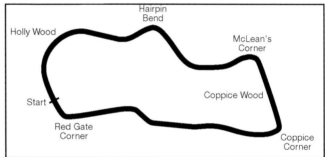

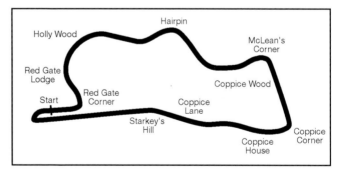

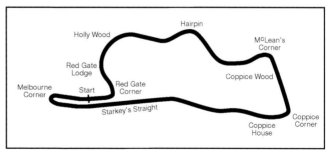

a hairpin; the start/finish line was relocated on to the new straight thus created before Red Gate Corner which was now a very sharp left.

In 1935, Donington Park came of age with Grand Prix cars competing at the opening meeting and culminating with the staging of the first Donington Grand Prix, by which time Fred Craner was established in Coppice House in the Park. Run on Saturday, 5 October under the International Sporting Code of the Association Internationale des Automobiles Clubs Reconnus (the forerunner of the Commission Sportif International of the Federation International des Automobiles), the General Competition Rules of the Royal Automobile Club and the supplementary rules of the Derby & District Motor Club, practice took place between the hours of 9am and 5pm on the three preceding days.

Left: Victory in 1937 went to Bernd Rosemeyer at the wheel of the V16 6-litre supercharged C-type Auto Union. The 16-cylinder cars were lighter on tyres than the Mercedes, which gave Rosemeyer sufficient advantage to beat von Brauchitsch by 38sec. Driving car number 5, the victor had started from second on the grid. *Archiv Auto Union*

Below: Two great masters at work at Donington Park a year apart: Germany's Rudolf Caracciola in the Mercedes-Benz W125 in 1937 . . . *Daimler-Benz Classic Archives*

Bottom: . . . and the little Mantuan, Tazio Nuvolari, at the wheel of the 3-litre supercharged D-type Auto Union on his way to victory in the 1938 Donington Grand Prix. *Archiv Auto Union*

Three Continental entries were received from Dr Giuseppe Farina driving a 4.5-litre Maserati (who set fastest lap in practice), a 3.7-litre Tipo 34 Maserati for Gino Revere, and Raymond Sommer with a 2.9-litre Alfa Romeo. There were 12 British-based entries including B. Bira — Prince Birabongse Bhanuban of Siam (the grandson of the King of Siam immortalised in Rogers and Hammerstein's musical *The King and I*) who had received the ERA which he raced as a 21st birthday present from his cousin and mentor Prince Chula Chakrabongse.

A study of the flag signals listed in the programme makes interesting reading today; a yellow flag indicated an immediate stop, while a *light* blue flag held horizontally informed the driver that he had to keep to the right as another competitor wished to pass him. The waving of a *dark* blue flag indicated danger ahead, and a green one marked the end of the race. A chequered flag with the competitor's number indicated he had completed the course. Beneath the list of 'Official Flag Signals' appeared the admonition, 'The driver of any machine who does not stop after a black or yellow flag has been displayed to him may be fined a sum not exceeding £5, and/or the machine may be excluded at the discretion of the Stewards.'

Fred Craner was both Secretary of the Meeting and Clerk of the Course; there were four Stewards (one appointed by the RAC) but one Judge was considered sufficient. Amongst the BBC broadcasting announcers was Graham Walker, father of the much-respected Murray who carried on the family tradition for the BBC *Grand Prix* programme, and does so for ITV at the time of writing. It is surprising to note that the Grand Prix was the only event on the programme until the times are looked at — the race took 4hr 47min 12sec to run at an average speed of 63.97mph. Victory went to Richard Shuttleworth driving his supercharged 2.9-litre Alfa Romeo from the 3.3-litre Bugattis of Earl Howe and Martin — none of the Continental entries appearing in the top six. Fred Craner had achieved his ambition of running a Grand Prix at Donington Park but this was just the beginning.

It was to be a busy season in 1936; the British Empire Trophy was run at Donington for the first time over 100 laps of the circuit, with victory going to the 23-year-old Richard Seaman

driving the ex-Whitney Straight Maserati. Later in the year he was to win the Junior Car Club 200-mile race by 51sec, collecting £350 prize money in the process.

The second Donington Grand Prix was run on 3 October over a distance of 307 miles; 23 entries were received, with 22 of them coming to the grid — which was decided by ballot. The race confirmed that this was Richard Seaman's year for he won with the Swiss driver Hans Ruesch in the latter's 3.8-litre supercharged Alfa Romeo — the car in which Nuvolari had won the Coppa Ciano earlier in the year. The time was 4hr 25min 22sec and the race average had risen to 69.23mph.

Donington Park really came of age in 1937 for it was in that

year that the truly terrifyingly awesome Mercedes-Benz and
Auto Union Grand Prix cars came to England for the first time
— their like had not been seen before and was not to be seen
again. But before the Grand Prix further changes were to be
wrought upon the circuit.

Craner's attitude was ever that better could still be achieved
and, with the continued agreement and support of the Shields
family, he produced his finest circuit. From Starkey's Corner the
track was extended over Melbourne Hill down to the famous
(infamous) Melbourne Corner hairpin taking the course just
into Derbyshire, the circuit now measuring 3 miles 220yd.

The new circuit was used for the first running of the RAC
Tourist Trophy on the mainland and for the Grand Prix but
before that there was a full season's racing, starting with
Raymond Mays winning the British Empire Trophy Race at a
speed of 62.96mph in his ERA before a crowd estimated to be
15,000. Coronation Day in June was marked with a special
meeting, Goodacre winning all four races — three five-lappers
and a 100-mile race in his Austin — while Pat Fairfield won
the Nuffield Trophy in June. This was followed by two club
meetings and a 12hr sports car race which was won by Prince
Birabongse (who raced as 'B. Bira') and Dobbs in a Delahaye.
The Royal Automobile Club's Tourist Trophy race was won by
Comotti driving a Darracq, while Arthur Dobson in an ERA
won the JCC 200.

For the third running of the Donington Grand Prix something
bordering upon the impossible happened; to the unbounded
delight of Fred Craner and the Derby & District Motor Club,
entries were received from Mercedes-Benz and Auto Union.
Forget the politics which gave birth to these leviathans — they
were and will remain almost unbelievable; Untertürkheim sent
W125s for Manfred von Brauchitsch, Hermann Lang, Richard
Seaman (the first Englishman to be asked to drive for a foreign
Grand Prix team) and Rudolf Caracciola (who was reputed to
be able to see in fog). From Auto Union came three of the
fearsome 6-litre supercharged V16s to be handled by Bernd
Rosemeyer, Achille Varzi and Hermann Müller; ranged against
them were seven ERAs, three Maseratis, an Alfa Romeo and
Maclure's Riley, the only normally aspirated car in the race.

Donington circuit was set amongst the woodland of the park
and the sight and sound of the Silver Arrows thundering
between the trees at speeds of up to 170mph must have been
awe-inspiring and electrifying to the 50,000 crowd who
attended. The Grand Prix was run over 80 laps (approximately
250 miles) and was won by Rosemeyer in 3hr 1min 22sec at
82.62mph from von Brauchitsch, Carraciola, Müller and Rudolf
Hasse with Bira a very creditable sixth aboard Chula's
Maserati.

Unpleasant things were happening in Europe and while the
winner was warmly applauded, the German National Anthem
was not played notwithstanding the fact that this had been an
International Grand Prix. With their white-clad mechanics, the
German teams demonstrated just what European Grand Prix
motor racing was all about and just how much had to be
learned at home.

Fred Craner was still the Clerk of the Course and Secretary of
the Meeting; he and the club had shown considerable courage
in paying £3,500 starting money to the German teams — but

The front cover
of the programme of the 1938
International Donington Grand Prix Car Race with
clear evidence of the late change of date of the meeting. There is no
claim that this was to be the British Grand Prix and reference to the
contents reveals that the Grand Prix was to be the only event of the
day. The illustration of the Mercedes-Benz and Auto Unions is from the
previous year's event. *Author's collection*

they were more than compensated by the £10,000 gate money.
The presence of a Judge was clearly considered unnecessary on
this occasion as none was listed in the programme but the flag
signals were more in line with those used at present except that
a white flag indicated the end of the race. Thus ended the
1937 season at Donington — there was to be one more Grand
Prix before war intervened and put an end to motor racing at
the Midlands circuit for a very long time.

The 1938 season opened with the annual running of the
British Empire Trophy which went to Arthur Dobson in his
Austin, while Raymond Mays won the 100-mile Coronation
Cup in his ERA; Bira won the Nuffield Trophy and Bob Gerard
the RAC TT in a Delage.

Following the unbounded success that the 1937 Grand Prix
had been it was announced very early that the exercise would
be repeated the following year but across Europe storm clouds
were gathering. The 1938 Grand Prix was scheduled for
1 October and the Mercedes and Auto Unions had arrived
three weeks early, only to be called home as the Munich Crisis
deepened and the Grand Prix was called off. Then Prime
Minister Neville Chamberlain returned from Munich declaring

'Peace in our time'; the GP was hastily re-scheduled for Saturday, 22 October and the German teams returned with four Mercedes-Benz and four Auto Unions. Mute evidence of the change still exists in the date change on the programme cover. The Mercedes W154s were to have the same drivers as the previous year except that Walter Baumer replaced the injured Caracciola (but some reports say that the latter did not like the Donington Park circuit) while the Auto Unions were to be driven by the great Tazio Nuvolari (replacing Rosemeyer who had lost his life in a record attempt), Müller and Hasse (who had been the reserve driver in 1937) with the addition of Christian Kautz. The Fourth Donington Grand Prix was run over 80 laps of the circuit totalling 250 miles before a crowd of 60,000 people. Victory again went to Auto Union, the winning car being in the hands of the little 46-year-old Mantuan, Tazio Nuvolari, from the Mercedes-Benzes of Lang and Seaman; the winner's time was 3hr 6min 22sec at a speed of 80.49mph. Fourth was the Auto Union of Müller with von Brauchitsch in the Mercedes fifth and Dobson's ERA sixth.

The 1939 British season commenced with the British Empire

Trophy on Saturday, 1 April. Craner had plans well in hand for a further Grand Prix on Saturday, 30 September but by then the world was engulfed in a war which was to last for six long, wearisome years. There exists on file at Donington Park a letter from Daimler-Benz written in the August entering three Mercedes-Benz cars for the fifth Donington Grand Prix in 1939.

The final race meeting at Donington took place on Saturday, 12 August, run by the Vintage Sports Car Club; it was abandoned after a serious accident and as competitors and spectators went home they could have little thought that they had witnessed what was destined to be the final race meeting at Donington Park for nearly half a century.

As with so many such properties, Donington Park was requisitioned by the Government for military use and was used for vehicle storage for up to half a million vehicles. Eventually, after the cessation of hostilities, the military had no further use for the park which now bore the marks of its wartime usage and as the years rolled on a number of attempts were made to reintroduce motorsport, but all came to nothing.

That is until a self-made millionaire (who had attended motorcycle meetings and seen the prewar Grands Prix after having ridden a pedal cycle to the circuit) purchased 300 acres of the park, including all the motor racing circuit, in 1971. He

Left: Alfred Neubauer ruled the Mercedes-Benz competitions department with a rod of iron for more than a quarter of a century: at Donington Park he stands atop a timing stand with stopwatch in hand while Rudolf Caracciola sits on the steps. The lady is probably Mrs Alice Caracciola who accompanied her husband to most of his races. *Daimler-Benz Classic Archives*

Below: For 1938 the International Formula for Racing Cars allowed an upper limit of 4.5 litres for normally aspirated engines and 3 litres supercharged: both Daimler-Benz and Auto Union had chosen a V12 layout, the Mercedes engine displacing 2,962cc and the Zwickau-built engine 2,968cc. Each team sent four cars to Donington and here the challengers are seen parading around the circuit: Manfred von Brauchitsch in the W154 beside Tazio Nuvolari in the D-type Auto Union lead the field. *Archiv Auto Union*

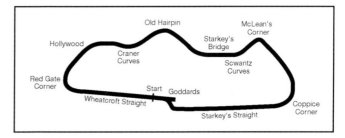

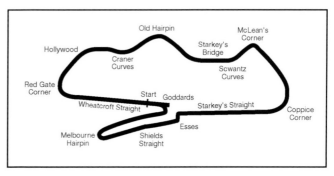

was F. B. 'Tom' Wheatcroft who first established a motor racing museum in a specially constructed building (he was, after all, a builder by profession) with 30 or so cars. Today the Donington International Collection comprises some 130 priceless cars and is justly world-famous.

Sadly, re-establishing racing did not come so quickly, partly caused by the protrusion of part of the circuit into Derbyshire. History repeated itself, for motorcycle racing was first to return to Donington, with cars following a fortnight after the first bike meeting. Action at this time was confined to the 1.957-mile National Circuit which, while still recognisable as the Donington of prewar days, was somewhat modified; the start/finish line was on Wheatcroft Straight before the familiar Red Gate Corner and Hollywood and the sweeping curves of old were now named Craner Curves and Hairpin Bend is now called Old Hairpin. Starkey's Bridge is still there but the circuit no longer passes under the narrow bridge of old but has been moved infield and the bridge extended to span the circuit. McLean's and Coppice Corner are still there but the latter has been somewhat re-aligned leading to Starkey Straight and Goddards, a sharp right and left taking the track back to the start/finish line.

Throughout this time Tom Wheatcroft cherished the dream of bringing a Grand Prix back to his circuit and in 1985 he took the bold step of increasing the circuit length to the optimum of 2.5 miles which was achieved by inserting the Esses on Starkey Straight before Goddards and taking the course down to the right-hand Melbourne Hairpin and thus making Goddards a left-hand hairpin.

On 22 September 1985 the final round of the European F3000 Championship was staged at Donington Park; March 85Bs filled five of the top six placings, with victory going to the eventual Champion, Christian Danner, from Mario Hytten, Ivan Capelli, Michel Ferté, Philippe Streiff (driving an AGS JH 20) and Alain Ferté. Wheatcroft's initial investment had been £2 million and this now had to be trebled. In 1987, he had bought out the rights to stage the British Motorcycle Grand Prix in that year and 1988 from Silverstone Circuits. The race was transformed and has since been an annual event. At around this time the Jim Russell Racing Drivers' School transferred from Snetterton to Donington Park.

On 28 June 1987 F3000 cars ran over 50 laps of Donington, making a race distance of 125 miles as the cars contested the fifth round of the Intercontinental F3000 Championship. Luis Perez Sala drove his Lola T87/50 to victory at 103.77mph beating Stefano Modena by just under 7sec, with Pierre-Henri Raphanel third — both were driving March 87Bs. Into fourth place came Roberto Moreno's Ralt, with the Lola of Michel Trollé and Ferté fifth and sixth.

The Silver Arrows returned to Donington Park in 1989 and 1990 as part of the World Sports-Prototype Championship when Mercedes-Benz won on both occasions — although that is not strictly true for in 1989 the cars were still running as Sauber-Mercedes, the Swiss team running their C9 cars. However, silver they most certainly were and history was repeated. The race was run over 120 laps of the full Grand Prix circuit, making a race distance of 300 miles; first home were Jean-Louis Schlesser and Jochen Mass in 2hr 57min 50.8sec at 101.12mph, just 51sec ahead of the second C9 in the hands of Mauro Baldi and Kenny Acheson whilst in third place was the Nissan R89C of Julian Bailey and Mark Blundell. Fourth place went to a Porsche 962C a lap down driven by Wollek and Jelinski with the identical car of Hyman and Larrauri fourth. The first British car home was the Aston Martin AMR1 driven by Leslie and Roe in sixth place on 118 laps.

The 1990 International F3000 Championship opened at

Left: Damon Hill took a great deal of effort in promoting the 1993 European Grand Prix at Donington Park, being present throughout the Press Day. Here he is seen with Max Turner and his Austin Seven which he and his brother entered in the very first motor race at Donington Park in 1933, Mr Turner riding as mechanic to his brother. *Author*

Below: On the day of which Tom Wheatcroft had dreamed so long, and that the weather tried unsuccessfully to spoil and which Ayrton Senna made his own, Senna is seen in the McLaren MP4/8 on his way to victory on the rain-soaked track. He had started from fourth on the grid and simply drove away from the opposition, setting the fastest lap in 1min 18.029sec, a speed of 114.975 miles per hour which compared with the existing lap record, set by Mauro Baldi at 113.416mph. However, Senna's fastest lap was set on a short one when he passed through the pit lane for a tyre change but did not stop. *Mike Dixon*

Above: Michael Schumacher had set third fastest lap in practice in the Benetton B193B but was eliminated on the 22nd lap in an accident. What battles there would have been had Senna not died so tragically!
Mike Dixon

Left: Having done so much to promote the European Grand Prix, Damon Hill was featured on the front cover of the programme.
Author's collection

OFFICIAL PROGRAMME
£5.00

Donington Park on 22 April with a 125-mile race over 50 laps of the full circuit; the first six places were evenly split between Lola and Reynard, the first three to Mugen-engined Lolas T90/50s, fourth to sixth to Reynard 90Ds. The winner, in 1hr 12min 15.3sec at 103.79mph, was Eric Comas from Chiesa and Jones; the first Reynard home was driven by Tamburini with Cosworth power, Dean with a Mugen engine and another Cosworth helped van de Poele take the final point.

And so to 2 September and the true return of the Silver Arrows, for by now the powers that be at Untertürkheim had decided that Peter Sauber and his team from Hinwil in Switzerland had done such a good job that the sports cars should no longer run as Sauber-Mercedes but as Mercedes-Benz. The Mercedes C11s driven by Jean-Louis Schlesser/Mauro Baldi won the Shell Donington Trophy, the second British round of the World Sports-Prototype Championship, the winner's time for the 300-mile race being 2hr 53min 40sec at 103.55mph. Second was the C11 driven by Heinz-Harald Frentzen and Jochen Mass; these were the only cars to complete the full 120 laps. Two laps down in third spot was a Spice SE90C-Cosworth driven by Tim Harvey and Cor Euser, with the Kenny Acheson/ Gianfranco Brancatelli Nissan 90C fourth, a further lap adrift. Fifth was another Spice in the hands of Bruno Giacomelli and Eric van de Poele, with Julian Bailey/Mark Blundell in a Nissan, sixth. Porsche 962Cs then filled the finishing board down to 17th place. The Jaguar XJR11s of Martin Brundle and Andy Wallace/Jan Lammers finished third and seventh on the road but were excluded from the results for refuelling infringements.

When the World Sports Car Championship returned to Donington Park in 1992 it was to a slightly longer race at 312 miles, 125 laps of the circuit. However, thanks to politics within the governing body who would not leave the sports cars alone, there were only 10 entries and only 5,000 spectators arrived but they did see the Peugeot 905s of Mauro Baldi/ Phillippe Alliot and Derek Warwick/Yannick Dalmas finish first and second, the winners' speed being 107.712mph in 2hr 54min. Third was the Lees/Brabham Toyota TR 010 (the only other car to complete the full distance) with the Andrews/ Frentzen Lola T92-Judd fourth on 119 laps. Fifth place went to the Sala/Caffi Mazda MXR-01, with DeLesseps and Hoy sixth in the Spice 89C. Gone were the Jaguars, gone were the Mercedes-Benz and soon, too, would be the sports cars, killed off by the sport's governing body.

Tom Wheatcroft's dream came true on Easter Sunday, 11 April 1993. The Asian Grand Prix had run into trouble and was to be replaced by the European Grand Prix and the new race was awarded to Donington Park which finally staged a round of the FIA Formula One World Championship. Sadly, the race was run in pouring rain (this was Easter in England!) over 76 laps of the Grand Prix circuit, making a race distance of 199 miles. Pole position went to Alain Prost from his Williams-Renault team-mate Damon Hill but victory went to Ayrton Senna (McLaren) from Hill, Prost, Johnny Herbert (Lotus), Riccardo Patrese (Benetton) and Fabrizio Barbazza (Minardi). Senna's winning time was 1hr 50min 46.57sec at a speed of 114.975mph, 1.23sec ahead of Hill. These two were the only competitors to complete the full race distance, the next three being a lap down, with Barbazza a further lap adrift.

It is interesting to muse upon the point that when the 1938 Grand Prix was run none of the manufacturers contesting the 1993 event even existed. Some interesting comparisons can be made with the 1938 Donington Grand Prix; the race in 1993 was some 50 miles shorter but run in under two hours whereas Nuvolari took over three hours in the Auto Union, and the race speed had risen from 80mph to 114. Some 50,000 spectators attended in 1938 and 40,000 in 1993, which serves to prove the point that motor racing is as great a draw as it has ever been, the attendance at the later event no doubt being affected by the weather.

Rather less than a month later the International F3000 Championship opened at Donington with the first of two rounds run in England less than a week apart — six days to be precise when the contingent moved south to Silverstone. In 1993 it might have been assumed that the F3000 Championship was a one-make affair, all the contestants using Reynard 93s, but this was not the case; it was simply that this was seen as the best chassis available, but there was some difference of opinion over power units, the majority choosing Cosworth with a few opting for Judd. The Donington race was over 46 laps of the Grand Prix circuit, making a race distance

of 115 miles which Beretta covered in 1hr 3min at 110.7mph from Lamy, Panis, Papis, Stewart and Simoni.

A form of sports car racing returned to the international calendar in 1995 in the shape of the International BPR Series run over 12 rounds, the fifth of which was run at Donington Park on 8 May. It was something of a McLaren F1 benefit as these cars filled the first three places in the hands of John Nielsen/Thomas Bscher, Raphanel/Owen Jones and Andy Wallace and Derek Bell. The next three places were taken by Porsche 911s driven by Mastropietro/Konig, Kaufmann/Albera/ Ligonnet (a Bi-Turbo car) and Bryner/Calderari. It was a welcome return.

International Sports Car Racing then received a new lease of life via the FIA/GT Championship whose contenders converged upon Donington Park on 14 September 1997. It was a Mercedes-Benz benefit, the factory CLK GTRs filling three of the first six places, with McLaren F1s taking the other top six placings. Victory went to the Mercedes of Bernd Schneider and Alexander Wurtz from the similar car of Nannini and Tieman, with the J. J. Lehto/Steve Soper McLaren third. The third works Mercedes took fourth place in the hands of Ludwig and Laylander from the McLarens of Kox/Ravaglia and Raphanel/ Gounon.

And the oldest race on the British motor sporting calendar, the RAC Tourist Trophy, has returned to Donington Park. The wheel has come full circle upon the only privately owned Grand Prix circuit in the world.

It is, perhaps, fitting that the outright lap record on the prewar Donington TT Course should stand equally to the credit of Mercedes-Benz and Auto Union. On 2 October 1937 it was set at a speed of 85.62mph 2min 11.4sec. The drivers were Manfred von Brauchitsch, who had started from pole position in the Mercedes, and Bernd Rosemeyer, whose Auto Union had started from second spot. The record will, of course, stand for ever. At the close of the 2000 season the outright lap record on the Grand Prix Circuit stands to the credit of Ayrton Senna at 115.33mph in 1min 18.029sec driving a Marlboro McLaren at the European Grand Prix on 11 April 1993. The outright lap record on the National Circuit was set by Johan Rajamaki at 120.92mph at the wheel of a Footwork-Judd FA13 in 58.27sec in August 1996.

Above: The Formula One engines used by McLaren-Mercedes in the last decade of the 20th century have been engineered and built by Ilmor Engineering but the co-operation between the two companies goes back some time. In 1994 Ilmor Engineering took full advantage of the rules in force at the Indianapolis Motor Speedway to take victory in that year's Indy 500 with the Marlboro Penske Mercedes PC23. The rules then in force allowed more supercharger boost power for two-valve push-rod engines with the result that the M-B5001 engine delivered no less than 1,023hp: with this phenomenal power-house behind him Al Unser Jnr took pole position and won at the engine's debut, hitting 254mph on the back straight at the Brickyard. The rules were changed for the following year! In addition to the Mercedes-Benz W154 the crowds at Donington Park on 23 May 1999 were also entertained by some demonstrations by this remarkable car which was in the capable hands of John Watson; it was the first occasion that it had been seen in action on a British circuit and is seen passing the pits. *Author*

Right: The third car demonstrated on 23 May 1999 was the 1998 West McLaren-Mercedes MP4-13 which was driven by Mario Haberfeld and is seen here about to pass under the starting gantry after exiting Goddards. *Author*

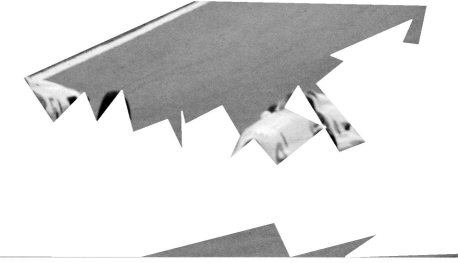

Above: Notwithstand the caption to the picture of John Surtees in the Mercedes Benz over the weekend of 19/20 May 2001 the Vintage Sports Car Club surpassed its previous efforts in persuading Audi to bring two of its Auto Unions back to Donington Park. The drivers entered the spirit of the weekend clad, as they were, in white overalls with brown leather helmets just as Rosermeyer and Nuvolari had been clad sixty-two and sixty-three years previously. The D Type was driven by Thomas Franck who is Head of Audi Tradition and Managing Director of Auto Union GmbH the C Type by Franz Peter. Both cars (in company with a not inconsiderable collection of other Audi competition cars) were demonstrated twice on both days and are seen at the Craner Curves. *Author*

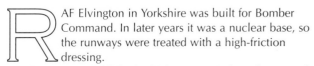

ELVINGTON
EXCESSIVE TYRE WEAR

RAF Elvington in Yorkshire was built for Bomber Command. In later years it was a nuclear base, so the runways were treated with a high-friction dressing.

A circuit was established which appears to have been used by the British Racing & Sports Car Club. The inaugural meeting took place on 8 July 1962 and was reported in the following week's *Autosport*, which said that the BRSCC hoped to run a further meeting in the September, but this appears not to have taken place. A second race meeting did take place a year after the first on 7 July 1963 but these two appear to have been the sum total of motor racing at Elvington. The high-friction dressing on the runways resulted in prodigious tyre wear on competing cars. At one of the two meetings a long-nose D-Type Jaguar ran through a set of green spot Dunlop R6 racing tyres in a 10-lap race, which was a mite inconvenient as the car had been driven to the circuit!

Photographs at Elvington have proved elusive in the extreme.

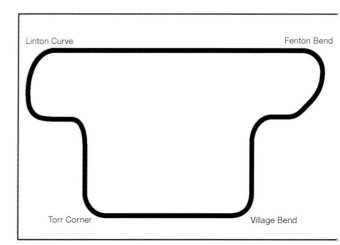

Save for pure ovals, the track on the airfield at RAF Elvington was probably the most symmetrical anywhere in the world, as can be seen from this map of the circuit. Four corners were named and four were not and no indication has been found as to the situation of the start and finish line, though it is fair to assume that it was on the main straight.

FERSFIELD
FIRST ATTEMPTS IN EAST ANGLIA

RAF Fersfield was opened in 1944 and was used by the USAAF and the US Navy for Operation 'Aphrodite'. This was an ingenious scheme whereby 'war-weary' bombers were loaded with explosives, taken into the air by crews who then baled out and were then guided by remote control from an accompanying manned aircraft to their targets. (It appears that the local populace were none too impressed when they heard of these operations.) It was also from RAF Fersfield that fighters set out to make the famous low-level attack on the Shell House Gestapo HQ in Copenhagen on 21 March 1945. Fersfield's active service came to an end when it closed in December 1945.

The Eastern Counties Motor Club was formed early in 1950 and was soon turning its attention to organising competitive motoring, the first speed event being speed trials at RAF Bentwaters on 23 April. The club's first race meeting took place exactly a year later on 22 April 1951 at Fersfield which is situated near Diss in Norfolk. Prior to that first race meeting the members had spent many weekends preparing the old airfield and cleaning the runways of rubbish and unwanted growth. That first meeting was a 'closed-to-club' affair but just two months later an invitation meeting (to which seven clubs were invited) was organised on 17 June at which seven races were run and which were effectively nine as the sixth race was run as two heats and a final. The RAC Steward requested that the fourth race be stopped as spectators had encroached into a restricted area; the red flag was shown but some of the drivers declined to obey it and were reprimanded for their colour blindness — not much changes! The race was re-run at the end of the meeting.

Further race meetings were run in 1952 but at the end of the

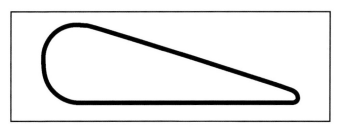

Above: It has proved particularly difficult to establish the plan of the circuit used by the Eastern Counties Motor Club at RAF Fersfield. On 22 June 1951 *Autosport* carried a report of the second race meeting at the new venue and said of the 2-mile-long circuit that it 'may be best described as a long thin "V" with a real Melbourne-type corner at the bottom of the "V" and a sharp right-hand bend followed by a rapidly tightening sweep at the top end.' From contemporary reports it is known that one of the runways and parts of the perimeter track were used and reference to the airfield map produced this outline of the circuit which was to the eastern side of the airfield, with the hairpin pointing almost due south. Location of the start and finish line is not known but contemporary photographs indicate that races at Fersfield were run clockwise.

Left: The front programme cover from the second Fersfield race meeting. *C. M. S. Abbott collection*

year the RAC requested that certain improvements be carried out which would have cost £10,000. This being beyond the club's resources, the venue was abandoned. However, the Eastern Counties Motor Club was not to be outdone and turned its attention to Snetterton where it successfully ran the Eastern Counties 100 meeting for many years.

The RAC Steward once insisted that everyone present at Fersfield should sweep the track clean of rubbish before he would allow racing to continue. As with most circuits there is always the lighter side and Fersfield was no exception, for the story goes of the road sweeper which did two laps to clean the track without the brushes working.

Lap records are, unfortunately, lost in the mists of time.

This picture comes from the second race meeting organised by the Eastern Counties Motor Club at Fersfield on 17 June 1951 and is of the Bentley Race, showing the cars of S. J. Laurence (39) and G. G. Macdonald (36) negotiating the long right-hand bend at the northern end of the circuit. The scant regard for safety is worthy of note, none of the three drivers in view having the benefit of a crash helmet although Laurence does appear to be wearing some overalls. The race had benefited from just four starters. *C. M. S. Abbott collection*

FULL SUTTON
COURTESY OF THE ROYAL AIR FORCE

The village of Full Sutton lies to the East of York on the A166, the airfield bearing the name seeing motor racing in 1958 when still in use as an operational Royal Air Force station. Permission to race had to be obtained form the Air Ministry and appears to have been organised entirely by the British Racing & Sports Car Club.

The circuit was 3.2 miles in length and used part of both runways and a considerable amount of the perimeter track. The start and finish line was situated on one of the runways and ran to a right-hand bend followed by a short straight and another right-hander on to the perimeter track. A straight of about half a mile led to another right-hand bend of somewhat tighter nature than the preceding two. There then came two straights nearly a mile in length with a left-hand kink about half-way along; two long right-hand corners with a very short straight between them led to another short straight and a right-hander, leading on to the second runway, and a sharp left brought competitors back on to the start and finish straight.

It would appear that the British Racing & Sports Car Club organised four race meetings at Full Sutton in 1958. The first meeting took place in April, when it snowed, causing Jimmy Clark to go off in the Scott-Watson Porsche; the car narrowly missed a flag marshal who had not been warned by his fellow flag marshal of the impending danger as he departed. The meeting on Saturday 27 September saw a six-race programme for Formula III racing cars, saloon cars, Sports Racing Cars (a term which has fallen out of fashion) and Production Sports and Grand Touring Cars. All races were over 10 laps, with the exception of the saloon car event, which was over five laps, and the main event of the day, which started at 4pm with a Le Mans start and ran over 16 laps for Sports Racing Cars of unlimited capacity. In this no less than 17 Lotus Elevens were entered, all powered by 1098cc Coventry-Climax engines with the exception of M. Dickens' example, which had a 1460cc Climax power unit. No 34 was driven by Innes Ireland.

It was the first airfield circuit to be lapped at more than 100mph by a sports car, the car in question being a D-Type Jaguar entered and owned by Border Reivers and driven by Jim Clark. The calculations in respect of the fastest lap were made in the pub after the meeting and initially showed a speed in excess of 120mph but when the alcohol and euphoria wore off the true figure was established!

Full Sutton was distant from centres of population and when RAF Rufforth became available the BRSCC moved there for convenience. The site of Full Sutton is now an industrial complex and a maximum security prison. It has not proved possible to glean the lap record.

Above: The 3.2-miles-long circuit at Full Sutton.

Left: Two programme covers from 1958 British Racing and Sports Car Club race meetings at Full Sutton, featuring cartoons which gently inform the public of the sponsorship being received from the *Daily Mirror.*

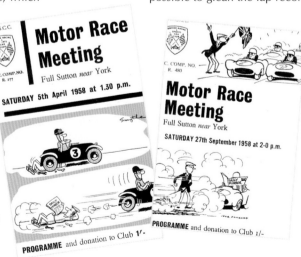

GAMSTON
NOTTINGHAMSHIRE'S ONLY
MOTOR RACING CIRCUIT

Gamston was one of the few Nottinghamshire sites selected as a bomber station by the Royal Air Force and was built to the usual wartime pattern of three runways, with the main one parallel to the B6387 road. It opened in December 1942 as satellite to No 14(P)AFU Ossington, and transferred to Bomber Command in May 1943 but was destined to play only a role in operational training. After the cessation of hostilities in Europe the station became a major holding unit, playing host to members of the Royal Australian Air Force awaiting repatriation. Between 1 July and 1 September 1945 1,841 Australians arrived at Gamston but by the end of the year the station had closed. It lay idle until May 1953 when it reopened as a satellite to Worksop, flying Meteors and Vampires, and finally severed its links with the RAF in 1957 when it closed down and became an inactive station.

Between closing in 1945 and re-opening in 1953, some motor racing took place in 1950 and 1951, organised by the Nottinghamshire Sports Car Club. It would appear that motor racing first took place at Gamston in 1950 but no proof has been found. However, a huge crowd attended a meeting on Whit Monday 1951 and *Autosport* of 27 July 1951 carried a report of a meeting run the previous Saturday by Sheffield & Hallamshire Motor Club. Reference was made to improved amenities.

Proceedings opened with a couple of five lap sports car races, the first of which saw Colin Chapman winning in his Lotus. Main event of the day was the 50-lap Formule Libre race which saw victory go to Bob Gerard in his 2-litre ERA who led from flag to flag. His only opposition appears to have come from Denis Poore's Alfa Romeo until it had plug trouble. Lap times were 77sec, indicating a lap speed of close to 90mph. For his efforts Gerard won the golden Kenning Trophy.

Why racing ceased in 1951 is unclear but, perhaps, there were rumours of the return of the Royal Air Force.

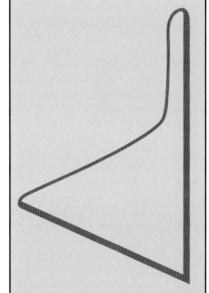

Left: This plan of the circuit at RAF Gamston comes from the programme of the meeting organised there by the Nottingham Sports Car Club on 7 August 1950. The length is put at '2 Miles Approx'.

Below: This circuit map is from the programme of a meeting also organised by the Nottingham Sports Car Club on 6 October 1951. The configuration is somewhat different and it has not been possible to ascertain whether the track did, in fact, differ as these two maps suggest.

Bottom: This third version is from the programme of a meeting run by the Sheffield and Hallamshire Motor Club on an unspecified date. The circuit length is stated to be 1.9 miles but, there being very little difference between this and the second outline from the NSCC meetings, it is likely that this circuit map is the definitive version.

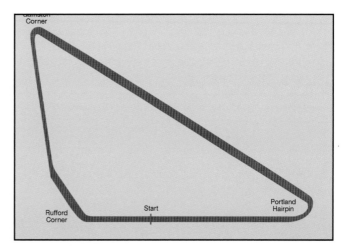

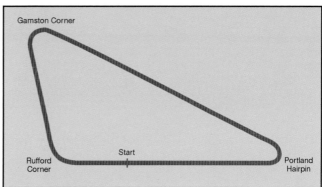

GOODWOOD
GLORIOUS GOODWOOD!

With the final cessation of hostilities in August 1945 minds across Europe turned to the resumption of motorsport and not least in England — but where could it take place? Of the three prewar circuits in England two were simply no longer available; Donington Park was still in the hands of the Government being used as a storage depot for military vehicles, while Brooklands had been 'sold down the river' and was used for aircraft production and the third, Crystal Palace, was in a state of disrepair. So eyes were cast elsewhere — and lit upon the many now-disused airfields, one of which was Westhampnett at Goodwood.

To tell the story of Goodwood requires a step back in time to 1938 when the Duke of Richmond and Gordon had been summoned to the Air Ministry where he was appraised of the serious situation in Germany, whereupon he agreed to part of the farming land at Goodwood being given over to the construction of a satellite airfield, the documents effecting the transfer being signed on 7 December 1938. Initially, the airfield was operated as a satellite to Tangmere but in July 1940 it became Westhampnett Aerodrome and was home to Hurricanes, but was always left to grass.

By 1946, the Duke was still in uniform and serving with the Royal Air Force when he was approached by some fellow

enthusiasts with a view to running motor races at Westhampnett. Whilst feeling that the idea of running cars so close to the 150-year-old horse-racing course might upset the neighbours, he warmed to the idea and took his Lancia Aprilia around the 2.4-mile perimeter track. It was 30ft wide, cracked and in poor condition with grass growing wherever it could get a foot-hold — but that there was potential was beyond question. The Duke summoned Tommy Wisdom (still a Wing Commander), racing driver and journalist, and together they toured the embryonic new track and decided in principle that if it was at all possible, Westhampnett would become the motor racing circuit at Goodwood.

As has been told in earlier pages, since 1907 Brooklands had been the Mecca of motor racing enthusiasts, with most events organised by the Brooklands Automobile Racing Club. Immediately after the war, this club became part of the Junior Car Club whose members had elected the Duke of Richmond and Gordon as its President at the early age of 42. Some time later it was decided that the title 'Junior Car Club' was somewhat restrictive and self-effacing, and that the use of the initials BARC, but changing 'Brooklands' to 'British', would convey the intentions of the organisation more accurately, although the change did not take place until the January 1949 annual general meeting. With such a lineage it was obvious that if racing was to take place at Goodwood it would be to 'his' club that the Duke would turn for someone to run the meetings.

Following the discussion with Tommy Wisdom the club's council members were summoned to inspect the facilities, the

Below: From Goodwood's early days comes this picture of the start of a single-seater race with a gaggle of ERAs about to take on a Gordini and a Maserati. *National Motor Museum Photographic Library*

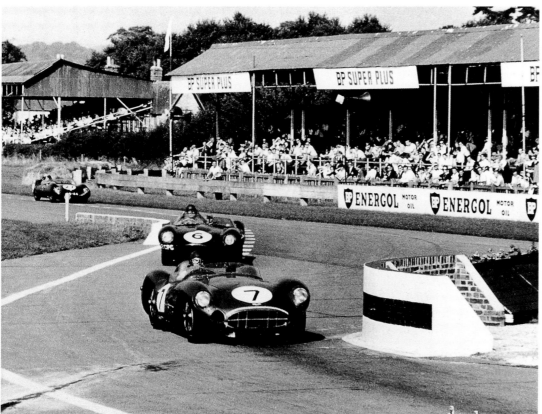

Above: Goodwood in 1952 with a works Jaguar C-type passing the main grandstand beside an Aston Martin DB3. Crowd protection is somewhat scant; the wooden barriers would not have given much protection against an errant car. *Jaguar Daimler Heritage Trust*

Left: During the 1958 RAC Tourist Trophy race, Tony Brooks, in the Aston Martin DBR1 which he shared with Stirling Moss, leads a works Jaguar D-Type and a Lotus Eleven through the famous chicane on his way to victory. *National Motor Museum Photographic Library*

sport's governing body in the United Kingdom (the Royal Automobile Club) being represented by the Earl Howe. Official approval was received and the headaches began in earnest for much work had to be done.

The first requirement was the erection of three miles of chain-link fencing around the circuit along with chestnut fencing between the still government-owned buildings to create enclosures. A paddock area was fenced off but there were no pits, no grandstands or yet paddock buildings. By virtue of its airfield origins, Goodwood had wide run-off areas all around it and there was some antipathy to this from certain quarters in authority who felt it would lead to the wilder elements taking extra risks rather than treating it as a safety-valve for drivers in trouble. Ironically, it was the lack of run-off areas which eventually brought about the closure of the circuit for racing.

The start/finish line was situated on a straight which led to a long double-apex climbing right-hand bend with an unsettling hump between the apexes known as Madgwick Corner because the old aerodrome ran very close to Madgwick Lane at this point. There followed another straight leading to Fordwater which started as a right flick, straightened slightly, before becoming a long right-hand curve which then tightened on itself — it was one of the most demanding and deceptive high-speed curves on any British circuit. Fordwater Curve was

named after a local road, Fordwater Lane, which runs up to the circuit from the village of Lavant. Following Fordwater the circuit turned right and then sharp left at St Mary's, the exit being downhill via a plunging dip: it was named after the two St Mary's churches on the Goodwood Estate at Lavant and Boxgrove. A short straight led to Lavant (named after the nearby village), which is the slowest natural corner on the circuit — it is actually two right-handers connected by a short straight, with the second turn faster than the first. This led to Lavant Straight, which was not quite telling the truth, for it was two straights with a left kink known as Lavant Kink rather less than halfway along it, but it was straight-lineable after the left-hand kink. This lead to Woodcote Corner, two sharp rights with a brief straight in between named after Woodcote Cottage which stands on nearby Claypit Lane, leading back to the start/finish line. This was the original circuit but in 1952 the final feature was introduced to slow competitors down past the pits and was variously known as Paddock Bend, Club Corner or the Chicane — all self-explanatory names.

The inaugural race meeting at Goodwood took place on Saturday, 18 September 1948, the circuit being officially opened by the Duke and Duchess of Richmond and Gordon in a Bristol 400. Entries had poured in but were restricted to 12 per race, for the RAC had sanctioned one car per 0.4 miles

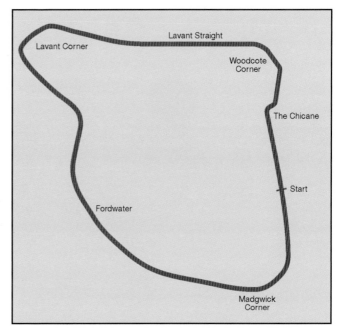

(later increased to one per 0.1 miles); this meant that 96 drivers were allowed for the eight-race programme but the entry list was heavily over-subscribed, although on the day 85 drivers actually competed. History was to repeat itself 50 years later.

Paul de Ferranti C. Pycroft driving his special-bodied Jaguar SS100 had the honour of winning Goodwood's first ever race. The main event of the day, the Goodwood Trophy, went to Reg Parnell driving his Maserati 4CLT/48 by the narrowest of margins from Bob Gerrard's ERA who became the new circuit's first outright lap record holder at 88.56mph. Reg Parnell's car had been purchased with the British Grand Prix in mind which was scheduled for 2 October — those were the halcyon days when anyone with the wherewithal could buy a Grand Prix car and race it in Grands Prix. The BBC broadcast the event in full; there was still petrol rationing but none the less in excess of 15,000 people attended the races, many coming by coach. The meeting had been a resounding success. And a 19-year-old novice called Stirling Moss won his first ever major motor race — the first of 22 at Goodwood, including four consecutive victories in the RAC Tourist Trophy.

This is not the place to recount the trials and tribulations of the supercharged V16 BRM which was the fruition of the dream of Raymond Mays and Peter Berthon to create a British Grand Prix car capable of beating the world. The car was fiendishly complicated and stupendously powerful but took a long time to develop; sadly, by the time that it was working well the 4.5-litre normally aspirated/1.5-litre supercharged Formula One was coming to its end and most Grands Prix were run to Formula Two regulations. It was, however, at

Above: During the St Mary's Trophy Race on 11 April 1966, Peter Proctor tries very hard to destroy his Team Broadspeed Ford Anglia; the Anglia taking avoiding action is in the hands of Mike Young. There must have been something *very* interesting going on to the left! *Mike Dixon*

Right: Following upon a tradition set by his grandfather in 1935, Lord March has opened his home to motor racing enthusiasts and Goodwood has been the venue for the Festival of Speed from 1992, a glorious occasion when enthusiasts have run exotic cars up the hill past his front door. On one such occasion John Surtees launches the factory-owned Mercedes-Benz W125 up the hill. *Richard Styles*

Goodwood that this fabulous car had its first victories on 30 September 1950 when Reg Parnell won two races in the day, the Woodcote Cup and the Goodwood Trophy. 1950 was also the year in which Bira brought his OSCA-engined San Remo Maserati to Goodwood and won the five-lap Formule Libre Richmond Trophy race.

By 1951, those who had had misgivings about the wide grass verges on ex-airfield circuits were vindicated when the Duke began to show concern over the high lap speeds which were being achieved at Goodwood; the result was the insertion of the now-famous chicane officially named Paddock Bend. Before the commencement of racing in 1948, the circuit had been surfaced with a non-skid material known as Resmat and

in the winter of 1951 the decision was taken to resurface Goodwood.

In August 1952, the BARC returned to its tradition of running long-distance motor races; in Brooklands' days the JCC/BARC had run the Double Twelve Hours and Thousand Mile races but Goodwood saw the first-ever night racing England with the advent of the Goodwood Nine Hours which started at 3pm and finished at midnight. Until the coming of the Willhire 24 Hours at Snetterton, the Nine Hours was the longest motor race held in post World War 2 Great Britain. It became a regular feature of the Goodwood calendar, attracting entries from the world's major manufacturers and becoming a round of the World Sports Car Championship.

Above: Goodwood was always been regularly used for testing and private practice, an activity which continued even after the circuit had been closed for racing. Here Graham Hill takes the prototype Ford GT40 through the chicane which was, shall we say, somewhat substantial and claimed not a few victims over the years, amongst them Jean Behra who took the left front wheel off his BRM P25 against it, fortunately without injury to himself.
Ford Motor Company

Right: Same driver, same car, same corner on the same circuit but the pictures are separated by three decades. Jack Sears brought his mighty 7-litre Ford Galaxie to Goodwood on only one occasion: it was on 30 March 1964 when he contested the BRSCC Saloon Car Championship in the Team Willment-prepared car. He won the race outright and it is believed to have been the first victory in a straight race for a pure Ford product at Goodwood. *Ford Motor Company*

Below right: Then, at the Revival Meeting over the weekend of 18 to 20 September 1998, Jack brought the Galaxie back to Sussex and drove it in the Dream Grid. The structure of the new chicane is not as rigid as its predecessor and will give way if struck forcibly. *Author*

The RAC Tourist Trophy had not been run since 1955 and as the Irish circuit at Dundrod was not considered usable and it was desirable that the race should not be dropped from the championship calendar, it was decided to run the event at Goodwood in 1958 on 13 September. The 23rd running of the race did not attract a Continental entry in the shape of Ferrari or the Belgian equipes for none confirmed their entries — perhaps the disinterest from Maranello was due to a shortage of drivers and the fact that their victory at the Sarthe circuit had given them the Championship for the year. Of the 29 starters, only the three Aston Martin DBR1 factory cars, two Lotuses, two of the four Jaguar D-Types and two Lister Jaguars could be considered as potential winners. It was anticipated that the Astons would win and so it proved as they finished in the first three places, won the Team Award and Stirling Moss set a new sports car record in 1min 32.6sec at a speed of 93.3mph. It was the fourth TT win for Moss; he completed the race in 4hr 1min 17sec for the 148 laps which made a race distance of 355 miles. The victory gave Aston Martin second place in the Championship equal with Porsche.

A year later, Aston Martin was to triumph again on 5 September when the combination of Carroll Shelby/Jack Fairman/Stirling Moss brought the DBR1 home in first place, but Joakim Bonnier and Wolfgang von Trips were second for Porsche from Olivier Gendenien/Phil Hill, followed by Tony Brooks and Cliff Allison in a Ferrari. This does not quite tell the full story for at Salvadori's first pit stop in the number one Aston, which he was sharing with Moss, the car caught fire during refuelling, destroying it along with the pit et al. Whitehead sportingly retired his privately entered Aston Martin so that the works cars would have a home and Moss was transferred to the number two car; as a result of this win Aston Martin became the World Champions.

Early in 1960 a young man who had done rather well on two wheels made his debut on four, driving a BMC A-Series-engined Formula Two Cooper T52; his name was John Surtees and he lost only narrowly to Jim Clark in a Lotus 18.

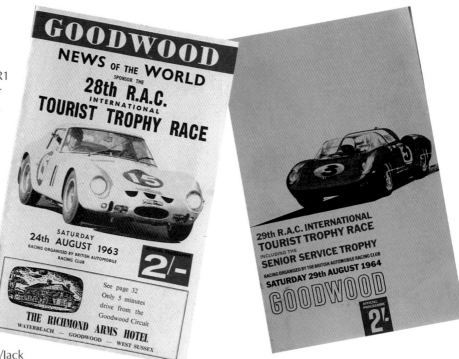

Above left: The cover of the programme for the 28th RAC Tourist Trophy, the world's oldest and most historic race held at Goodwood on Saturday, 24 August 1963, showing a Ferrari 250 GTO, three of which featured prominently in the results. The race was sponsored by the *News of the World*. *Author's collection*

Above right: A year later the cover is somewhat less 'busy' with just an artist's impression of a Ferrari 330 — and details of the meeting; sponsorship has switched to Senior Service cigarettes. *Author's collection*

Below: No fewer than four V16 BRMs came to Goodwood for the first Revival Meeting in 1998, three to compete and one on static exhibition. The sight of four of these incredible cars together again was something which few had ever expected to witness. Three were finished in the familiar dark British Racing Green of BRM but this Mk1 P15 from the Donington Collection, driven by Rick Hall, was in the light green used by ERA, out of which BRM was born. *Author*

In August 1966 Goodwood closed its gates after nearly 18 years of very special motor racing; in the interests of safety, cars had been restricted to 3 litres in the previous season. The official reason for closure was cited as being economic due to a restricted calendar but the truth was concern over spectator safety, speeds having risen by 2mph per year. The final event at Goodwood was a handicap race which was won Christopher Le Strange Metcalfe.

But it was not the end for the old road circuit and pits road were maintained in good condition and continued to be used for testing and sprints on a regular basis.

In 1935 one of Freddie March's first actions on becoming Lord March was to hold a fun day at Goodwood House which included driving tests and a run up the hill past Goodwood House. This was to be the inspiration for the present Earl of March to run the Festival of Speed which has been held from 1992 in Goodwood park, with spectacular cars once again running up the hill past Goodwood House. The festivals have attracted thousands of visitors over three days at weekends in June.

As with all motor sport venues Goodwood has had its high and low spots; it has been host to the oldest motor race in the British calendar, the RAC Tourist Trophy, but it was here that Stirling Moss had the crash which ended his Formula One career and it was also here that Bruce McLaren died in a private test.

In September 1996 came the news that, after five years hard work, protesters had been overruled and motor racing would be allowed to return to Glorious Goodwood for five historic days' racing a year. The first Revival Meeting at the Sussex circuit took place over the weekend of 18-20 September 1998, the first day of the meeting being the 50th anniversary to the

Right: A further year on from the 1964 programme and the cover is a little more fussy for the Easter Monday meeting, the *Sunday Mirror*-sponsored International Trophy meeting for Formula One cars.
Mike Dixon Collection

Left: This is another of those rare racing cars: Lance Reventlow was the heir to the Woolworth fortune and had the dream of an American car competing in Formula One and International sports car racing. His dream came to life in the shape of the Scarab: just four cars were built — two Grand Prix cars and two sports cars. The Scarab Formula One car suffered the same fate as the Aston Martin DBR4/250 in that it came too late in the life of 2¹/₂-litre Formula One, the rear-engined cars from Cooper and Lotus having taken centre stage by the time that it arrived on the scene. However, clothed in the American International racing colours of blue and white, the Scarab was a lovely-looking car, beautifully engineered. One was driven in the Dream Grid at the inaugural Revival Meeting by its original *pilote* Chuck Daigh and then in 2000 *both* of them raced, No 26 driven by Don Orosco and No 48 by Brian Redman. *Author*

Right: The 'Thin Wall Special' was a 4¹/₂-litre Ferrari which Tony Vandervell purchased as a test bed for his lead indium bearings prior to building his own Grand Prix cars. The car is now part of the Donington Collection and is seen negotiating the chicane ahead of Duncan Ricketts' E-Type ERA at the first Revival Meeting. *Author*

day of the opening of Goodwood Circuit. The Earl of March and Kinrara performed the opening ceremony on the Friday morning and then drove round the circuit in a Bristol 400 as his grandfather had done in 1948.

In order to achieve this miracle 270,000 tonnes of earth were moved into the site by a fleet of 200 lorries from all over southern England to create the required acoustic banking. A new safety barrier has been laid around the circuit using 20,000 lorry tyres and a further 7,000 car tyres, and six miles of fencing have been erected around the perimeter. Twenty thousand new trees have been planted with 18,000 ivy plants used to cover the tyre walls, and there are 40 acres of newly seeded grass. And the hydrangeas have also been renewed.

The weekend was like being in a time warp: 1,500 entries were received of which 300 were selected to compete in the Revival Meeting. Those who returned to Goodwood must have felt the memories flooding back and those who came for the first time will have received some idea of what motor racing was like when it really was a sport, for Goodwood was always about tradition, good manners and 'doing things right', which is, sadly, forgotten by an element in the sport today. There were four V-16 BRMs, three Vanwalls, seemingly countless C- and D-Type Jaguars, Aston Martins, Ferraris and bird-cage Maseratis. There were Maserati 250Fs, BRM P25s, Dino Ferraris and a Super Squalo; there was a full field of 500s, Ken Tyrrell driving one in the Dream Grid. No less than four World Champions raced over the weekend: Phil Hill, John Surtees, Sir Jack Brabham and Damon Hill (released by Jordan Grand Prix for the weekend). Damon Hill drove the Ferrari 250 GTO, which his father had raced in the original Tourist Trophy, in the recreated RAC Tourist Trophy race, and also rode a Manx Norton. Jackie Stewart drove a BRM in the Dream Grid. And, of course, the master was there, Stirling Moss driving everything he could lay his hands upon. Dan Gurney came from across the pond to join Tony Brooks and Roy Salvadori, and Barry Sheene came to ride a Manx Norton for the first time in his life.

Victory in the first race at Goodwood for 32 years, the Woodcote Cup, went to Ludovic Lindsay at the wheel of one of the most famous of the ERAs, the ex-Bira R5B 'Remus'.

The dream of Lord March has come to fruition, for Glorious Goodwood has been returned to us — along with our sport — and what better place is there to be than Goodwood on a

Left: Stirling Moss was ever an integral part of Goodwood and such was the case at the first and subsequent Revival Meetings. Here he brings Tim Samway's Aston Martin DBR1 through the chicane in the Lavant Cup race. *Author*

Below: This book is about motor racing but two motorcycle races were included in the Revival Meetings and due credit must be given; the 1996 World Champion Damon Hill raced a Manx Norton in the Lennox Cup, giving a good account of himself. He also drove two cars which his late father had raced at Goodwood: in The RAC TT Celebration he shared a Ferrari 250GTO with Willie Green and drove the BRM P578 in the Dream Grid. *Author*

Bottom: Bruce McLaren lost his life in a testing accident at Goodwood and he is for ever remembered in the Brooklands Garden. *Author*

summer's day? The great Roy Salvadori is on record as saying: 'Give me Goodwood on a summer's day and you can forget the rest.' But let it not be forgotten that had the circuit not closed it could not have been returned to us as it has been for it would, undoubtedly, have been changed in later years.

The outright lap record on the original circuit prior to the installation of the chicane in 1952 stands for all time to the credit of the World Champion Giuseppe Farina driving an Alfa Romeo 159 at 97.36mph in 1min 28sec. Before Goodwood closed in 1966 the outright lap record on the revised circuit stood jointly to the credit of Jackie Stewart in a BRM and Jimmy Clark in a Lotus Climax in 1min 20.4sec at 107.46mph — an increase of 10mph in just 14 years. It was set at the Easter Monday Meeting in 1965; upon the closure of the circuit this record was destined to stand in perpetuity but who knows what future meetings may bring? The fastest lap at the initial Revival Meeting was set in the Richmond Trophy by Rod Jolley driving his Cooper-Climax T45/51 in 1min 26.885sec at 99.44mph. At the second Revival Meeting, run on the weekend of 17-19 September 1999 the lap record was broken, but by only the smallest margin, by Geoff Farmer driving the Rob Walker Lotus 49 in the Glover Trophy. Farmer circulated in 1min 20.09sec at 107.87mph and the race was run at 103.50mph. It was the first time that the 3-litre Formula One cars had appeared at Goodwood. At the close of the 2000 season this stands as the outright lap record. The third Revival Meeting held 15-17 September 2000 was marred to a degree by the public-created fuel shortage, but once more was an outstanding success. No doubt the best is yet to come.

GRANSDEN LODGE
FIRST RACING AFTER THE WAR

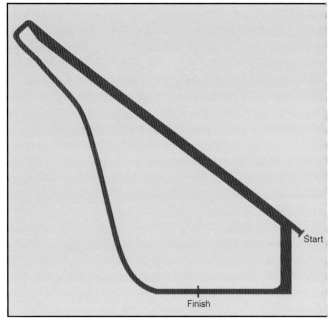

Above: The map of Gransden Lodge circuit shows that it used most of the main runway, much of the perimeter track and a small section of another runway. All of the races were run anticlockwise.

Below: The programme cover from the first race meeting at RAF Gransden Lodge on 13 July 1947 — barely two years after the cessation of hostilities.

Situated 12 miles west of Cambridge, Gransden Lodge was one of the few East Anglian airfields from which Canadian squadrons flew, being, for two years, the home of No 405 (Vancouver) Squadron. Gransden Lodge opened as a satellite to RAF Tempsford early in 1942 and saw active service throughout the war. The final active squadrons moved out in February 1946 and the station then lay vacant but the main runway remained in use for emergency landings into the 1950s.

In 1946, there was only one motor racing event held on English soil and this took place at Gransden Lodge, organised by the Cambridge University Automobile Club in a somewhat clandestine manner. It turned out to be a very successful venture and proved the feasibility of running motor races on airfields.

Gransden Lodge is probably unique in being the only British circuit to be planned with the start and finish lines at different points on the track; the standing lap measured 1.84 miles and the full lap 2.23 miles, which meant that no race distance was ever the multiple of the number of laps covered. Just how the timekepers coped is not recorded! Gransden had three runways and the start line was a short distance along the main one, the main straight being very nearly a mile in length, leading to a sharp left-hand hairpin bend on to the perimeter track and a straight of about a quarter of a mile followed by a right flick and another straight of about half a mile. There then followed a tight left on to another straight of half a mile or so, on which was situated the finish line. At the end of this straight was a 90° left on to another runway leading in a few hundred yards to a left on to the main straight. The circuit was run anticlockwise.

On Sunday, 13 July 1947 the Cambridge University Automobile Club combined with the Vintage Sports Car Club to run another meeting at Gransden Lodge to which 15,000 spectators came. Starting at noon, it was billed as a Joint Invitation Race Meeting in aid of the RAF Flood Victims Relief Fund; apart from members of the two promoting Clubs, members of the Bugatti Owners' Club, The 500 Club, the Hants & Berks Motor Club and the Midland Motoring Enthusiasts Club were invited. The programme consisted of no fewer than 10 races, including a Vintage Racing Car event , most of which were over 10 laps of the 2.23-mile circuit. The two exceptions were the race for 500cc cars, which ran over just four laps, and the main event, the Gransden Trophy, which was run over 20 laps and attracted an entry of 19 and was described in the August issue of *Motor Sport* as 'quite the finest race we have seen, or shall see, in England this year and the massed start a sight for the gods!' The race was won by Dennis Poore in his 3.5-litre Alfa Romeo 8C-35 at

86.3mph. This was the car that had won the Donington Grand Prix in the hands of Dick Seaman a decade earlier when it had been owned by Hans Reusch. Second was George Abecassis in a 3.3-litre Grand Prix Bugatti from Roy Salvadori in a 2.9-litre Alfa Romeo; the only other cars to cover the full distance were also 2.9-litre Alfas in the hands of Rolt and Hutchinson.

Half of the races were scratch events and half were handicaps, but the meeting was notable in that it contained the first race for 500cc racing cars to be held: it attracted just four entries, of whom three finished, with victory going to Eric Brandon's Cooper at 60.25mph. *Motor Sport* opened its report of the meeting with the words, 'Would that we in England could have this kind of racing every Bank Holiday, instead of once a year.' It was the last race meeting to be held at Gransden Lodge. The success of Gransden Lodge made the RAC look towards airfield sites as a stopgap measure and was, no doubt, influential in their decision to choose Silverstone.

CAMBRIDGE UNIVERSITY AUTOMOBILE
CLUB AND VINTAGE SPORTS-CAR CLUB

**JOINT INVITATION RACE
MEETING**

Held under the General Competition Rules of the R.A.C.

**IN AID OF THE
R.A.F. FLOOD VICTIMS RELIEF FUND**
AT
GRANSDEN LODGE AERODROME
on
SUNDAY, 13th JULY, 1947, Start 12 noon

R.A.C. Permit No. A/31

*

STEWARDS:

| Major L. A. BAUDLEY, M.C. for the R.A.C. | Major J. M. B DOVE for the V.S.C.C. | F. K. DYKES, Esq. for the C.U.A.C. |

Scrutineers : L. C. McKENZIE, F. R. PROCTOR.

Judges : E. K. KARSLAKE, T. GERALD ROSE

Timekeepers : A. J. GIBBONS, P. MAYNE

Clerk of the Course : D. HODKIN.

Secretary of the Meeting :

Mrs. CARSON, "Melfolm," Pack Lane, Kingsclere, Basingstoke, Hants.

PROGRAMME 1/-

IBSLEY
TWO CIRCUITS IN SHORT ORDER

RAF Ibsley in Hampshire was situated two miles north of Ringwood near the western edge of the New Forest and had an active life of five years, from 15 February 1941 (when it was opened as a satellite to Middle Wallop) until March 1946. Notwithstanding its closure date, work on a new station HQ had started in January 1946; the station became inactive in 1947 and was soon derequisitioned.

The circuit at Ibsley, situated on the Fordingbridge to Ringwood Road in Hampshire, was used on two occasions for races by the Bristol & District Light Car Club. It was exactly two miles in length and resembled the end-on view of a loaf of bread. It was roughly square with the start/finish line on a straight which led to a sharp right named Court Corner followed by another straight leading to a left flick and a long right named Samson's Curve which became a long curving right tightening into Church Corner and another straight leading to the only other left of any description, and Paddock Bend and the start/finish line. Not, perhaps, the most exciting circuit but one which was much needed at the time it was used; *Autosport* has said it was used from 1950 until 1955.

The first meeting at Ibsley circuit was held on Saturday, 4 August 1951, organised by the West Hants & Dorset Car Club on a track which *Autosport* described as 'tricky enough to have good spectator appeal'. The programme consisted of

Left: The cover of the programme for the national race meeting at Ibsley on Saturday, 18 April 1953 organised by the West Hants & Dorset Car Club. Note the Ecurie Ecosse D-type Jaguars and the oil drums marking the circuit.

Below right: By 1954 the circle containing details of the meeting had changed to white and the featured car on this occasion was an Ecurie Ecosse C-Type Jaguar.

races for sports cars, Formula III and Formule Libre. The lap record for the day was set by Ray Merrick's Cooper-Norton-JAP in 1min 39.2sec at 79.83mph; the car consisted of a Cooper 500 chassis with an 1132cc engine made up of a JAP crank case with single overhead-cam Norton heads on the twin cylinders. The engine capacity qualified it as a Formula Two car.

On Saturday, 19 April 1952 the WH and DCC ran 'The Second Ibsley Car Race Meeting' which attracted over 100 entries and with multiple starts made a total of over 160 starters. Twenty being the highest number of starters listed in the programme for any race, it is reasonable to assume that this was the maximum the RAC would allow. The programme consisted of 11 scratch and handicap races with distances varying from five to 15 laps; all were for sports cars or racing cars (Formula Two being referred to as Formula B) and one exclusively for Bentleys. The Formula III race was run in two heats and a final, such was the demand for entries. Ecurie Ecosse had come a very long way to give their C-Type Jaguars an airing and the Formula Two race attracted entries from George Abecassis in an HWM, Connaughts for Ken McAlpine and W. B. Black, David Murray was

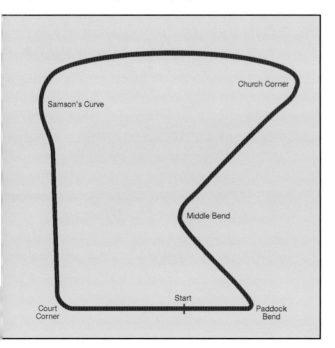

Left: The original Ibsley circuit as used in 1953, utilising parts of two of the runways.

Right: 1955 saw a complete change, as this cover of the programme for the National race meeting at Ibsley on Saturday, 30 April 1955 shows. Race organisation was still in the capable hands of the West Hants & Dorset Car Club. The Ecurie Ecosse C-Type Jaguars are featured once more but note the oil drums marking the circuit.

Right: The circuit as used from 1955, using only the perimeter track.

Below: On a chilly day in 1955 Don Beauman adjusts his goggles at the wheel of his Connaught 'A' Type whilst he and his fellow competitors await the start. From this distance in time it seems incredible that a circuit such as Ibsley could attract a field of what were current Formula One cars, there being at least three other Connaughts on the grid, Nos 151, 157 and 159, diagonally behind Beauman on the next row of the grid. Where are these cars now? Just look at the size of the crowd! *Ferrett Fotographics*

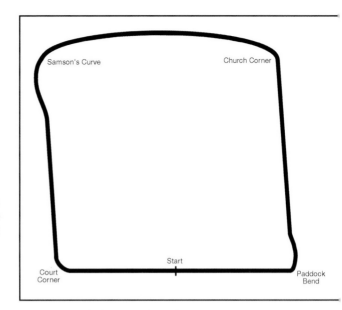

down to drive a Ferrari and a young man named Mike Hawthorn was entered in a Cooper Bristol.

Two years later the Club was back on Saturday, 8 May to run on the shorter circuit. The main event was a Formule Libre race which had attracted a remarkable entry including the V16 BRM in the hands of Ron Flockhart who won at 83.48mph and set the fastest lap at 87.39mph from Jimmy Stewart and Ninian Sanderson in C-Type Jaguars. The Formula III race was won by Les Leston from Don Parker, respectively Cooper and Kieft mounted. The meeting started with a race for 'closed' cars in two classes up to and over 1500cc: the smaller class was won by C. A. Leavens driving a somewhat unlikely mount in the shape of a Jowett Javelin; the larger class went to Roy Salvadori in an Aston Martin from Gylie Tyrer's Jaguar and Capt R. L. Woods in another Aston Martin.

Racing at Ibsley appears to have continued until 1955.

LINTON-ON-OUSE
RACING ON AN OPERATIONAL RAF STATION

The perimeter track and parts of two runways were used to form the Linton-on-Ouse circuit in 1960 and 1961, on what was still an operational RAF base, with the racing organised by the Northern Centre of the British Racing & Sports Car Club. It would appear that one meeting was held in each of the two years in question, on 10 July 1960 and 9 July 1961.

The 1960 meeting was held in torrential rain and Tony Hodgetts recalls blue sparks coming off his fingers as he cranked the field telephone which was used by the marshals to communicate with race control. The meeting was dominated by Jimmy Blumer's Cooper Monaco.

The meeting in 1961 was marred by a fatal accident to a flag marshal. The driver of the Formula Junior car involved was a serving RAF officer and, following the inquest into the death of the marshal, the venue was no longer available. After this sad incident and a near fatality to another flag marshal at Full Sutton, Tony Hodgetts and Garth Nicholls started a campaign which resulted in flag marshals working face to face instead of back to back, a system which is still in use and is considerably safer.

Below: The programme cover from the first race meeting held at RAF Linton-on-Ouse on Sunday, 10 July 1960. As was common at the time, it features a cartoon — no doubt the artist was on the *Daily Mirror* staff. Racing organisation was in the hands of the British Racing & Sports Car Cub with proceeds going to the Soldiers, Sailors & Airmen Association. *Motor Racing Archive*

Below right: The programme cover from the second and final race meeting held at Linton-on-Ouse RAF station on 9 July 1961. Race organisation was in the hands of the British Racing & Sports Car Club with sponsorship from the *Daily Mirror*. Whilst it was commonplace in the 1950s and 1960s, sponsorship from daily or Sunday papers is now a rarity. As was so often the case, the cover shows a splendid disregard for portraying what might be seen in action on the day, for the illustration is of Juan Manuel Fangio taking the flag in a Formula One Ferrari! *Doug Winton Collection*

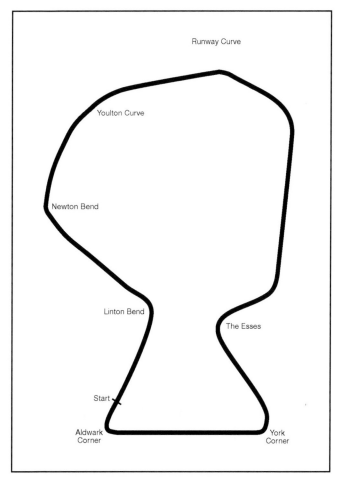

Above: Looking for all the world like a deflating balloon this is the 1.7-mile circuit at RAF Linton-on-Ouse in Yorkshire as used in 1960. The section between York Corner, Aldwark Corner and Linton Bend was on two of the runways, with the rest of the track on perimeter roads. With its considerable right-hand bias, it was probably quite a challenging circuit.

LONGRIDGE
MOTOR RACING IN A QUARRY

L ongridge in Lancashire may be unique in the world in being the only motor racing circuit situated in a quarry. The roads used for the extremely short circuit were already in place when motor racing commenced in 1973 although there had been sprints earlier than that. Motor racing continued until 1978 when the site was sold, which caused considerable ill-feeling amongst those who organised the sport on both two and four wheels for they were not informed of the impending sale and consequent loss of the venue and had laid in plans for the 1979 season when they heard the news.

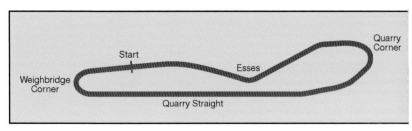

Above: Longridge was a strange circuit: just 0.43 miles long, it had a tarmacadam surface and was set in a quarry. A maximum of 10 starters were permitted due to its restricted length: it was, to say the least, tight.

Left and below: By 1998 Longridge was a residential caravan park. *Graham R. Heath*

LULSGATE
AERODROME TO RACING CIRCUIT TO AIRPORT

This was another ex-RAF airfield circuit and was situated on the Bristol-Bridgwater road, being just two miles from the former and 22 miles from the latter. The circuit was host to just two race meetings, both of which were organised by the Bristol Motorcycle & Light Car Club; the first was held on Saturday, 16 April 1949 and the second exactly a year later on 15 April 1950.

At the 1949 meeting all but one of the races were for sports cars, divided into classes by engine capacity and by the categorisation 'Sports' and 'Super Sports'. The first race was for sports cars up to 1,100cc and the Super Sports up to 850cc; race two: sports cars 1,101-1,500cc and Super Sports 851-1,100cc; race three: 1,501-2,000cc sports and Super Sports 1,101-1,500cc; and race four: sports cars over 2,000cc and Super Sports over 1,500cc. Race five was exclusively for members of the promoting club, apparently without restriction. Race seven was a Bugatti handicap and race eight a handicap for Bentleys. The only non-sports car race was the sixth which catered for

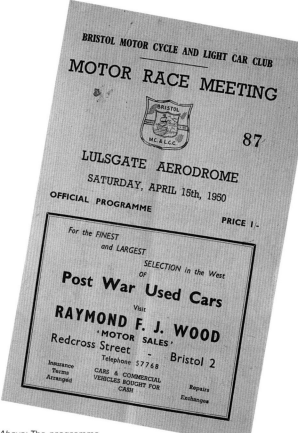

Above: The programme cover of the very first race meeting organised by the Bristol Motorcycle & Light Car Club at Lulsgate Aerodrome on Saturday, 15 April 1950. No frills and a form of sponsorship from the local used car trader.
G. Millington collection

Left: This is the track plan of Lulsgate — it was a typical airfield circuit, making use of the runways and perimeter track.

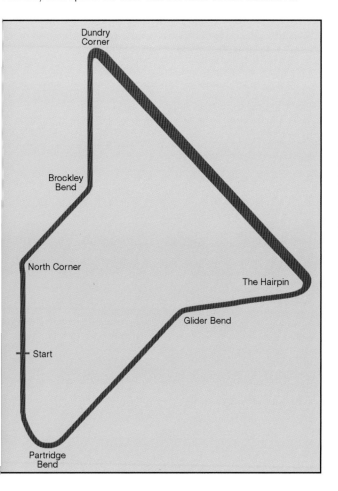

'500cc Racing Cars (National Formula)'. Given that at the time this race meeting was held petrol rationing was still very much the order of the day, the question is raised as to where all the competitors (nearly 100 of them) found the necessary fuel. A name which was to be heard much in the future, Les Leston, entered in the largest capacity race driving a Jaguar.

The following year's race meeting was run to the same format except that the single-seater event was now designated International Formula Three and the two one-make handicap races had been replaced by a race on handicap for sports and Super Sports of all capacities. All the races were over five laps with the exception of the Formula III which was of 10 laps' duration.

Lulsgate is now Bristol International Airport.

Above: A grid of five Formula III 500cc racing cars prepares for the dropping of the Union Flag at Lulsgate on 16 April 1949: closest to the camera is W. C. Cuff driving *Hell's Hammer V,* with Gerry Millington beside him in the Milliunion. Next to him is J. N. Gibbs No 57 in his MAP500, while No 3 is F. Westcott. Behind them is No 3 W. Messenger. The interest in and support for motor racing is evident from the size of the crowd which has come to watch; many a circuit would like to see such a crowd for a Club Meeting today. *G. Millington collection*

Below: Gerry Millington (note the lack of protective clothing!) is seen running in second place at the hairpin ahead of No 57 J. N. Gibbs in his MAP500. At this time, Millington's Milliunion was powered by a Rudge engine. *G. Millington collection*

LYDDEN HILL
KENT'S 'OTHER' CIRCUIT

Kent is one of the few counties in the United Kingdom to boast two motor racing circuits and it cannot have been easy to survive in the shadow of Brands Hatch but Lydden Hill, a few miles from Canterbury, has managed to do so. Lydden was the brainchild of Bill Chesson who was a showman and a promoter: grass track motorcycle racing took place from around 1957 — the land on which this took place was owned by one Barry Skinner who sold it to Bill. By 1962 Bill wanted to progress and laid a tarmac track in order to be able to promote motor and motorcycle road racing. The original plan was for a 1-mile circuit but this scheme had to be put on hold when the tarmac ran out at what is now known as the Devil's Elbow; the result was the short circuit which is sometimes used for Legends!

Once the current circuit was complete Lydden became extremely popular to the point that in 1967 a meeting featuring Formula Three was televised and included such up and coming hot shoes as Andy Sutcliffe, Roger Williamson and one Tom Walkinshaw. By 1986 the RAC MSA was pressurising Bill Chesson to erect Armco barriers which he steadfastly refused to do so on the grounds that they would be dangerous to the

motorcycle racing fraternity and, when the governing body threatened to refuse him a new circuit permit, he put the circuit up for sale. He did not actually want to get rid of it so put on it a price of something over one million pounds. His bluff was called when Tom Bissett came up with the asking price and Bill sold — who could seriously refuse that kind of money? Sadly Bill Chesson died in June 1999 following a long illness.

Lydden was the birthplace of Rallycross, in which branch of the sport the new owner was a competitor, and his plant hire business was an outstanding asset, enabling him to make immediate improvements to the circuit.

In March 1991 Mr and Mrs Bissett entered into a joint venture with McLaren. McLaren subsequently acquired Mr and Mrs Bissett's shares in Lydden circuit and became the sole owners. Lydden is currently leased by McLaren to the British Motorcycle Racing Club which organises and manages an active programme of motor sport at the circuit. McLaren is currently in discussion with Dover District Council as to the future of the circuit.

At the close of the 2000 season the outright lap record stands at 99.74mph in 38sec dead. It was set by Rob Cox driving a Lola DFZ in October 1989.

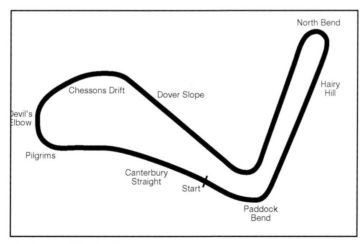

Circuit map of Lydden Hill.

MALLORY PARK
The Friendly Circuit

The estate at Mallory Park has many historical connections, the oldest being the unique Anglo-Saxon defended moat which is now known as Kirkby Moats, while a Roman road passes through the estate. It is probably safe to say that Mallory Park is the only motor racing circuit which can trace its ancestry back to the Domesday Book, for records go back as far as the Norman Conquest when the Manor was known as Cherchebi and was held by one Hugh de Cherchebi. In 1174, in the reign of Henry II, it was vested in the Mallory family, the then owner being in rebellion against the King, but the estate appears to have remained in the family until 1389 when Sir Ankitill Mallory sold it to the Abbot and convent of St Mary de Pratis at Leicester; the lordship remained in the family's possession until 1540 when it fell into the hands of King Henry VIII upon the dissolution of the monasteries. By 1593 it had passed to John Noel who had married Ann Harvey, Henry having granted it to her father Thomas. By 1600 the Noels had become one of the leading families in the area, Vernon Noel having been made a Baron, and his son, Sir William, married the daughter of John, Lord of Lovelace. In 1762, Sir Cleoberry Noel became Viscount Wentworth, the title having descended on the distaff side. Lord Byron married into the Wentworth family and it is said that on his visits to Mallory he wrote beneath the shade of the Lebanon cedar tree which still stands in the grounds. The last occupant of Kirkby Hall was Herbert Clarkson who died in 1941, when it was sold.

During World War 2 the hall was occupied by the Pioneer Corps; Kirkby Mallory Hall was a large house which was, sadly, demolished in 1952, leaving only the stable block and the coach house which now form the circuit offices, workshops, Coach House hotel, pub and restaurant.

The estate of 300 acres was auctioned in 1953 and was purchased by a Mr Moult of Derby who planned to have horse racing on the disused Pony Trotting track but his plans did not come to fruition. From September 1949 until 1954 the Leicester Query Motorcycle Club had held grass track

The publicity leaflet for the 1958 season at Mallory Park.

Right: During the 100-lap (two 50-lap sections) John Player Formula 2 Championship Race at Mallory Park on 12 March 1972, Niki Lauda rounds the hairpin in the STP March-entered March 722. *Fred Scatley*

Below: Mallory Park from the air on a glorious summer's day; sadly there are no cars on the track but judging from the number of people on the grid it is being formed but it is masked by the building which contains Race Control. The long, seemingly never-ending sweep of Gerards Bend is seen to great advantage in this view, as are the two lakes and the island set in the main one. In the top left-hand corner is the almost unbelievably tight hairpin with the trees still growing on the inside of the circuit. *Mallory Park Circuit*

The original Mallory Hall which was destroyed by fire. *Mallory Park Circuit*

consultancy capacity until the end of September. Over the next two years a considerable amount of money was spent on Mallory Park with the building of new spectator stands and new commentators', press and timekeepers' boxes. Under the control of Grovewood Securities Mallory Park enjoyed its golden days in the 1960s and 1970s with some of the greatest names in motor racing competing there. Amongst these a young Austrian who arrived for the Whit Sunday meeting in 1964 for his first race in England in a new Formula Two Brabham, which he had ordered at the Racing Car Show in January — Jochen Rindt. He asked Denny Hulme if he could follow him round to learn the circuit and then proceeded to set fastest time in practice; despite being delayed by an incident during the race, he finished third behind the reigning World Champion Jim Clark and his experienced team-mate Peter Arundell.

After a little over 20 years the owners of Mallory Park decided that enough was enough and offered the estate for sale; no doubt the expense of bringing Brands Hatch (which the company also

motorcycle races at Mallory Park. In 1955, the estate was purchased by an Earl Shilton-based builder named Clive Wormleighton under whose influence the present tarmac circuit was constructed at a cost of £60,000 in 1956. The circuit length is 1.35 miles without the chicane and 1.37 with it and there is a one-mile oval which cuts out the hairpin and the chicane. Upon completion of the construction work a circuit test was held on Wednesday, 26 April when local Grand Prix driver Bob Gerard and Maurice Cann respectively conducted a Cooper-Bristol Formula Two car and a Moto Guzzi motorcycle around the new circuit, Gerard managing an 81mph lap. The very first race meeting was held on the following Saturday when the Leicester Query Club organised a motorcycle meeting, cars appearing for the first time on Whit Monday, the meeting being organised by the Nottingham Sports Car Club. The first race was won by D. Rees in an Austin and on 7 July the British Racing & Sports Car Club began its long association with the circuit.

Mallory Park is an interesting circuit and a challenge to any driver; from the start/finish line the track passes along Kirkby Straight (named after the local village) to the long sweep of Gerards Bend (named after Bob Gerard) which seems to go on for ever and then on to Stebbe Straight which takes its name from the local slang name for the nearby village of Stapleton; now comes the fast right-left of the Lakes Esses leading to Shaw's Hairpin (named after Jack Shaw, the late secretary of the LQC), a famous feature and a favourite spectator spot. This is followed by the Devil's Elbow to complete the lap. The chicane was added in early 1986 to reduce speeds through Devil's Elbow but is used only for motorcycles. The oval was introduced in 1964 and when in use competitors continue right at Lake Esses cutting out Shaw's Hairpin; within the oval lie two very attractive lakes.

Clive Wormleighton continued to run the circuit very successfully until 1962 when ownership passed to Grovewood Securities in the July, the previous owner remaining in a

In 1997 this life-size statue of Jim Clark was unveiled at Mallory Park in memory of the great Scottish driver. *Author*

Left: The Mallory Park oval; the circuit map may give the impression of a dull circuit but it most certainly is not! This circuit was used anticlockwise for Eurocars.

Below: This is the full Mallory Park circuit, taking in the fearsome Shaws Hairpin which is approached up quite a steep hill, with another hill immediately following the corner on the back to the start and finish line.

Bottom: This version of Mallory Park was used in the 1950s and 1960s, incorporating the Castrol Chicane.

owned) up to current Grand Prix standards had some effect on the decision, and the opening of Donington Park, which was only some 20 miles distant, may have also influenced the decision. Whatever the reasons, Mallory Park was once more on the market but, reportedly, with a restriction on its future use for motor racing, although planning permission had been obtained for the erection of 30 dwellings on the estate.

Enter a very determined lady, Edwina Overend, who was the competitions secretary of the Midland Centre of the British Racing & Sports Car Club. As time passed and the 1982 season drew to its close, the expected cessation of racing at Mallory Park loomed large and various time wasters had come and gone, Mrs Overend approached Chris Meek with a view to his purchasing the estate. Chris was a well-known racing driver and Leeds-based businessman who effected the purchase late in 1982 and reopened the circuit on 29 May 1983, the first race meeting of the new era being organised by the 750 Motor Club. There had been no interruption to the programme and Mallory Park went from strength to strength, apart from a hiccup in December 1985 when the local borough council served a Noise Nuisance Order which restricted use of the circuit to 40 days a year. On Sundays there is an absolute curfew and no racing engine must be run after 6pm, and as the village church can be seen from the circuit that stipulation does not seem unreasonable. And Edwina Overend? As these words are written she is managing director of Mallory Park (Motorsport) Ltd and is probably the only lady to hold such a position.

Mallory Park has hosted all the major motor racing formulae be to contested in postwar Britain — European Formula Two, Aurora Formula One, Group 7 sports cars, Formula 5000 and Formula Three. In a 1981 programme the name of Damon Hill appears as one of the 'Ams' in the Yamaha RD 350 Pro-Am series.

The history of the 100mph lap at the Leicestershire circuit is interesting; the first one was a long time coming, for it was not until 1966 that it finally happened when, on Sunday, 29 May, the late Denny Hulme took a Lola T70 round in 47.6sec at a speed of 102.10mph. Two years later, in the June, Roy Pike established the first Formula Three 100mph lap in a Titan which he propelled round in 48sec at 101.25mph. With the coming of Formula 5000 and Formula One cars the outright record continued to fall until, in 1979, Riccardo Zunino took an Arrows A18 round in 40.065sec at an incredible 121.32mph. Twelve years after the first 100mph lap, Vincenzo

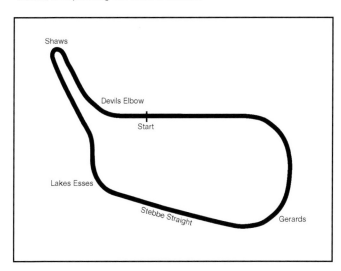

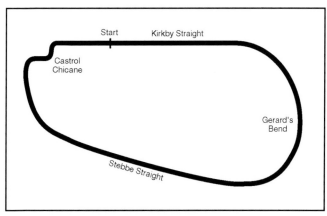

Sospiri established the first such lap in a Formula Ford when he drove a Van Dieman RF88 at 100.41mph in 48.44sec.

From the mid-1990s the British Racing & Sports Car Club promoted EuroCars, V6 and V8 saloon-outline cars which had graduated from the stock car circuits. At Mallory Park they ran anticlockwise on the oval circuit.

Mallory Park is prospering — it calls itself the Friendly Circuit and justifiably so. Apart from the regular car and motorcycle race meetings, the track hosts the Everyman Driving Centre which covers racing cars, rally cars, 4 x 4 off-road vehicles and for those brave (or mad!) enough, the Tank Commando Course. There are Corporate Activity Days and there is Junior Drive for the under-17s. And the fishing in the lakes is said to be pretty good too! But it is probably true to say that the days of running Internationals at Mallory Park are over.

At the close of the 2000 season the outright lap record on the full circuit stands to the credit of Johann Rajamaki driving a Formula One Footwork Judd in the BOSS Formula at 127.12mph in 38.23sec. It was set on 5 May 1997. On the oval circuit the outright record has stood since May 1995 to the credit of a V6 Ford Mondeo Eurocar driven by Ian Fewings at 106.51mph in 33.84sec.

Right: The programme cover from the Historic Sports Car Club meeting at Mallory Park on 24 May 1998. The car pictured is a Bolwell GT owned and raced by Chris Camp. The car emanates from Australia and is built around Holden components; it is the only one in the United Kingdom and just may be the only one in the Northern Hemisphere. There is a V8-engined Bolwell in the United Kingdom — which is also owned by Mr Camp. *Charlie Wooding*

Below: 'Mike the Bike' in action — even after all these years the number of motorcycle racers who have successfully made the transition from two to four wheels can be counted upon the fingers of one hand. One of these few was Mike Hailwood, seen here at the 12 March 1972 meeting at the wheel of the Matchbox-Team Surtees Ford-powered Surtees TS10. In his wheel-tracks is the only man to have achieved World Championships on two and four wheels — John Surtees. *Fred Scatley*

MALLORY PARK
THE FRIENDLY CIRCUIT

Historic Race Meeting

24th MAY 1998

Organised and promoted by

HISTORIC SPORTS CAR CLUB

For conditions of entry see inside

OLIVER'S MOUNT
JUST TWO RACES

The history of Oliver's Mount near Scarborough starts prior to World War 2 when members of the Scarborough & District Motor Club attempted to persuade the local council to support the construction of a circuit at Seamer Moor, initially of 14 miles and then a 10-mile one on the town's former racecourse. All seemed to be progressing well until rumours that some £25,000 of ratepayers' money would be needed to fund the construction which resulted in the shelving of the project, and then the actions of an Austrian Corporal already referred to elsewhere caused the total abandonment of any thoughts of motor racing until the cessation of hostilities.

It is, perhaps, poetic justice that Hitler was instrumental in the eventual creation of Oliver's Mount; Scarborough Corporation planned a 'Welcome Home Week' for returning servicemen and the local motor club was approached to put on some form of 'entertainment'. It is said that everything comes to he who waits and this was just the opportunity that the SDMC had been waiting for, so it soon set about finding a suitable venue to stage the required 'entertainment'. Their eyes set upon the picturesque wooded slopes of one of the town's most famous landmarks and when the Corporation's surveyor produced the modest estimate of just £920 to prepare a track, Oliver's Mount circuit was born and the first motorcycle meeting took place on Tuesday,

17 September 1946. The new circuit was run anticlockwise.

The original circuit was 2 miles 780yd long but in July 1954 the Esses were realigned resulting in the circuit being reduced by 52yd and it was on this course that cars raced on just two occasions in 1955 and 1956. These cars were 500cc Formula IIIs and, apparently on both occasions, were part of the 'Cock o' the North' meeting in July of each year. Victory in 1955 went to Cliff Allison driving his Cooper-Norton, from Tom Dickson (Staride-Norton) and W. Howard (Cooper-JAP). Allison set fastest lap in 2min 18.6sec at a speed of 62.69mph which was (of course) the lap record.

The following year, Tom Dickson (this time driving a Cooper-Norton) won from Robinson (Cooper-Norton), W. G. Harris (Flather Special) and Harry Stillborn (Cooper-JAP). Dickson set fastest lap in 2min 19.2sec at a speed of 62.42mph which means that Allison's fastest lap from the previous year still stands as the outright lap record for cars.

The very tight, twisty nature of the circuit meant that the 500cc FIII cars were the only ones which could use it. There were later attempts to use it for cars of other categories but the circuit was adjudged to be too narrow, and widening it would have destroyed its character.

Oliver's Mount continues to flourish as a motorcycle circuit with the occasional car rally and a car hill-climb course, and in September 1996 the circuit celebrated its Golden Jubilee.

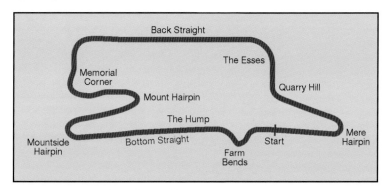

This map of the circuit at Oliver's Mount, while showing the twisty nature of the track, cannot impart its hilly nature. Having seen car racing on only two occasions it must qualify as one of the least used circuits in the British Isles.

OULTON PARK
NOT FOR THE FAINT-HEARTED!

I t is said that if one wishes to test the abilities of a new driver one sends him to Oulton Park with the car to demonstrate his prowess. If this statement does not strike a chord, go to the Cheshire circuit and see!

By the early 1950s Britain had a goodly number of motor racing circuits but the northwest was not well served. The members of the Mid-Cheshire Car Club took it upon themselves to rectify the situation. In 1953 they decided to create one of their own at Oulton Park near Tarporley, this being the property of Sir Philip Gray-Egerton. With his permission, a circuit was mapped out starting early in 1953 and by August the new track was in existence, measuring a sinuous 1.504 miles, almost rectangular in shape. The first meeting took place on 8 August but the RAC would not allow

the public to attend, wanting an opening meeting to be run successfully before allowing spectators to attend; none the less some 3,000 members of the organising club and its guests attended as spectators. The main event of the day was the 33-lap 49.6-mile Formula 2 race which was won by Tony Rolt driving Bob Walker's Connaught A Type. The Formula III event was divided into three 10-lap heats (won by Don Truman, Charles Headland and Don Parker) and a 17-lap final which went to Les Leston.

Oulton Park has a vast catchment area which includes Liverpool, Manchester, Chester and Crewe so it is little surprise that the second and last meeting of 1953 on 3 October attracted a crowd of 40,000. It was a joint motorcycle and car meeting, the Wirrall 100 Motor Club joining the Mid-Cheshire Car Club in organising it. The car side of the day was confined to three Formula III races and a final which was won by Glaswegian Ninian Sanderson from Ken Tyrrell.

By April 1954 the Oulton Park track had grown to 2.23 miles in length and within a year of the opening meeting had grown again to 2.761 miles. At Easter 1975 another circuit measuring 1.654 miles came into use. Oulton Park is unique amongst the

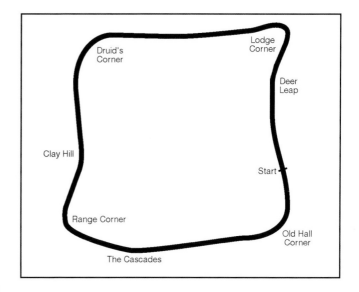

Right: This is the original Oulton Park circuit as used at the very first motor race meeting on 3 October 1953, measuring 1 mile 887yd 2ft. Built in parkland, it was completely unlike other circuits which had emerged following the World War 2, all of which had been built upon redundant airfields and thus were almost totally flat. This one plunged up and down the hills as it followed the natural contours of the land. This circuit was used only in 1953 and Range Corner did not survive beyond that first season.

Below right: For the start of the 1954 season Oulton Park circuit was extended by the track turning sharp left at Cascades and running to a right-handed hairpin named Island Corner, returning to the old circuit at what had been Range Corner and was now called Kinckerbrook. The circuit now measured 2.23 miles.

new post-World War 2 circuits in that it is a true road circuit whilst its contemporaries were, with one exception, converted from airfields, the exception being the short-lived Blandford. It has something in common with Mallory Park in that it can trace its history back a very long way (possibly as far as Roman times) and is mentioned in the Doomsday Book as 'Aleton'.

The British Racing Drivers Club brought the British Empire Trophy to Oulton Park in 1954 and ran it for sports cars on the new 2.23-mile circuit. Alan Brown won the race in a Cooper-Bristol from Roy Salvadori, driving a Maserati A6GCS, who set the new lap record at 74.73mph in 1min 48sec.

In August Oulton Park saw its first International Meeting when the *Daily Dispatch* sponsored the Oulton Park Gold Cup. Apart from the 11-year period when Aintree ran International Formula One races, it fell to Oulton Park to bring the major formulae to the northwest of England and the Gold Cup was run for all the major formulae: Formula One, Formula Two, Formula 5000 and the big sports cars. Its first running was over the second new circuit of the year, the 2.761-mile version, and was for Formula One: the entry was entirely British with the exception of Jean Behra in his Gordini. There were 19 starters, Stirling Moss starting from the back of the grid in his new Maserati 250F which had only arrived from the factory on the morning of the race. By the end of the first lap he had passed twelve of his rivals and took the lead from Reg Parnell's Ferrari 625 on the fourth lap to win by 1min 14.4sec at the end of the 36-lap race. Bob Gerard's Cooper Bristol and Don Beaumann's Connaught were the only other cars not to be lapped. This was Moss' first victory in the Gold Cup — he was to win it a total of five times, repeating the win in 1955, 1959, 1960 and 1961. Jack Brabham won the Gold Cup four times, John Surtees three and Roy Salvadori and Jim Clark twice each. 1955 saw the Gold Cup run three months after the Le Mans disaster which spoke volumes for the relative safety of British circuits. Whilst the Continentals were cancelling their Grands Prix (Switzerland banned motor racing for ever!), the phlegmatic British got on with the job.

1956 saw the Vintage Sports Car Club bring the Richard Seaman Memorial Trophy Race to Oulton Park from Silverstone but the BRSCC's Daily Herald Trophy for sports cars was almost rained off. The race was reduced from 56 to 40 laps and the Le Mans-winning Ecurie Ecosse team was withdrawn. Stirling Moss won in the works Aston Martin DB3S from his team-mate Tony Brooks.

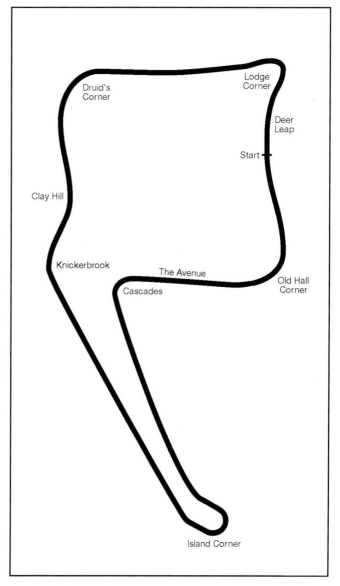

Prior to the 1957 season Moss and Brooks tested the Vanwalls at Oulton and advised that the surface should be replaced at Island Bend. Their advice was acted upon.

There was a new look to the Cheshire circuit for the 1961 season, the pits being rebuilt into a two-storey affair with a concrete wall to protect the pits crews when working on their charges. The Oulton Park Trophy was a televised event for GT cars which was won by Mike Parkes in the Maranello Concessionaires Ferrari 250GT from Graham Hill in an E-Type Jaguar and Tony Maggs in an Aston Martin DB4GT; Innes Ireland fought his way through to fourth in another 250GT after a poor start, setting a new class lap record on the way. On 4 May a young man named John Young Stewart raced an E-Type Jaguar but failed to finish.

Oulton Park was bought by Grovewood Securities in 1964 to increase the Company's motor sport empire and later in the year Grovewood also acquired the freehold, thereby ending nearly 500 years of ownership by the Egerton family. Grovewood's takeover coincided with the increase in required safety measures. Being set in parkland Oulton Park was more difficult and more expensive to bring up to standard than other circuits but the decision was made that it was to be motor circuit first and parkland second.

The spring meeting that year had a distinctly Scottish flavour, Jimmy Clark winning the sports, GT and saloon car races and Jackie Stewart, starting out on his International career, won the Formula Three race in Ken Tyrrell's Cooper-Austin. Jimmy Clark was the reigning World Champion yet had time to enter a relatively minor meeting at an English circuit — how times change! 1965 saw the revival of the world's oldest motor race when the Royal Automobile Club Tourist Trophy came to the Cheshire circuit. It was run for Sports and GT cars in two 2-hour heats and was won by Denny Hulme in a 2-litre Brabham.

2 April 1966 saw prospective spectators at the British Automobile Racing Club's Oulton Park 200 being turned away because the circuit was blanketed in snow! Good Friday 1969 saw the birth of Formula 5000 in Europe: Peter Gethin had a runaway win driving the Church Farm Racing McLaren M10A-Chevrolet.

The last RAC Tourist Trophy to be run at Oulton Park took place on Whit Monday 1969 and ended in tragedy. Paul Hawkins lost control of his Lola T70 at Island Bend and hit a tree; he was killed instantly and the race was stopped, Trevor Taylor (who had bravely tried to save Hawkins from the blazing wreck) being declared the winner. Paul was Australian and hugely popular and known as Hawkeye; the son of a gentleman of the cloth he was a colourful character with a wide and colourful vocabulary.

Programme cover from the International Spring Cup Meeting on 15 April 1967.

Good Friday 1971 saw Formula One return to Oulton Park to contest the Rothmans Trophy. Victory went to the diminutive Mexican Pedro Rodriguez driving a Yardley BRM P160; he set a new highest race average speed at 115.13mph. The fastest lap was shared with Peter Gethin driving a McLaren M10A (who had harried Rodriguez throughout the race) in 1min 25sec at 116.93mph.

Until 1973 racing had always been restricted to Saturdays and Bank Holidays but that year the council gave permission for four Sunday Meetings — but it was to last for only a year. That first Sunday meeting on 13 May was to feature F5000 as the top race of the day and it saw a 1-2-3 win for Chevron, victory going to Teddy Pilette.

At the start of the 21st century Oulton Park is still as popular as ever and still as demanding as it ever has been on drivers but, in common with so many other circuits, it no longer hosts major International meetings. Gone are the glory days when all the major Formula One teams came to Cheshire, now the major event on the circuit's calendar is the twice-yearly visit of the British Touring Car Championship. This is no fault of the circuit management — it is just the way the sport has gone (some might say, degenerated!). But Oulton Park is still the great challenge it always was.

At the close of the 2000 season the outright lap record on the International Circuit stands to the credit of Gareth Rees driving a Super Nova Formula 3000 Reynard 95D in the British Formula Two Championship on 6 July 1996. He circulated in 1min 24.68sec at a speed of 117.91mph. The outright lap record on the newly-sponsored Fosters Circuit stands to the credit of Luca Riccitelli in a Formula 3000 car in 50.09sec at a speed of 119.30mph.

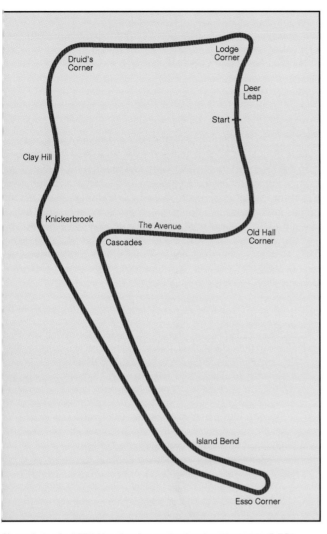

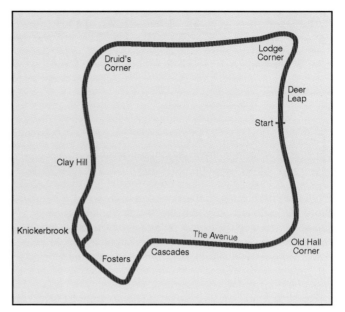

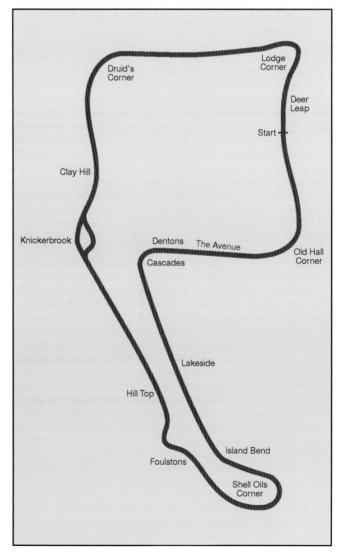

Above: Later in 1954 the circuit was further lengthened to 2.761 miles by extending Island Bend to another hairpin which was called Esso Corner. Island Corner now became Island Bend.

Above right: In 1975 a new 1.654-mile circuit was introduced and the long version was used somewhat less. The corner names are as used in the 1980s and 1990s. This circuit is used by the British Touring Car Championship.

Rght: Finally, the Oulton Park of today. Little has changed apart from the insertion of a left-handed kink following the hairpin at Shell Oils Corner, which has been named Foulstons in honour of John Foulston who bought the Brands Hatch Leisure Circuits and who sadly lost his life at Silverstone in private practice and whose daughter Nicola now runs the circuits in his stead.

Left: How times change! It is 21 September 1971 and Dave Walker's Novamotor-powered Gold Leaf Team Lotus is prepared for the Shell Oils Formula Three event in a very rural paddock with the public looking on. This was in the days when a factory team would quite happily consist of Formula One and Formula Three teams — and the drivers would quite likely drive both on the same day. In the 21st century factory cars are hidden away in garages and the enthusiast cannot get near them.
Mark Lowrie collection

OUSTON
FURTHEST NORTH IN ENGLAND

RAF Ouston in County Durham is approximately 12 miles from Newcastle upon Tyne city centre. A fighter base during World War 2, RAF Ouston no longer exists and is now a small industrial estate but it does have Army connections and is known as Albermarle Barracks. There is a possibility that racing first took place at Ouston as early as 1961 but it is certain that the Newcastle & District Motor Club organised race meetings there on 24 June 1962, 23 June 1963 and 21 June 1964, the last named being a joint car and motorcycle meeting. Jackie Stewart was a competitor at the 1963 meeting driving an E-Type Jaguar; he won the race and this is believed to have been his first victory.

Jim Clark attended the meeting in 1964 and was driven round the circuit in an open-topped car and then presented the prizes. It would appear that this was the last meeting at Ouston as Croft (which was 'just down the road') had reopened in 1964.

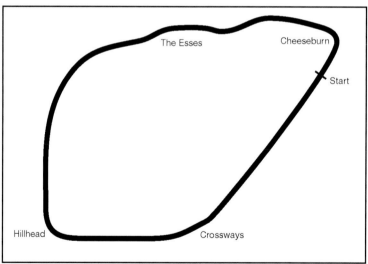

Above: This is the map of Ouston Race Circuit at RAF Ouston near Newcastle-upon-Tyne. In common with so many of the airfield circuits, it used parts of two of the runways and the perimeter track. It was approximately 1½ miles in length, with the start and finish line about a quarter of the way along the main straight, which took a right at Crossways at the intersection of the two runways used. Another straight led to Hillhead and a continuous right which tightened upon itself before reaching the Esses. Cheeseburn was a sharp right leading back on to the start and finish straight.

Top: From June 1964 comes this shot of Jimmy Clark performing the opening lap of honour at Ouston as passenger in an E-Type Jaguar. It serves to show the wide, open nature of the circuit.
Robert R. Davidson

PEBSHAM –
THE ONE THAT NEVER WAS

Perhaps this one should not be included at all; in 1956/7 Hastings and Bexhill Town Councils were giving consideration to allowing two circuits to be built on and around Pebsham Airfield which lay between the two towns. The envisaged Grand Prix circuit would have been three miles in length and the club circuit would have been exactly two miles long. It would appear that the plans did not receive approval.

Below right: The one that never was: this would have been the Grand Prix circuit had the plans to develop Pebsham ever come to fruition.

Below: This would have been the Club circuit at Pebsham.

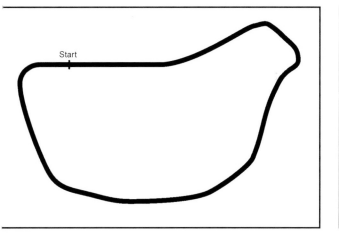

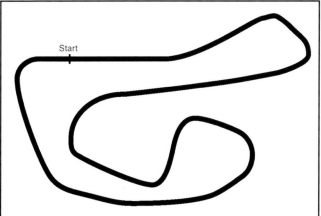

ROCKINGHAM
MOTOR SPEEDWAY
OVAL RACING RETURNS TO ENGLAND

Of all the motor racing circuits which have existed in England, just two have been purpose-built with a view to racing cars upon them and their respective creations are separated by nearly a century. Construction at Brooklands commenced in 1906 with the opening in 1907; construction of England's newest circuit started late in 1999, with the opening meeting planned for May 2001.

Rockingham Motor Speedway near Corby in Northamptonshire has been constructed upon a 'brown field' site as a banked oval, with the intention of bringing American oval racing across the Atlantic for the first time and the opportunity has been taken to use the infield for further circuits.

In all, there are six circuits at Rockingham: the main oval measures a mile and a half, the International Circuit is 2.6 miles long and 39ft wide; the motorcycle circuit measures 2.05 miles; the Historic Circuit 2.246 miles and the Club and Schools Circuits 1.7 miles. All are run anticlockwise.

There is Grandstand seating for 20,000 people at Turns One and Four and a further 7,500 in Rockingham Building. There are 36 pit garages.

Over the weekend of 20-22 September 2001 the fastest cars in the world made their debut at Rockingham Motor Speedway – the Champ cars came to England for the first time to contest the Rockingham 500, a round of CART (Championship Auto Racing Teams) Fedex Championship Series. For various reasons the race distance had to be reduced to 300km and victory was snatched on the exit of Turn Four of the last lap by Gil de Ferran driving the Marlboro Team Penske Honda-powered Reynard at a race average speed of 153.41mph from Kenny Brack at the wheel of the team Rahal Ford-engined Lola and the Newman Haas Racing Lola Toyota driven by Cristiano da Matta. The fastest lap and, therefore, the outright lap record was set by Patrick Carpentier in 25.551sec at 210.59mph in the Player's Forsyth Racing Cosworth-powered Reynard. Carpentier is the only Canadian ever to hold the outright lap record at an English circuit.

Below left: This is the 1¹/₂-mile-long banked oval at Rockingham which is 60ft wide and banked at between 3.1° and 7.9°. It is surfaced with nearly 151,000sq yd of tarmac. Strictly speaking, the Motor Speedway is not an oval, consisting as it does of two long and two shorter straights, linked by four corners of differing lengths. Turn One is 0.13 miles long, Turn Two 0.52 miles, Turn Three 0.096 and Turn Four 0.169 it therefore follows (as can be seen) that none of the straights is of equal length. The radius of the Turns is 617ft.

Below right: The Historic Track measures 2.246 miles and uses the whole of Turn Four: that part of the track which lies on the infield of the oval is 39ft wide.

Bottom left: The International Circuit has much in common with the Historic Track and has 13 'turns', to use American parlance.

Bottom right: The 'Link' Circuit will probably be used for motorcycle racing. It is possible that the final configuration of the circuits may vary from these outlines when Rockingham commences operations.

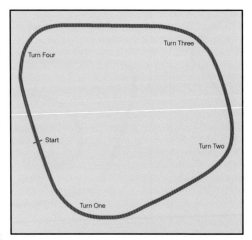

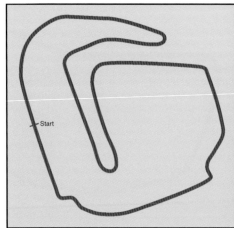

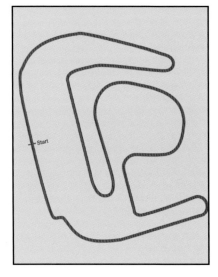

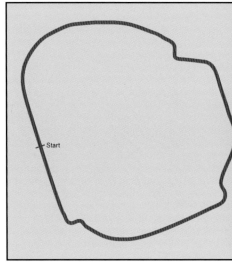

RUFFORTH
RACING AFTER THE BOMBERS LEFT

RAF Rufforth was built three and half miles west of York and was a typical standard pattern heavy bomber airfield being formally opened in November 1942. Following the cessation of hostilities, the airfield remained in active service until finally closing in 1954 when it was used for gliding, and motor racing commenced on 28 March 1959 following the loss of Full Sutton.

The original Rufforth circuit was 2.1 miles long, utilising most of the main runway (which resulted in a main straight the best part of a mile in length), some of the perimeter track and a piece of another runway. The start and finish line was situated about two-thirds of the way along the main straight and led to The Hairpin which was a right-hander which almost doubled back upon itself on to the perimeter track. The subsequent straight led to the right-hand Fosse Curve and on to the left-hand Grange Curve. A short straight led to the left-handed Boundary Bend, followed by another straight and the right-hand Becketts Hairpin, which also doubled-back on itself on to the runway. At the intersection of the runways the course turned right at Runway Bend on to the main straight. This circuit was used on four occasions in 1959.

Rufforth mark two was 1.7 miles long and somewhat different to its predecessor. The start and finish line was moved to halfway between Fosse Curve and Grange Curve, and The Esses had been inserted between Becketts Hairpin and Runway Bend. Because it ran towards a main road, the main straight had been

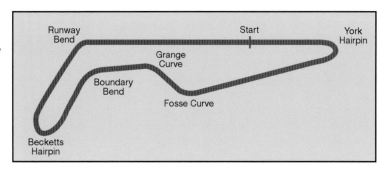

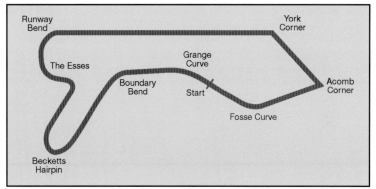

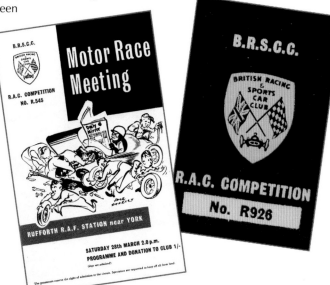

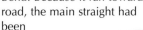

Top: This is the circuit outline of Rufforth mark one, measuring 2.1 miles, as originally used in 1959. The start line was situated two-thirds of the way along one of the main runways, terminating at York Corner, where the course turned right on to the perimeter track. It then made its way to Fosse and Grange Curve, Boundary Bend and thus to the right-hand Becketts Hairpin, where it joined another runway and then turned back on to the start and finish straight at the intersection of the two runways at Runway Bend. It was probably used on only four occasions, with the first meeting taking place on 28 March 1959.

Above: Rufforth mark two was used from 1960 and was somewhat shorter at 1.7 miles. The original start/finish line had gone completely, for the circuit now turned right off the original main straight at a runway intersection, at what was now called York Corner, taking another right at the new Acomb Corner a little short of Fosse Curve. The start line was now situated between Fosse and Grange Curves and the circuit was now as before until after Becketts Hairpin, the Esses having been inserted before Runway Bend which was still recognizable as the original location.

Far left: The programme covers for many of the Yorkshire circuit's meetings in the 1950s carried a cartoon and were sponsored by the *Daily Mirror*

Left: This programme cover comes from a Saturday meeting in June, probably during the 1960s, but the year is not mentioned. The use of yellow reproduces the BRSCC badge in a style which is familiar to motor racing enthusiasts. *Motor Racing Archive*

somewhat truncated and now turned right at York Corner on to part of the runway which had not hitherto been used and right again at Acomb Corner leading to Fosse Curve. A typical meeting was run by the Northern Centre of the British Racing & Sports Car Club on Saturday, 30 May 1959 and consisted of a seven-race programme principally for sports cars but with one race for modified saloon cars, one for Formula III and the main event of the day for Racing and Sports Racing Cars run over 16 laps. It was the Yorkshire Evening Post Trophy Race and, strangely, was the last race of the day; a notable entrant was one J. Clark driving the Lister Jaguar of Border Reivers — another was T. Lanfranchi driving an Austin Healey 100S entered by Huddersfield Motor Racing Team, whilst Tim Parnell drove his father's Formula Two Cooper and Trevor Taylor a Beart Cooper Formula Two.

At some point in time the site was sold to a farmer and racing ceased in 1978.

From April 1962 comes this shot of David Bridges' Formula Junior Merlyn, which appears to have had a disagreement with the control bus. Neither the car nor the bus has fared too well from the altercation. *Ferret Fotographics*

Below: Upon a date lost in the mists of time, at a meeting organised by the British Racing & Sports Car Club, Tony Lanfranchi is presented with his rewards for winning the Daily Mirror Trophy Race. *Mark Lowrie Collection*

SILVERSTONE
THE HOME OF THE BRITISH
RACING DRIVERS' CLUB

Silverstone claims to be the home of British motor racing; over the years much energy has been put into the circuit and it is hard to refute the claim.

With the termination of hostilities in Europe in 1945 the first motorsport event on English soil was held at Gransden Lodge in 1946 and the next on the Isle of Man in 1947, but there was nowhere permanent on the mainland which was suitable. As has been recounted under the story of Goodwood, Brooklands was owned by Vickers Armstrong, Donington Park was a storage depot for military vehicles, and Crystal Palace was somewhat overgrown.

In 1948, the Royal Automobile Club set its mind upon running a Grand Prix and started to cast around for a suitable venue. There was, of course, no possibility of closing public roads on the mainland as could happen on the Isle of Man or the Channel Islands; it was a time of austerity and there was no question of building a new circuit from scratch so some viable alternative had to be found.

What was available was a considerable number of ex-RAF airfields and it was to these that the Competitions Committee of the RAC turned its attention with particular interest being paid to two near the centre of England — Snitterfield near Stratford-upon-Avon and one behind the village of Silverstone in Northamptonshire. The latter was still under Air Ministry control (a squadron of Wellingtons had left only the previous year) but a lease was arranged in August 1948 and plans put into place to run the first British Grand Prix since the RAC last ran one at Brooklands in 1927, those held at Donington Park in the late 1930s not having benefited from the title 'British'. Apart from the village from which it takes its name, the story of Silverstone commences on 20 March 1943 with the opening of the airfield; during World War 2 the site was host to many squadrons flying a wide variety of aircraft.

As is the case with so many stories of British motor racing circuits, when Silverstone is discussed one name stands out: in August 1948 the Royal Automobile Club employed one James Wilson Brown on a three-month contract to create the Grand Prix circuit in rather less than two months. Nearly 40 years later Jimmy Brown died virtually in harness.

The prospect of running a Grand Prix in England as late in the year as October is one which would not be countenanced today but the idea was relished in 1948 for it was, after all, only continuing a tradition handed down from Brooklands and Donington Park. So it was that on Thursday, 30 September Silverstone first reverberated to the sound of Formula One motor racing engines and on 2 October the new circuit saw its first motor race. The prewar Donington Grands Prix had all been held in October, so Silverstone was but following tradition — but it was a pretty austere place then.

The new circuit was marked out with oil drums and straw bales and consisted of the perimeter road and the runways running into the centre of the airfield from two directions. It was pointed out that this would provide the unnerving prospect of cars approaching each other at racing speeds before suddenly turning left, so canvas screens were erected at the centre of the circuit — surely a classic case of 'out of sight, out of mind'! Spectators were contained behind rope barriers and the officials were housed in tents.

The names given to the corners and features of the circuit deserve some explanation: Abbey Curve derives its name from the ancient Luffield Abbey, while the ruins of the Chapel of Thomas à Becket lie on the other side of the circuit, hence Becketts Corner and Chapel Curve. Stowe Corner is derived from Stowe School to the south, while Maggotts and Copse come from two local landmarks, Maggotts Moor and Seven Copses Wood. Finally, the RAC named two corners after the Club in Pall Mall and the Country Club at Woodcote Park in Surrey. Hangar Straight was so named because of two large aircraft hangars which still stood along the straight. All of these names are retained today with the addition of some suitable names for new features created with the rebuilding of the circuit. It was 3.67 miles in length and the start/finish line was on Abbey Straight between Abbey Curve and Woodcote.

The entrance to Silverstone in 1997.

Below: Of all the circuits in England, none has changed so much nor so often as Silverstone. This is the original Silverstone circuit on which the Royal Automobile Club ran its first international Grand Prix on 2 October 1948; the basic overall outline is recognisable as Silverstone but it is very different to what is known today. It is inconceivable that Segrave and Seaman Corners would be even contemplated now, allowing cars to approach each other at racing speeds. Screens were erected so that they would not be able to see each other! A truly classic case of 'out of sight, out of mind'. The start/finish line is on the straight before Woodcote; it was 3.67 miles long.

nobleman the Baron Emmanuel de Graffenried in the Enrico Plate-entered Maserati 4CL exactly one second slower. Third on the front row was 'Phi-Phi' Étançelin in another 26C from Bob Gerard in ERA R14B/C and Leslie Johnson driving the E-Type ERA GP2.

Victory went to Villoresi at the wheel of the Maserati 4 CLT in 3hr 18min 3sec at 72.28mph from his team mate Ascari who was just 14sec behind. Third was Bob Gerard whilst into fourth place came Rosier's Lago-Talbot followed by 'Bira' in a Maserati 4CLT/48, with John Bolster sixth in arguably the most famous ERA, R5B 'Remus'.

Starting at noon, there was a supporting race for 500cc racing cars which became Formula Three but which was then

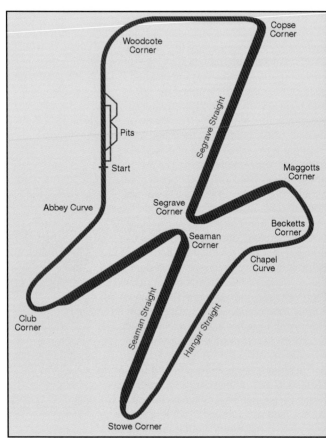

An Official Opening Ceremony was performed at 11.45am on Grand Prix day by John Cobb who was the current holder of the Land Speed Record escorted by three famous motorcycle racers — A. J. Bell, Freddie Frith and Maurice Cann. An estimated 100,000 people arrived to witness the first postwar Grand Prix on English soil which started at 2pm and was expected to last for three hours.

There were no factory entries but Scuderia Ambrosiana sent two Maserati 4CLT/48s (called San Remo, for that was where they first appeared) for Luigi Villoresi and Alberto Ascari who finished in that order (notwithstanding having started from the back of the field of 25 starters) ahead of Bob Gerard in his ERA R14B/C. The race was 239 miles long and was run at an average speed of 72.28mph. Ecurie France, under the guidance of Paul Vallee, sent no less than four 4.5-litre Lago-Talbot Type 26Cs for Louis Chiron (who had driven in the 1927 Brooklands Grand Prix and who was now 48 years old), Louis Rosier, Philippe Étançelin and the Italian Franco Comotti who had won the TT at Donington Park in 1937. The field, which totalled 25 starters, included a veritable horde of ERAs, started from a five-four-five grid. There were an additional seven entrants who either did not arrive or simply did not start.

Fastest lap was set in practice by Louis Chiron in the Lago-Talbot 26C in 2min 56sec at 75.8mph from the Swiss

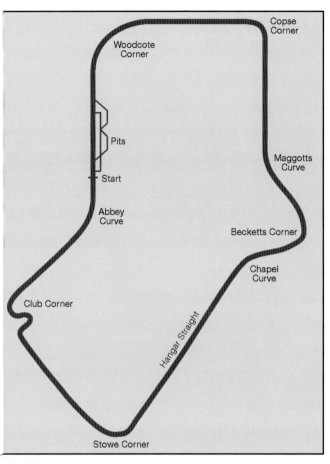

As in the previous year the Grand Prix was preceded by a 500cc race which was won by a young man driving a Cooper-JAP. It was the slim youth who had retired from the previous year's race — he received £60 for winning the 17-lap race; the Baron won £500 for his victory in the Grand Prix. Once again the competitors had started from a five-four-five grid.

In 1949 the first running took place of what was to become an institution at Silverstone, the International Trophy sponsored by the *Daily Express* and which became virtually a second Grand Prix. The sponsorship by the newspaper had the added bonus of allowing the famous cartoonist Giles (who was no mean racer himself) to have free rein. The first International Trophy was run on 20 August in two heats and a final; victory in the first heat went to Prince Birabongse and the second to

invariably referred to as Formula III. This race was won by 'Spike' Rhiando from John Cooper, driving two of the latter's cars after a slim youth named Stirling Moss had retired.

The second Grand Prix at Silverstone was scheduled for 14 May 1949 and was officially designated the British Grand Prix. It was to use the full perimeter track with a chicane inserted at Club Corner since it had been realised that the use of a canvas screen in the centre of the circuit to shield approaching cars from sight could not be allowed to continue. The length of the second Silverstone Grand Prix circuit was exactly three miles and the race was run over 100 laps, making it the longest postwar Grand Prix held in England. There were 25 starters and victory again went to a 'San Remo' Maserati, this time in the hands of 'Tulo' de Graffenried (who finished ninth the previous year) from Bob Gerard in his familiar ERA, and Louis Rosier in a 4.5-litre Lago-Talbot; fourth was the prototype ERA R1A driven by David Hampshire and Billy Cotton from the Lago-Talbot of 'Phi-Phi' Étançelin, with Fred Ashmore sixth in a Scuderia Ambrosiano Maserati 4CLT/48. The race average had risen to 77.31mph. Bira set the fastest lap in 2min 11sec at 82.44mph — the inexorable rise had already started. The attendance was estimated at anything up to 120,000. During the race John Bolster rolled his ERA which brought to an end his racing career. The attendance figures at the first two Grands Prix pose a question: if 100,000 people could be accommodated in the late 1940s, why does Silverstone restrict attendance on Grand Prix day today to 90,000?

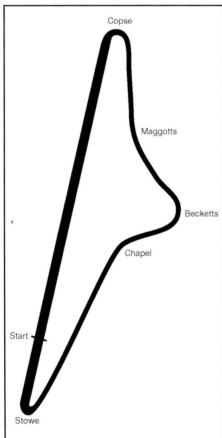

Left: On Saturday, 2 July 1949 the Vintage Sports Car Club used this configuration for its 10-race programme. No mention was made in the programme of the length of this circuit and it is not known whether the layout was used again. At Copse and Becketts the course was marked out in oil drums and at Stowe with straw bales. Spectator protection on the main straight consisted of a post and rope fence.

Right: By 1950, Silverstone had acquired the configuration with which everyone who knows the circuit is familiar; just one major change was two years away. The removal of the chicane reduced the circuit length to 2.889 miles.

Far right: In 1952, the pits and the start/finish line were moved to just beyond Woodcote - with the reprofiling of some corners the circuit length was increased to 2.927 miles. Silverstone was now to remain unchanged for nearly a quarter of a century.

Dr Giuseppe Farina — both were driving Maserati 4CLT/48s, but the final went to a Ferrari Tipo 125 driven by Alberto Ascari from Farina, with Luigi Villoresi third in another Ferrari.

For 1950, Silverstone was graced by the presence of Royalty as Their Majesties King George VI and Queen Elizabeth attended the Grand Prix accompanied by HRH the Princess Elizabeth on a lovely day in May, the only occasion that the Monarch has attended a motor race in the United Kingdom. Perhaps this has been due to the fact that even Royalty cannot avoid the traffic jams.

The year saw the institution of the World Championship for Drivers and Silverstone was the very first qualifying event, with the British Grand Prix carrying the courtesy title European Grand Prix. The race was the first time that the Alfa Romeo 158 'Alfettas' had been seen in England and they took the first three

Left: In this scene from the 1950 Daily Express Trophy Race Dr Giuseppe Farina in an Alfa Rome 158 leads Whitehead (Ferrari), Reg Parnell (Maserati) and Cuth Harrison (ERA) through Woodcote Corner. Note the variety of headgear and the primitive manner of marking out the course. *National Motor Museum Photographic Library*

Right: From 1952 comes this evocative shot of three works Jaguar C-Types passing the pits at Silverstone, having negotiated Woodcote Corner, in the hands of Ian Walker driving No 41, Stirling Moss in No 41 and Tony Rolt handling No 42. International flags fly from the flagpoles atop the pits but the lack of protection for those working there is quite alarming. *JDHT Ltd*

places in the hands of Dr Giuseppe Farina, Luigi Fagioli and Reg Parnell with the race average having increased by a staggering amount to 90.96mph, but the distance had been reduced to 205 miles. In fourth place came Yves Giraud-Cabantous driving a works-entered Lago-Talbot, from Louis Rosier in another Lago-Talbot with Bob Gerard sixth in ERA R14B/C; the race had started from a four-three-four grid of 21 starters.

This race featured the first public appearance of the BRM V16 which had barely been finished in time and was flown to Silverstone on the morning of the Grand Prix. When the flag dropped, the new car was left on the line, the half-shafts breaking when the colossal horsepower was fed to them.

The start line was still in its original place but the chicane had been removed from Club Corner reducing the length to 2.889 miles; it was now to remain unchanged for 25 years.

The 1950 British Grand Prix was to mark the end of an era, for it was the last time that an ERA was to feature in the results of a major Grand Prix.

At Silverstone on Saturday 29 July the Aston Martin Owners' Club organised its first ever race meeting under the title of The St John Horsfall Race Meeting, in honour of the great Aston Martin supporter who had been fatally injured at the circuit the previous year whilst contesting the International Trophy race in an ERA. Some notable names were in the programme, amongst them Dudley Coram, who was Clerk of the Course and Secretary of the Meeting, and is remembered for the work he

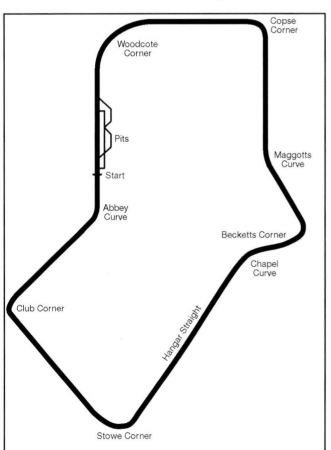

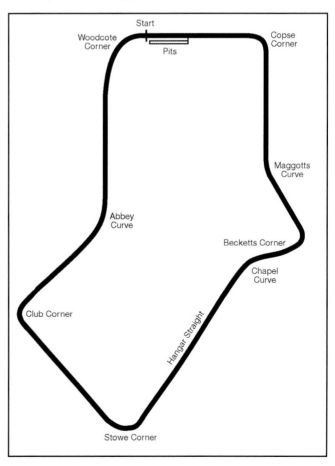

Right: The glorious D-type Jaguar in full flight at Silverstone: Tony Rolt at the wheel of OKV 2 is on his way to third place in the International Trophy. This car, chassis number XKC403, is one of the original 1954 factory team cars. On the day in question, Mike Hawthorn brought XKC404 (OKV 3) home in fourth place, with XKC406 in the hands of Duncan Hamilton, fifth. Note the 'GB' plate on the rear of the car for the works C- and D-type Jaguars were fully road legal and were (on occasion) driven to the circuits. At this time the cars ran with the wrap-round windscreen on the driver's side only - it was in 1956 that the rules specified that if a car was to call itself a sports car for racing purposes it must have a full-width windscreen and at least some semblance of a passenger seat. It was also in 1956 that the D-type achieved its final flowering in the shape of the long-nose finned version. In those halcyon days you could - provided you had the wherewithal - pop into the local Jaguar dealer and order a C- or D-type. A total of 67 'production' D-type Jaguars were built or commissioned; of these 42 were delivered while nine were destroyed in the fire at Browns Lane in February 1957 or subsequently dismantled, while 16 were converted and delivered as the XKSS road car. In either case, they are truly rare — and highly desirable! *Jaguar Daimler Heritage Trust*

Below: For the 1954 British Grand Prix, Daimler-Benz sent two of its streamlined W196 Mercedes-Benzes to Silverstone for Juan Fangio and Karl Kling. It appears to have been a typical English summer as the W196s are worked on in the rain in Silverstone's paddock. *Daimler-Benz Classic Archiv*

did in establishing Snetterton. Amongst the competitors in The David Brown Challenge Cup was Holland Birkett driving an Austin 750. Entries came from members of the Vintage Sports Car Club, The Bugatti Owners' Club, The Bentley Drivers' Club, The Lagonda Car Club, The MG Car Club, The Lancia Car Club (just two of them), SUNBAC and, of course, the Aston Martin Owners' Club.

1951 was memorable for it saw the defeat of the all-conquering Alfa Romeos at Silverstone, with victory going to José Froilan Gonzalez (the Pampas Bull) driving Ferrari 375/50-

2 from Fangio in an Alfa Romeo 159B and Luigi Villoresi in Ferrari 375/51-3; fourth was Felici Bonetto for Alfa Romeo (159A) from Reg Parnell in the V16 BRM, with Consalvo Sanesi collecting the last World Championship point in another 159B Alfetta. The race distance had increased to 263 miles and the average speed had shot up to 96.11mph — in just four years the race speed had increased by nearly 24mph. The V16 BRMs performed better this year, Parnell's fifth place being supplemented by Peter Walker bringing his car home in seventh place.

It was in 1951 that the 750 Motor Club first ran a race which was to become the stuff of legend and a traditional part of the British motor racing calendar when they instituted a six-hour relay race for clubmen driving teams of cars on a handicap basis; the first one was won by a team of vintage Bentleys. In later years the race was to become known as the Birkett Six-Hours.

The International Trophy attracted the cream of Formula One and included the invincible Alfa Romeo team whose cars won the preliminary heats in the hands of Fangio and Farina. However, the heavens opened for the final and visibility was almost nil, and in those conditions the supercharged Alfettas were at a distinct disadvantage. When the race was abandoned after only six laps Reg Parnell was in the lead in Tony Vandervell's 'Thinwall Special'; no official winner was declared, so it was not until two months later in the Grand Prix referred to above that Alfa suffered their first real defeat.

By 1952, the RAC had decided it no longer wished to run the circuit, and on 1 January the lease was taken over by the British Racing Drivers' Club with Jimmy Brown continuing as track manager but now employed by the BRDC. The lease covered only the track perimeter and the right to use other areas at specific times. The start/finish line was moved from Abbey Straight to just after Woodcote Corner and with some reprofiling of corners the lap distance was extended to 2.927 miles.

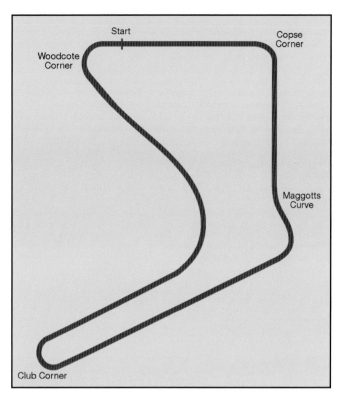

Above: Silverstone has changed considerably and several times over the years, but who remembers this configuration? It is the 'long' Club circuit of the mid-1950s.

Below: In their early days the 500cc/Formula III brigade did not confine themselves exclusively to Brands Hatch and on 22 August 1953 the Half-Litre Car Club ran its first race meeting at Silverstone. The basis of the British Racing & Sports Car Club badge is in evidence in the club badge used on this programme cover. *Motor Racing Archive*

Coinciding with the BRDC taking over the running of the British Grand Prix there was a little unrest within the sport which led to the downgrading of Grands Prix to Formula Two, having an adverse effect upon the 248-mile race which was won by Alberto Ascari in runaway fashion at 90.9mph from his Ferrari team-mate Piero Taruffi — both were driving the Tipo 500. Third place went to Mike Hawthorn driving a Cooper-Bristol Mk 1 from Dennis Poore driving Connaught A4, with Eric Thompson fifth in his Connaught A5, the final point going to Dr Farina in his Ferrari Tipo 500. There were no fewer than 32 starters, although Aston's Aston-Butterworth failed to leave the line.

The International Trophy was notable in 1952 in that it saw an all-too-rare victory for HWM when Lance Macklin had a superb win.

The same situation pertained in 1953 with the World Championship again being run for Formula Two cars. The race distance was back to 263 miles and was a straight fight between the Maserati and Ferrari teams, with victory going to Ascari at 92.9mph aboard a Ferrari Tipo 500 from the Maserati A6GCM/52-2048 of Fangio and another Tipo 500 driven by Farina. Fourth was Gonzalez, in Maserati A6GCM/53-2041, with Hawthorn fifth aboard a Tipo 500 Ferrari from Bonetto's Maserati A6GCM/53-2044.

The programme included a Formule Libre race which really put the Grand Prix into perspective; Farina drove the Thinwall Special to victory at a higher average speed than that at which the Grand Prix had been won and set the first lap record at over 100mph, at 100.16mph.

The 1954 Grand Prix season was the first for the new 2.5-litre Formula One (2.5-litre normally aspirated engines or 750cc supercharged) and had attracted interest from some major players. Lancia had joined the fray with the D50 and Daimler-Benz were back; the appearance of Lancia meant that there were no fewer than three Italian teams competing in Formula One, the others being Ferrari and Maserati. British interest was catered for by the Owen Organisation with the BRM, the Vanwall of Tony Vandervell and Connaught still fighting the good fight, while Cooper-Bristol were not to be

Below: The streamlining of the W196 had proved extremely effective on the long straights at Reims, but at Silverstone in 1954 it proved to be an embarrassment as the drivers were unable to see the drums which marked the circuit. Here, we see Fangio neatly clipping one of them and sending it spinning; he had started from pole position but at the expense of the bodywork and even his genius, could only manage fourth in the race. This was one of those rare occasions when the might of Untertürkheim went home with their tails between their legs. *Daimler-Benz Classic Archive*

forgotten. At the start of the season Mercedes-Benz had swept all before them, but Silverstone was a debacle for the team which returned to Untertürkheim with their tails very much between their legs, notwithstanding Fangio starting from pole position. The 263-mile race was won by Gonzalez from Hawthorn in the works Ferrari 625s, with Onofre Marimon third in the works Maserati 250F (2506) a lap down after starting from the last row but one of the grid. Fangio was fourth in the W196 followed by Maurice Trintignant in a Ferrari 625 a further two laps adrift, and Roberto Mières who started from the back row was sixth driving 250F number 2502.

The winner's average speed for the 263-mile race was 89.69mph in two hours 56min 14sec. Fastest lap in 1min 50sec at 95.78mph was shared by Gonzalez, Hawthorn, Moss, Ascari, Jean Behra and Fangio. Included in the programme was a 1,500cc sports car race; until now the smaller British manufacturers had not had the opportunity to test their mettle against the Continentals, but Hans Hermann had entered a Porsche 550 which was pushed into third place by the Lotuses of Colin Chapman and Peter Gammon.

The following year, 1955, was the first in which the Grand Prix alternated with Aintree and the Mercedes team made up for 1954 by coming home in the first four places on the Merseyside circuit, but by the time the race returned to Silverstone in 1956 they had gone, as had Lancia, as an independent entrant, the cars having been handed to Ferrari who ran them as Lancia-Ferraris. The great Juan Manuel Fangio scored his only British Grand Prix win in one of these cars. The Grand Prix had been extended from 90 to 101 laps increasing the race distance to 295 miles which Fangio won at 98.65mph in 2hr 59min 47sec, this being the second-longest Grand Prix held at Silverstone. Second, a lap down, was another Lancia-Ferrari which had started the race in the hands of the Marquis Alfonso de Portago but was taken over at half distance by Peter Collins and in third place was Jean Behra in a Maserati 250F number 2521, a further lap down. Another lap behind in fourth was Jack Fairman in a works Connaught B5, followed on 97 laps by Horace Gould in a privately entered 250F (2514) and in sixth place on 96 laps was Luigi Villoresi driving another works 250F (2519). The fastest lap was set by Stirling Moss, who started from pole position on the four-three-four grid, in his privately entered Maserati 250F (2522), in 1min 43.2sec at 102.1mph.

Matters were somewhat happier for the British enthusiast at the International Trophy; a quality field had been attracted, including the Lancia-Ferraris of Fangio and Collins, but the first 13 laps of the race were led by the lovely new BRM P25 driven by Mike Hawthorn. When the engine of the BRM expired, Stirling Moss in the Vanwall took over, going on to win, breaking the Lancia-Ferraris in the process. The British Cup of Joy overflowed, with Connaughts coming in second and third in the hands of Archie Scott Brown and Desmond Titterington.

The writing was on the wall! The first victory for the new Frank Costin-designed aerodynamic Vanwall in the capable hands of Stirling Moss was but the beginning. By the middle of the season the Vanwall had proved itself the fastest car in Grand Prix racing, if not yet the most reliable.

For 1958 drastic changes were introduced into Formula One; race distances were reduced from three to two hours, and oxygen-bearing and alcohol fuels were banned to be replaced by 100-octane petrol. This downward spiral of race lengths has

continued over the years to the point where today it is very rare for a Grand Prix to be more than 200 miles. Fangio had retired, Maserati had withdrawn due to financial difficulties so the glorious 250F would be seen no more as a factory entry. The new rules had the effect of producing smaller and lighter cars which meant that Vanwall and BRM had to modify their designs but, as is so often the case, Ferrari was a jump ahead and contested the season with the Dino 246, having abandoned the Lancia-Ferrari and its V8 in favour of a straight six. Throughout the 1958 season the battle was between Ferrari and Vanwall and it was fervently hoped that Tony Vandervell would succeed on his home track but it was not to be; on this occasion the green cars fell apart, Lewis-Evans and Brooks coming home fourth and seventh, and even Moss could not challenge the Dino 246, retiring his Vanwall on the 26th lap with engine problems. Victory went to Peter Collins from Mike Hawthorn, both driving Dino 246s; the joker in the pack was John Cooper whose minute rear-engined Coventry-Climax-powered cars harried the established marques, with Roy Salvadori coming home third in a 2.2-litre example. Lewis-Evans was driving Vanwall VW6, while in fifth spot was the American Harry Schell driving BRM P25-257 from Jack Brabham in the 2-litre Cooper-Climax T45.

The crowd of 120,000 spectators would dearly have loved to see a British Racing Green car victorious on its home ground but must have been heartened to have had four British drivers in the first four places. The race average was increasing year on year and in 1958 was 102.05mph but the race distance was a mere 219 miles.

The 2.5-litre Formula One (which had produced some truly beautiful racing cars) came to an end in 1960 after a mere six years but by now the mid-engined revolution had taken place with only Ferrari and Aston Martin still placing the engine ahead of the driver (which many contended was the proper place for it!). Aston Martin had been late on the scene with the DBR4/250 and, sadly, it was never a success. At Silverstone on 16 July 1960 the front-engined cars were completely outclassed, the first three places in the race going to Coventry-Climax-engined cars, with victory for Jack Brabham in the works Cooper-Climax T53 from John Surtees (Lotus-Climax 18 373) and Innes Ireland (Lotus-Climax 18 371). In fourth place came Bruce McLaren in the works Cooper-Climax T53 from Tony Brooks in the Yeoman Credit-entered Cooper-Climax T51, with the final World Championship point of the race going to Wolfgang Graf Bergh von Trips of Cologne in the Ferrari Dino 246. The race distance was 225 miles and the race average was 108.6mph. Of the 25 starters 16 finished and amongst the retirees was Gino Munaron driving a Cooper-Ferrari T45.

In 1961, the BRDC took the bold step of acquiring the lease to the agricultural land within and around the circuit and Jimmy Brown found himself a farmer as well as track manager. This was also the year of the new 1.5-litre Formula One introduced by the governing body on safety grounds — it met strong opposition in Great Britain which gave birth to an alternative but short-lived 3-litre 'Inter-Continental Formula' which extended the life of the now-obsolete Formula One cars. The International Trophy was run for this Formula and produced a notable first and last — the first (and only) British

Silverstone is owned by, and is the home of, the British Racing Drivers Club whose badge is probably the most coveted in the world by all who follow and love the sport, for membership and the right to wear the badge cannot be bought. Membership is by invitation and then only on qualification. *Author*

appearance of the American Scarab team and the final appearance of a works Vanwall, on this occasion a rear-engined car driven by John Surtees. The race was wet and Stirling Moss demonstrated his supreme prowess in Rob Walker's Cooper by lapping the entire field at least twice except for Jack Brabham who suffered the ignominy only once.

Within a year the despised 1.5-litre cars would be as fast around Silverstone as their predecessors but the intransigence of the British manufacturers meant they were late in building competitive engines. However, by 1962 (the second year of the Formula) they had caught up and the International Trophy was run for the 1.5-litre cars. It was the last race before the commencement of the World Championship and attracted a very healthy field. This was the classic occasion when Graham Hill in the BRM crossed the finishing line almost sideways to snatch victory from Jimmy Clark's Lotus; both drivers were credited with the same time.

The British Grand Prix did not return to Silverstone until 1963, the RAC having broken the alternating policy with Aintree by awarding the race to the Merseyside circuit two years in succession. The 1963 race was run over 240 miles at an average of 107.75mph; the increase in race length was due to the fact that the nimbler cars were travelling quicker and in order to make the race last for two hours the race distance had to be increased. The increase in speed was due more to improvements in the braking area and

cornering power than to vast increases in horsepower; the day of the special builder had come, with BRM and Coventry-Climax happy to sell their power units to anyone who wished to purchase them. Even Ferrari had succumbed to the rear-engined layout, but sent only one car to England for John Surtees (Dino 156/63 0001). He finished second behind Jim Clark's works Lotus-Climax 25 R4 and ahead of three BRMs driven by Graham Hill (P57-5785), Richie Ginther (P57-5784) and Lorenzo Bandini (P57-5781), with sixth place going to a Lotus-BRM (24 945) driven by the American Jim Hall. There were some notable cars on the grid such as the two Scirocco-BRMs of Tony Settember and Ian Burgess, Ian Raby's Raby-BRM and the Dutch nobleman Count Carel Godin de Beaufort in his Porsche 718.

For the 1965 season, BRM took a chance and signed a young Scottish driver straight from Formula Three; the International Trophy was only his fourth Formula One race but in a top class field he qualified second and won handsomely from John Surtees in the Ferrari. The name of this newcomer was John Young Stewart and the world came to know him as Jackie, and he placed his BRM fourth on the grid for the Grand Prix. This was the final year of the 1.5-litre Formula One and when the circus came to Silverstone it was notable for the appearance in third place on the grid of a V12 Honda driven by the American Richie Ginther; it retired on the 27th lap but it was the precursor of much that was to come. Poleman was Jimmy Clark in the V8 Lotus-Climax 33 R11, with Graham Hill second in the BRM P261-2616; Clark won the 234-mile race from Hill and Surtees in Ferrari 1512-0007 at a speed of 112.02mph. And the newcomer who had placed his BRM (P261-2617) fourth on the front row of the grid? He came home a very creditable fifth behind Mike Spence's Lotus-Climax 33 R11 and ahead of Dan Gurney's Brabham-Climax BT11.

The following year the new 3-litre Formula One was heralded as the 'Return of Power', and apart from a short aberration when 3.5-litre engines were permitted, that Formula has lasted for more than 30 years. However, Brands Hatch hosted the first British Grand Prix for the new Formula so it was not until 1967 that the big-engined cars came to Northamptonshire. The race distance was unchanged but Jim Clark's winning speed in Lotus-Cosworth 49 R2 had risen to 117.6mph; second was Denny Hulme aboard the Repco-Brabham

Above left: Programme cover from the 1952 5th RAC British Grand Prix. The lack of advertising is refreshing.

Left: Eight years later the programme cover for the Grand Prix is still free of sponsorship.

from the Ferrari 312 (0003) of Chris Amon. Fourth was Brabham in his own Repco-powered car ahead of Rodriguez in the Cooper-Maserati T81B, with John Surtees taking the final Championship point in the Honda RA 273-F102.

There was a frightening increase in the race average speed in 1969, for it rose by 10mph to 127.2mph when Jackie Stewart won in the Matra-Cosworth MS80/01 from Jacky Ickx (Brabham-Cosworth BT26-4) and Bruce McLaren driving one of his own Cosworth-powered cars (M7C/1). The race distance had been extended to 245 miles. For the Grand Prix in 1969 the grid was changed from its four-three-four to three-two-three due to the increase in the road space occupied by the cars, occasioned in no small part by the huge tubeless racing tyres which they now sported. The costs of Formula One were rising inexorably and the days of the private entrant were fast receding — the Silverstone grid in 1969 seeing just 17 starters — and the lap record was raised dramatically to stand at 129.61mph. In fourth place was the Lotus-Cosworth 49B/R6 driven by Austrian Jochen Rindt which had started from pole position, while home in fifth place came the Brabham-Cosworth BT26-1 driven by Piers Courage and entered by Frank Williams Racing, so the day of the private entrant was not quite dead. The final point went to Vic Elford in McLaren-Cosworth M7A/3 entered by Antique Automobiles just to press home the point.

A high spot of the Grand Prix meeting was the Formula Three race for the then current 'screamer' cars which saw eight contestants running nose to tail for the whole race, but Allan Rollinson broke clear to win by 10 yards.

By 1971, the 3-litre Formula was five years old and many would have liked to have seen a change but none was forthcoming (nor has there been subsequently!): it was also the year when sponsorship came to the fore and international racing colours finally disappeared — with the sole exception of Ferrari who remain faithful to Rosso Corsa. Race lengths were reduced to 200 miles — Silverstone's Grand Prix was just 199 miles and was to get even shorter as the years progressed.

Ken Tyrrell became a constructor and Jackie Stewart won at Silverstone driving the Tyrrell 003 on his way to a double World Championship. Ronnie Peterson was second in March 711/6 from Emerson Fittipaldi in Lotus 72D/R5: all were Cosworth-powered in what was fast becoming Formula Super Ford; the race average was 130.5mph. Fourth was Henri Pescarolo in March-Cosworth 711/3, from Rolf Stommelen and John Surtees driving respectively Surtees TS9/002 and TS9/001;

these three were a lap down and also Cosworth-powered. Thirteenth home but not classified as he had not covered 90% of the total distance, was Reine Wisell driving a Lotus 56B powered by a Pratt & Whitney turbine.

It had become relatively easy to build a Formula One car around the package of the Cosworth engine and the Hewland gearbox as witnessed by the grid of 28 for the 1973 British Grand Prix. If the quantity was there, quality was not necessarily so evident; of the entries 23 were Cosworth-powered, there were three BRM V12s, a Tecno flat-12 and a singleton Ferrari. This was the year that Jody Scheckter lost control of his McLaren at the completion of the first lap, spinning into the pit wall and setting in motion the biggest accident ever seen on a British motor racing circuit. The race was stopped at the completion of the second lap and the carnage cleared away; it speaks highly for the construction of the cars that only one driver was injured. Twenty-eight cars had started the race but only 19 took the restart and the race was won by Peter Revson (McLaren-Cosworth M23/2) from Ronnie Peterson (Lotus-Cosworth 72/R6) and Denny Hulme (McLaren-Cosworth M23/1). The race average had risen little in two years as it was run at 131.75mph; it was only 195 miles long.

It was in 1973 that Lord Alexander Hesketh started entering March-Cosworth 731/3 in Grands Prix for James Hunt who finished fourth at Silverstone ahead of François Cevert in the Tyrrell-Cosworth 006 and Carlos Reutemann in a Brabham-Cosworth BT42/3. The approach of the Hesketh equipe was refreshing but there was a serious side to the venture for the Hesketh 308 appeared in 1974.

The 1973 débâcle wrought changes upon Silverstone as it was deemed necessary to slow the cars through Woodcote, for it had become evident that bits of damaged cars could have entered the grandstands and injured spectators. A chicane was inserted at Woodcote, increasing the circuit length to 2.932 miles and a two-two-two grid formation introduced for the 1975 Grand Prix. Some enquired when a one-one-one grid would be introduced — little could they have known how close their joke would come to the truth!

'Formula Super Ford' reached its zenith in 1975 when 26 of the 28 entries were Cosworth-powered, there being just two Ferraris to challenge them. FIA rules now stipulated a maximum of 26 cars could start the race, so the slowest two in practice were eliminated.

At the 1971 British Grand Prix, Gold Leaf Team Lotus entered two cars: one was a 72 which Emerson Fittipaldi brought home in third place, the other was the Pratt & Whitney turbine-powered 56B with which Reine Wisell struggled manfully. It finished 13th on the road but was not classified as a finisher as it completed only 57 laps of the 68-lap race, which was less than the required 90%. Wisell is seen here taking the car through Copse Corner. *Fred Scatley*

Tom Pryce set fastest lap in practice, placing Shadow-Cosworth DN5/2A on pole in 1min 19.36sec, but an accident on lap 20 destroyed his chances for the 1975 race was run in appalling weather and it was stopped at two-thirds distance (164 miles). Victory went to Emerson Fittipaldi (McLaren-Cosworth M23/9) from Carlos Pace (Brabham-Cosworth BT44/B2) and Jody Scheckter (Tyrrell-Cosworth 007/6); not surprisingly, the race speed was reduced to 120.01mph. Fourth was James Hunt in Hesketh-Cosworth 308B/2, fifth Mark Donohue in March-Cosworth 751/5 and sixth was Vittorio Brambilla in March-Cosworth 751/3. Of the first six finishers only the first and sixth were actually running at the end, the others having retired but had covered sufficient distance to be classified.

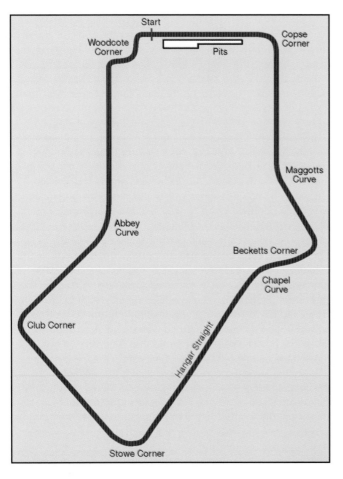

International motor racing at Silverstone is not concerned solely with Formula One, however, and 1976 saw one of the closest finishes ever seen in endurance racing at the Silverstone Six-Hour race which was Britain's round of the Group 6 World Championship for Makes. The series was almost a German benefit that season as the main contenders were the Porsche 935s and BMW 3-litre CSLs (commonly known as the 'Batmobiles'). Porsche had had the upper hand in the opening rounds but at Silverstone things were different. John Fitzpatrick and Tom Walkinshaw kept their BMW ahead to win by 197yd (1.18sec!) from the Wollek/Heyer Porsche 935 Turbo. Third was a Porsche 934 Turbo in the hands of Kinnunen and Evertz with another CSL fourth, driven by Grohs and de Fierlant; fifth place went to a Porsche Carrera Turbo driven by Lombardi and Martin, while a Ford Escort BDG was sixth, driven by Finotto and Grano.

The 1977 British Grand Prix saw the beginning of a revolution in Formula One, for towards the back of the grid was the product of Règie Renault which was exploiting a rule in the Formula One regulations that allowed the use of 1.5-litre enforced induction engines. The new, turbocharged car expired early in the race but those in the know marked the arrival of the new contender for they had witnessed a revolution which was to have as great an impact as the coming of Cooper. In second position on the grid was a Brabham in the hands of Ulsterman John Watson powered by a V12 Alfa Romeo engine. The car had an early battle with James Hunt in the McLaren but the fuel system let Watson down and the winner was Hunt at a speed of 130.36mph, with Niki Lauda second for Ferrari from Gunnar Nilsson in a Lotus; Jochen Mass brought his McLaren home fourth, with Hans Stuck fifth in the second Brabham-Alfa Romeo and sixth place went to Jacques Laffite in a Ligier-Matra. The race distance was 199 miles.

The International Trophy attracted World Championship contenders for the last time in 1978 but the race witnessed the debut of the epoch-making Lotus 79 in the hands of Mario Andretti. Such events as the International Trophy gave the Formula One also-rans a chance to start which they were normally denied in Grands Prix; two such were the Theodore and Fittipaldi. Keke Rosberg won in the former in atrocious conditions from Fittipaldi in his namesake car.

14 May witnessed the running of the Silverstone Six-Hours, a round of the World Championship for Makes, run in two classes up to and over 2 litres. It was contested by Porsche, de Tomaso, Lancia, Chevrolet, BMW, Fiat and Renault but in

Above: By 1975, speeds had increased so much that something had to be done to slow the cars as they passed the pits and the timekeepers; in order to achieve this, a major chicane was inserted at the entry to Woodcote. It had the effect of increasing the circuit length to 2.932 miles.

Right: In October 1978, Indycars came to England to race once at Brands Hatch and once at Silverstone. In this picture, Wally Dallenbach is seen at Silverstone in his McLaren-Cosworth on the first of the month; unfortunately, the idea did not excite British enthusiasts greatly and it was an experiment which was not repeated for the rest of the century. *B. Grant-Braham/Motor Racing Archive*

Northamptonshire there was evidence only of the two German manufacturers. A 3.2-litre Porsche 935 won in the hands of Ickx and Mass from a 3-litre version driven by Bob Wolleck and Pescarolo; third and fourth were BMW 320s handled by Grohs/Joosen and Kottulinsky/Hotz and from sixth to tenth it was an all-Porsche affair. The race was run over 235 laps of the Grand Prix circuit to make a total of a little over 689 miles which the winning car covered at 114.914mph.

Come the 1979 Grand Prix and the passage of two years had made a great difference to the performance of the turbocharged Renaults; the car which had started from the rear of the grid in 1977 was now on the front row beside Alan Jones in the Williams. When Jones's Cosworth expired, his team-mate Clay Regazzoni moved into the lead, going on to win from René Arnoux in the Renault with Jean-Pierre Jarier third in the Tyrrell. The race distance was again 199 miles and the winner's average speed was 138.80mph. Speeds were steadily increasing and this phenomenon would, in due course, have a dramatic effect upon the face of Silverstone.

In 1980, Great Britain hosted two rounds of the sports car World Championship for Makes — sports cars, in other words — at Brands Hatch in March and at Silverstone on 11 May in the form of the Silverstone Six-Hours which was won by Alain de Cadenet, driving a car bearing his own name, with Wilson, the 235 laps (687 miles) being completed at 114.602mph. The only other car to complete the full race distance was the Brun/Barth Porsche 908/3, with a Porsche 935K Turbo driven by Paul and Redman third, a lap down.

The passage of a further two years saw the arrival of the one-one-one grid in 1981, albeit staggered in two rows. The turbocharged era had arrived for not only did Renault occupy the first two places on the grid but turbo-engined Ferraris were fourth and eighth. More and more major manufacturers were entering Grand Prix racing and BMW-powered Brabhams made their first appearance in practice but did not qualify; the four-cylinder BMW turbo engine was interesting in that it was based upon a production unit from the 316 but BMW Motorsport did not accept an engine for Grand Prix use until it had done 50,000 miles in a road car, the theory being that by then it would be known whether or not it was a porous block!

The Renaults dominated the race but total reliability was still lacking and the day went to John Watson in a McLaren, following which he was awarded the MBE. Second place went

to Clay Regazzoni in the Williams from Jacques Laffite in the Talbot-Ligier a lap down; the race speed was down a little at 137.64mph and the distance was again unchanged at 199 miles. In fourth place was Eddie Cheever in the Tyrrell from Hector Rebaque driving the Brabham-Cosworth and Slim Borgudd in the ATS.

For 1982 endurance sports car racing entered a rejuvenated phase with the coming of Group C; the British Racing Drivers' Club and l'Automobile Club de l'Ouest instituted a joint Silverstone/Le Mans Challenge Trophy. The trophy eventually went to Jacky Ickx and Derek Bell in a Porsche 956, but at Silverstone they could not make maximum use of the fuel allowance and victory went to the Lancia-Martini Turbo of Riccardo Patrese and Michele Alboreto. The race was also the British round of the Endurance World Championship and was the Silverstone Six-Hours. The winning car completed the 240 laps in 6hr 0min 15sec at a speed of 128.5mph, with the second-placed car three laps adrift. Third went to the Wollek/Martin/Martin Porsche 936C Turbo with the Francia/Taruffo Osella-BMW fourth from Pescarolo and Spice in a Rondeau. A welcome return to competition was Aston Martin whose Nimrod was placed sixth in the hands of Mallock and Salmon.

The big sports cars returned to Northamptonshire on 8 May 1983 to contest the Silverstone 1000 Kilometres which was a round of the newly instigated World Endurance Championship. It was a Porsche benefit with Derek Bell and Stefan Bellof bringing their 956 home ahead of Bob Wollek and Stefan Johansson in an identical car — in fact 956s filled the first five places, with a Kremer CK5 sixth, but the Ray Mallock/Mike Salmon Aston Martin Nimrod was seventh.

By 1983 a Formula One team without the backing of a major manufacturer was having great difficulty in keeping up as the Grand Prix scene had become a high-pressure technical exercise with research and development on engines being the keynote. Clearly the time had come for a major change in the regulations but none was forthcoming and the 3-litre normally aspirated/1.5-litre forced-induction Formula continued seemingly ad infinitum.

In the 1983 British Grand Prix the first Cosworth-powered car was in 13th place on the grid, all the cars in front of it

being powered by turbocharged engines. Renault and BMW were now supplying their power units to other constructors but down in 14th place on the grid history was repeating itself. Just as the first appearance of the Turbo Renault in 1977 had started a revolution, the Spirit was powered by a turbocharged V6 Honda engine. Fuel consumption of the turbos was heavy and refuelling in the races became *de rigueur,* the mechanics now playing as important a part as the driver. With the ever-increasing power available, speeds were continually on the increase and in practice René Arnoux put in a lap at over 150mph in the Ferrari. In the race the lap record was raised to over 140mph by a relative newcomer from France named Alain Prost who won the race in the Renault at 139.218mph for the 196 miles, from Nelson Picquet in the Brabham-BMW and Patrick Tambay in a Ferrari. The next three places were filled by Nigel Mansell (Lotus), Arnoux (Ferrari) and Lauda (McLaren). The sport was on the threshold of three years of

development which almost got out of hand and had to be curbed by major rule changes.

A little more history was written in October on the Grand Prix circuit in the Formula Three Championship when a late charge saw Martin Brundle challenge Ayrton Senna for the title. In the 'Finals' meeting Brundle led from start to finish, beating Senna by half a second to lead the Championship by a single point. Three weeks later at Thruxton the title went to Senna but on a cold day in November they were both back in Northamptonshire for Formula One testing. As a result Senna was signed by Toleman and Brundle by Tyrrell and two young men entered Grand Prix racing, of whom a lot more was to be heard.

The 1985 International Trophy (run on 24 March) saw the race again making history as it was the first under the regulations for the new International Formula 3000. Every new formula sets new questions and this one was no exception; some teams ran ex-Formula One machinery, while the Lola T950 was based upon an Indycar design, whereas Ralt and March drew upon their Formula Two experience. Mike Thackwell wrote himself into the history books by winning the International Trophy for the third time and the first F3000 race in the process, driving a Ralt RT20 from John Nielsen in a similar car. The next three places were filled by March 85Bs in the hands of Michel Ferté, Christian Danner and Gabriele Tarquini, with sixth place going to a Formula One Tyrrell 012 driven by Roberto Moreno.

Six weeks later the big sports cars arrived in Northampton-shire for the first British round of the Endurance World Championship for Teams and the Silverstone Thousand Kilometres turned out to be a Porsche benefit, the German cars taking five of the top six placings in the shape of four 962s and a 956. The winners were Jacky Ickx and Jochen Mass from Derek Bell and Hans Stuck but third was the Lancia-Martini of Riccardo Patrese and Alessandro Nannini, then it was back to a 962 in the hands of Manfred Winkelhock/Marc Surer and Jonathan Palmer/Jan Lammers, with sixth going to the 956 of Ludwig, Barilla and Belmondo. The first four cars covered the full race distance of 138 laps.

The qualifying lap for pole position at the 1985 British Grand Prix was set at over 160mph by Keke Rosberg in the Williams-Honda and three other cars clocked over 159mph. Cars were now taking Woodcote faster than before the chicane had been inserted. The day of the non-turbo engine was over, there being only one normally aspirated car of the 26 starters. The engineers had agreed that it was impossible to equate turbo and non-turbo engines and approaches were made to the FIA to rescind the turbo part of the 1966 regulations!

Spectators' windscreen sticker for the 1964 BRDC International Trophy Meeting. *Author*

But through all this no one appeared to have noticed that somewhere along the line the ratio between normal and forced-induction had gone wrong. Under the 4.5-litre Formula One forced-induction engines of 1.5-litre were allowed (viz the V16 BRM) and under the 2.5-litre Formula One forced-induction was allowed at 750cc (although no-one ever took this route). In those two cases the ratio of forced induction to normal aspiration was roughly one third. But come 1966 and the 3-litre Formula One forced-induction was allowed at 1.5-litre — exactly a half. Had the former ratio been employed and forced induction engines been limited to 1 litre it might have been a very different story.

Whilst many were unhappy during the turbo era (which was, effectively, a new Formula One) it had had the undoubted benefit of drawing in the major manufacturers and produced open battles between Renault, Honda, Porsche, BMW, Alfa Romeo and Ferrari, with the bonus that three of them built the cars as well as the engines, which is what Grand Prix racing is all about. The 1985 race was a peak in the history of Silverstone and while Prost put the new lap record up to 150.035mph it was something of an economy run as the FIA (in a desperate move to curb the escalating horsepower) had put a limit on fuel tank capacities. Race distance was 190½ miles (due to the starter showing the chequered flag a lap early!) which Prost won in the McLaren-Porsche at 146.246mph from the Ferrari of Michele Alboreto and the Ligier-Renault of Jacques Laffite; in fourth place came Nelson Piquet in the Brabham from Derek Warwick aboard the Renault and Marc Surer in the second Brabham. Five constructors and four different engines in the top six.

The following year, 1986, was a non-Grand Prix season at Silverstone but it was enlivened by Denny Hulme deciding to celebrate his 50th year by racing for the Rover team in the FIA Touring Car Championship after 12 years of retirement. The Silverstone round of the Championship was the RAC Tourist Trophy, the oldest race on the British calendar. The season had not gone well for 'The Bear' but at Silverstone it all came together and he and his co-driver Jeff Allam came home to a popular win of the 50th running of the race. It was 80 years since Rover had won its first Tourist Trophy and it was the last

major victory for the Rover Vitesse and Denny's fourth Tourist Trophy win — a mere 21 years after his first.

The International season opened at Silverstone on 13 April with the first round of the Intercontinental F3000 Championship. By now entrants had decided that the only way to enter this formula was with cars built for it and the field consisted of Lola, March and Ralt with Cosworth power. The first home was Pascal Fabré with a Lola T86/50 from Pirro (March), Nielsen (Ralt), Thackwell, Kaiser (Lolas) and MacPherson (March).

In 1986, the Silverstone Thousand Kilometres run on 5 May was a round of the World Sports Car Championship which Jaguar won in a year when everything did not exactly go their way. However, the Derek Warwick/Eddie Cheever XJR9 was the only car to complete the distance of 212 laps, in 4hr 48min 55sec at a speed of 129.05mph. The Hans Stuck/Derek Bell Porsche 962C was two laps down in second place, with the second works Porsche a further three laps adrift in the hands of Joe Gartner and Tiff Needell.

The growing interest in classic cars led the Norwich Union insurance company to instigate the Norwich Union Classic Run on 25 May. Over 400 cars took part in that event which has since become established as an annual affair converging upon Silverstone.

Someone had become rather more than a little concerned over that 160mph lap in 1985, for by the time the Grand Prix

The FIA Cup for Thoroughbred Grand Prix cars was instituted in 1995 and is run in three Classes for 3-litre Formula One cars as follows: Class A caters for all cars built before 31 December 1971, Class B for all post-1971 non-ground-effect cars and Class C for all ground effect and flat-bottom cars. By definition, this means that nearly all competitors will be Cosworth DFV-powered but there are some exceptions, such as the BRM and the glorious Ferrari 312T5, seen here passing the pits in practice at Silverstone on 4 May 1997 driven by Mike Littlewood, who is overtaking the Trojan T103 of John Narcisi. One basic rule is that all cars must compete in the colours in which they ran when contesting Grands Prix, which serves to stir some memories. Responsibility for running the Championship was taken over from the Historic Sports Car Club by Thoroughbred Grand Prix Ltd from the beginning of 1997. *Author*

returned to Silverstone in 1987 a new corner was inserted before Woodcote which changed the character of the circuit and increased the length to 2.969 miles. With the incredible power output of the turbos this had little effect upon lap speeds, merely making the cars pass the pits on a slightly different line.

However, the first International meeting at Silverstone in 1987 was the initial round of the Intercontinental F3000 Championship on 12 April over 42 laps/125 miles of the Grand Prix circuit. The race was run at 103.96mph, the winner being Mauricio Gugelmin in a Ralt from Michel Trolle in a Lola and Roberto Moreno aboard another Ralt. Stefano Modena brought his March into fourth spot ahead of Pierluigi Martini's Ralt and Alfonso de Vinuesa's Lola.

Things went somewhat better for Jaguar in 1987 for they won no fewer than eight rounds of the FIA World Sports Car Championship, the Silverstone Thousand Kilometres (barely a month after the F3000 race on 10 May) being the fourth round and the fourth win, the XJR8s putting on a truly impressive demonstration to take a one-two finish. The first car home was that of Cheever and Boesel, followed by Lammers and Watson with the Porsche 962C of Stuck and Bell; these three covered the full race distance of 210 laps of the Grand Prix circuit, the winning car averaging 123.42mph. Into fourth place eight laps down came another 962C driven by Mass/Wollek with the Shafer/Brun/Pareja Porsche 962 fifth on 200 laps. In sixth place came the highest-placed C2 car, the Mallock Leslie Ecosse C287.

And so to the 1987 Grand Prix on 12 July, the event now firmly established at Silverstone. The first two placings were a repeat of the 1986 race, Mansell winning from his Williams-Honda team-mate Piquet over 193 miles at 146.208mph and Ayrton Senna in the Lotus-Honda. In fourth place came the second Lotus driven by Satoru Nakajima from Derek Warwick's Arrows and Teo Fabi's Benetton.

The 1988 race was won at 124.142mph for the same race distance as the previous year; the dramatic reduction in race speed is attributable to the truly appalling conditions, the entire race being run in pouring rain. Victory went to Ayrton Senna aboard the McLaren from Nigel Mansell (Williams) and Alessandro Nannini (Benetton). In fourth was Gugelmin (March) with Piquet (Lotus) fifth and Warwick (Arrows) sixth, a lap down. Berger and Alboreto had occupied the front row of the grid for Ferrari but the race was not a good one for Maranello, Alboreto running out of fuel on the 62nd lap and Berger finishing ninth. The Grand Prix was run on 10 July but a month previously, on 5 June, one of the three British rounds of the FIA F3000 Championship was run over 124.5 miles of the Grand Prix circuit (42 laps). The first three places were filled by Reynard 88D-Cosworths driven by Roberto Moreno whose race average was 132.27mph, second was Bertrand Gachot, with Pierre-Henri Raphanel third. Fourth was Foitek in a Lola T88/50, with Alesi fifth aboard a Reynard and Apicella sixth driving a Judd-engined March 88D.

The first international meeting of the year at

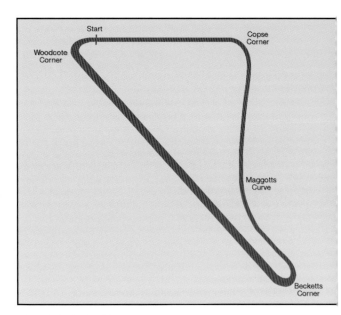

Above: This is the Silverstone Club Circuit of 1987: instead of sweeping on to Chapel Curve at Becketts Corner the circuit turned very sharp right on to a long straight which rejoined the Grand Prix circuit midway through Woodcote Corner.

Below: On 10 May 1987, the contenders in the World Sports Car Championship converged on Silverstone to contest the Silverstone Thousand Kilometres over 210 laps of the Grand Prix circuit. The Sauber-Mercedes C9 of Henri Pescarolo and Mike Thackwell is seen negotiating Woodcote; it was forced to retire on the 108th lap with suspension failure. This was before the Saubers turned silver and the car is running in the predominantly black livery of the team's main sponsor, Kouros. *Mike Dixon*

Silverstone was the first British round of the World Sports-Prototype Championship on 8 May. Run over 210 laps of the Grand Prix circuit, the Silverstone Thousand Kilometres saw victory go to the Jaguar XJR9 of Martin Brundle and Eddie Cheever who won at 128.02mph from the Sauber C9 Mercedes driven by Jo Schlesser and Jochen Mass. The second Sauber, driven by Mauro Baldi and James Weaver, was third, two laps down, while third on the road was the Porsche 962C of Derek Bell and Tiff Needell which was disqualified as its fuel tank

Championship had their turn in the third round of their championship, the first of two run in England that year. In the F3000 race Allan McNish led Eric Comas home from Apicella. The first two were Lola T90/50-Mugen-mounted, while the third placed car was a Reynard 90D-Mugen, the Japanese engine having virtually ousted the Cosworth. In fourth and fifth were Antonio Tamburini and Richard Dean driving Reynard 90Ds with Mugen and Cosworth power, whilst in sixth was one Eddie Irvine in a Reynard-Cosworth run by Pacific Racing. McNish won at 134.338mph in 54min 23.2sec.

The sports cars again ran over 300 miles of the Grand Prix circuit contesting the Shell British Racing Drivers' Club Empire Trophy. The first three places went to British cars, with Jaguar first and second from a Spice-Cosworth in the hands of Fermin Velez and Bruno Giacomelli. The winning Jaguar XJR11 of Martin Brundle and Michel Ferté was the only car to run the full distance of one hundred and one laps, lapping even the second-placed XJR11 of Jan Lammers and Andy Wallace. The winning car averaged 128.886mph and took 2hr 19min 33sec. Fourth to six places were occupied by Porsches, Bob Wollek and Frank Jelinski bringing their 962C in fourth, with the 962C of Bernd Schneider and Steven Andskar fifth from the 962C of Oscar

was 2.5 litres oversize. Porsche 962Cs driven by Wollek/Hobbs/Streiff and 'Winter'/Jelinski/Dick were fourth and fifth, with Coppelli and Thyrring bringing the first C2 car, a Spice SE 88C-Cosworth, into sixth position.

April at Silverstone is not the warmest place to be but none the less the F3000 contingent contested the first round of the 1989 International F3000 Championship on the 9th of the month over 41 laps of the revised Grand Prix circuit, a race distance of 121.72 miles which Danielsson completed in 55min 31sec at 131.56mph at the wheel of a Reynard 89D-Cosworth. Second by 0.5sec was Favre in a Lola T89/50-Cosworth from Blundell and Alesi in Reynards, Cosworth and Mugen powered respectively with the Mugen and Cosworth-engined Lolas of Comas and van de Poele taking the final points. The year saw further changes to the circuit at Woodcote in more attempts to slow the cars past the pits.

Mid-July is the traditional time for the British Grand Prix and on the 16th some 90,000 spectators converged upon the circuit to see Alain Prost score his 38th Grand Prix win in the 190-mile race at 143.694mph in 1hr 19min 22sec, driving the McLaren MP4/5-Honda. Nigel Mansell brought the Ferrari into second place from Nannini's Benetton and the Lotus-Judd of Piquet. Fifth and sixth came Pierluigi Martini and Luis Perez Sala for Minardi. Senna had taken pole position but spun off on the 11th lap. Such was the strength of the entry that nine entrants failed to pre-qualify and four failed to qualify — 39 entrants in all!

The weekend of 19/20 May 1990 was a busy one at Silverstone, for on the Saturday the second round of the FIA F3000 Championship was run on the Grand Prix circuit and on the Sunday the contenders in the World Sports-Prototype

Above: It was the year of Jaguar in 1987. Under the guidance of Tom Walkinshaw the 'Big Cats' took the Manufacturers' title and the Drivers' Championship, winning all but two of the rounds on the way. The Drivers' title went to Raul Boesel who shared his XJR8 at Silverstone with Eddie Cheever — it is seen here at Woodcote Corner. *Mike Dixon*

Right: Speeds continued to increase and the chicane at Woodcote had outlived its usefulness and something further was necessary, so in 1987 a new left and right corner was inserted before Woodcote which increased the circuit length to 2.969 miles. The character of Silverstone was now beginning to change.

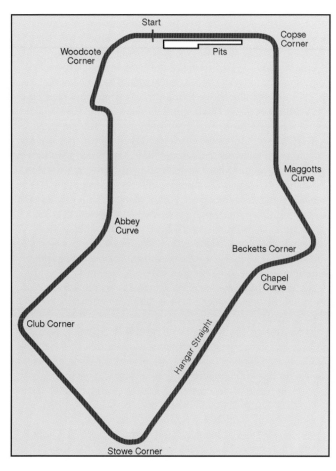

1991 saw further dramatic changes to Silverstone, wrought at the behest of the sport's governing body who decreed that speeds should be reduced. Instead of changing the rules of Formula One and reducing engine sizes (the 3-litre Formula has been with us since 1967!), the circuits on which Grands Prix were run had to change in order to accommodate the cars, and Silverstone was no exception! Gone were the glorious Maggotts Curve and Becketts Corner to be replaced by a complex of twists retaining the old names. At Stowe the circuit turned infield to Vale and a new Club Corner was created. The challenging sweep of Abbey Curve was replaced by a new double corner and an entirely new complex consisting of three corners named Bridge, Priory and Luffield was inserted before Woodcote.

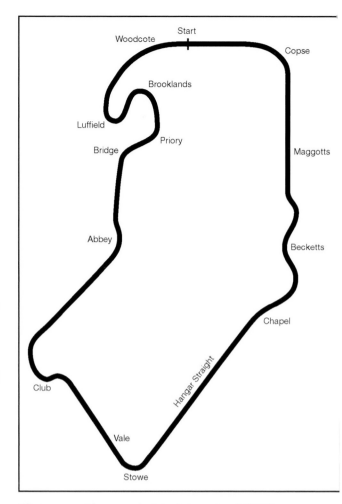

Larrauri and Harald Huysman sixth. The fourth to sixth placed cars hand all covered 99 laps, as had the Nissan R90C of Blundell and Brancatelli which was fourth on the road but was unclassified as the last lap took too long!

And so to July and the British Grand Prix: once again it was over 190 miles, and was won at 145.253mph; Prost was now driving for Ferrari and his was the victory from Thierry Boutsen in the Williams and Ayrton Senna's McLaren. Twenty-six cars were allowed to start but, as in 1989, such was the entry list, five entrants failed to pre-qualify and four did not survive official practice. One of these was Geoff Brabham driving a car bearing his own name — a sad reflection on the sport when compared with his father's day. Amongst those which failed to pre-qualify were marques now long gone — EuroBrun, AGR and Coloni and amongst those who did not survive official qualifying were Osella and Onyx. Perhaps the most interesting car technically was that driven by Giacomelli, the LIFE powered by a Rocchi W12 engine — it was the slowest car present. Fourth was Eric Bernard in a Lola-Lamborghini followed by Piquet's Benetton and the second Lola driven by Aguri Suzuki, a lap adrift.

Britain had only one round of the International F3000 Championship in 1991 so on the weekend of 19 May the sports cars had Silverstone to themselves. They now raced for the World Sports Car Championship and this, too, was the only round run in England. The race distance was reduced to 269 miles (83 laps of the 3.25-mile Grand Prix circuit) and it was a straight battle between Jaguar and Mercedes-Benz, with victory going to the Jaguar XJR14 of Teo Fabi and Derek Warwick in 2hr 12min 30sec at 122.048mph. In second place, four laps behind, came the Mercedes C291 of Michael Schumacher and Karl Wendlinger, followed by the singleton driver XJR14 of Martin Brundle from the Mercedes C11 in the hands of Jo Schlesser and Jochen Mass. Fifth place, on 78 laps, was the Spice SE90C of Piper and Euser, followed by the Baldi and Alliot Peugeot 905 — a presage of things to come.

July came, of course, and with it the Grand Prix on the revised 3.245-mile circuit — 59 laps of which made a race distance of 191.5 miles, with Nigel Mansell disposing of it from pole position in 1hr 27min 35.48sec at 131.227mph. The almost unbelievably popular victory was Mansell's 18th Grand Prix win, making him the most successful English driver ever. Two other drivers completed the full distance, Gerhard Berger for McLaren and Alain Prost for Ferrari. In fourth place a lap down was Ayrton Senna in the second McLaren who had retired but was classified as a finisher, while fifth and sixth were Nelson Piquet (Benetton) and Bertrand Gachot (Jordan).

1992 was once more a busy International season for

Silverstone with a round of the International F3000 Championship, the World Sports Car Championship and, of course, the Grand Prix. The first two were run on the same day, 10 May, which must have made for a busy time! The F3000 race was the first one of the year and the only appearance of the Championship in England; practice was spoilt by a hailstorm but the races were run in bright weather. The victor was Jordi Gene who completed the 37 laps/120 miles in 59min 21.7sec at 121.145mph in a Reynard 92D-Mugen from a similar Judd-engined example in the hands of Rubens Barrichello. Lola-Cosworths were third and fourth, driven by Olivier Panis and Marc Gounon, with Luca Badoer and Emanuele Naspetti taking the final points in Cosworth-powered Reynards.

The sports car race was a sad affair with but a handful of cars coming to the starting line; there were 11 starters and just five finishers. The race was 312 miles long and was won by the Peugeot 905 of Warwick and Dalmas at 122.661mph in 2hr 32min 29sec, two laps ahead of the Sala/Herbert Mazda MXR-01 which was four laps ahead of the Lola T92/10-Judd driven by Pareja and Johansson. The other two finishers were two Spice SE89C-Judds on 85 and 76 laps, driven by DeLesseps/Hoy and Randaccio/Sebastiani. At the end of the year the World Sports Car Championship was no more.

The Grand Prix on 12 July was a somewhat happier affair

with the Williams cars of Mansell and Piquet taking top honours from the Benettons of Brundle and Schumacher, Berger's McLaren and Hakkinen's Lotus. 'Our Nige' dominated practice and dominated the race, winning the 191-mile sprint in 1hr 25min 43sec at 133.772mph; the circuit had been changed again in an attempt to slow the cars but it was not working. At the end of the race the fans invaded the track oblivious of the fact that some cars were still racing and landing the organisers and circuit in hot water with the FIA.

Six days after competing at Donington Park the competitors in the 1993 International F3000 Championship converged upon Silverstone for the second round of the Championship on 9 May, over 37 laps of the Grand Prix circuit. Gil de Ferran won the 120-mile race at 119.462mph from David Coulthard, Michael Bartels, Franck Lagorce, Paul Stewart and Olivier Panis — all were driving Cosworth-powered Reynard 93s.

1993 was one of those very rare occasions when Great Britain staged two Grands Prix in a year; the first had been the European Grand Prix at Donington Park at Easter, while the British Grand Prix filled its usual mid-July slot. Prost had won his home Grand Prix at Magny-Cours for Williams-Renault and the British fans expected that Damon Hill would be allowed to win his home race. He set fastest practice time but with very little qualifying time left Prost set a time 0.128sec faster than Hill to take pole position and went on to win the race after Hill's engine exploded on the 41st lap — there was dark talk that the engine had been 'grenaded' from the pits. The race was over 59 laps, a race distance of 191.5 miles, the full distance being covered by the first four cars; second and third were the Benettons of Schumacher and Patrese, with Herbert's Lotus fourth. A lap down in fifth and sixth were Senna (McLaren) and Warwick (Footwork). It was Alain Prost's 50th Grand Prix victory, an achievement which was somehow lost due to the chauvinism of the crowd.

A year later, the British Grand Prix was run over 60 laps of a circuit which had been revised yet again to make a race distance of a mere 188.5 miles — does a race of such a distance really qualify for the title Grand Prix? It was a race of controversy which rumbled on for most of the rest of the season; Hill was barely ahead of Schumacher on the grid and on the green flag lap the young German sprinted ahead of the Englishman which is not allowed under the rules, cars being required to maintain station during the green flag lap. The race authorities informed Benetton that their man had been penalised 5sec for his transgression but they did not realise that it was a 'stop/go' penalty and did not call Schumacher in, so he was black-flagged, which he ignored for six laps. For failing to respond to the black flag Schumacher was disqualified, having finished second on the road; Benetton appealed but the stewards rejected the appeal. (The Clerk of the Course is

in control of the race and his word is law, and his word on this occasion was a black flag, which a driver ignored.).

Damon Hill won the race at 125.609mph in 1hr 30min 4sec from Jean Alesi in the Ferrari, Mika Hakkinen (McLaren), Rubens Barrichello (Jordan), David Coulthard (Williams) and Ukyo Katayama (Tyrrell). The fifth and sixth placed men were a lap down on the winner. The Pacific-Ilmors of Bertrand Gachot and Paul Belmondo failed to qualify.

Two months previously, on 2 May, the International F3000 Championship had started at Silverstone; it was an all-Reynard 94D affair with most of the cars powered by variants of the Cosworth V8, with some Judd and Zytek-Judd intervention. The race was over 38 laps, Franck Lagorce winning at 119.512mph for the 123 miles from David Coulthard, Gil de Ferran, Vincenzo Sospiri, Hideki Noda and Didier Cottaz — third and sixth were Zytek-Judd engined.

As had now become traditional, the International F3000 Championship started at Silverstone on 7 May. Forty laps, 126 miles run at 110.532mph in 1hr 8min 13sec by Riccardo Rossett driving Super Nova's Reynard 95D-Cosworth AC from his team-mate Sospiri; Allan McNish was third in a Zytek-Judd KV-engined 95D, with a Lola T95/50-Cosworth AC piloted by Marc Goossens fourth. Kenny Brack was fifth in another Reynard, with Zytek-Judd power from Pescatori in a Cosworth-engined Reynard.

Once more July brought the Grand Prix in 1995, over a slightly longer distance at 192 miles — 61 laps. Damon Hill and Michael Schumacher were not having a happy year and managed to take each other off after the final pit stops, leaving Coulthard in the lead which he lost when he had to take a 10sec 'stop/go' penalty for speeding in the pit lane. All of this left Johnny Herbert to take his debut Grand Prix win — he was euphoric and was held shoulder high on the podium by the second and third-placed men, David Coulthard and Jean Alesi. Olivier Panis was fourth for Ligier from Mark Blundell's McLaren-Mercedes, the powers that be at Untertürkheim having decided that the people at McLaren could make better use of their engines than Sauber. In sixth spot, a lap down, was Heinz-Harald Frentzen in the Sauber C14-Ford. In 12th and last place was the Pacific PRO2-Ford of Bertrand Gachot, making one of their all-too-infrequent Grand Prix finishes, three laps down on the winner.

On 12 May 1996 the Northamptonshire circuit hosted the fourth round of the International BPR Series which was very much a British affair. First was the McLaren Formula One GTR

Now into his seventies, The Master still races regularly and commands respect wherever he goes. At the wheel of a Maserati 250F, Stirling Moss rounds Copse during the Coys Historic Festival in 1997. *Author*

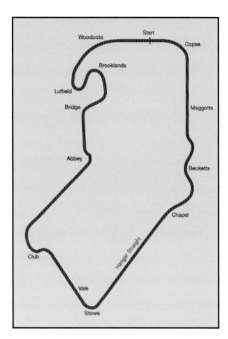

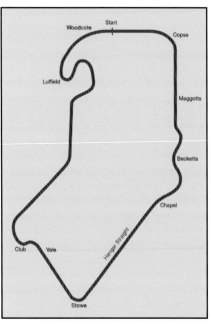

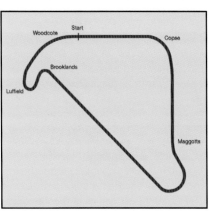

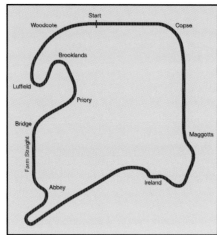

Above left: Further changes to the Grand Prix circuit came in 1994 with a dramatic redesign at Copse, making it a sharper corner, and there were also changes at the Priory/Luffield complex.

Above: From 1997 Silverstone could boast no less than six different circuits within its confines. Apart from the full Grand Prix Circuit measuring 3.194 miles, there is the International Circuit (show here) which measures 2.252 miles.

Left: The Historical Grand Prix Circuit runs to 3.144 miles.

Bottom left: The circuit most familiar to the Clubman is the National Circuit measuring 1.639 miles; it is today's equivalent of the old Club Circuit.

Below: To the southern end of the Silverstone empire lies the Southern Circuit measuring 1.969 miles, and within it the 0.796-mile Stowe Circuit.

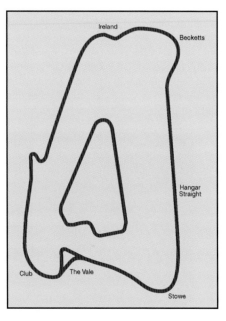

of Andy Wallace and Olivier Grouillard, followed by the Jan Lammers/Perry McCarthy Lotus Esprit and another McLaren in the hands of James Weaver and Ray Bell. Fourth were Steve Soper and Nelson Piquet in a McLaren, with the Ferrari F40 GTE driven by Jean-Marc Gounon/Éric Bernard/Paul Belmondo fifth, with sixth place going to another McLaren driven by Nielssen and Bscher.

At the Grand Prix on 14 July the pressures on Damon Hill as national favourite and son of a famous father were not inconsiderable but he responded well, setting pole from his team-mate at Williams, Jacques Villeneuve, and Michael Schumacher in the Ferrari. Unfortunately, Hill muffed the start and later spun out of contention when a front wheel nut became loose and Villeneuve went on to win at a fraction over 124mph in 1hr 33min from Gerhard Berger's Benetton, Mika Hakkinen's McLaren, the Jordan of Rubens Barrichello, David Coulthard in the second McLaren and Martin Brundle in the other Jordan, a lap down. August 17 saw the return of the International F3000 Championship over 40 laps of the Grand Prix circuit, the first 15 finishers completing the full race distance. The winner was Kenny Brack for Super Nova from Edenbridge Racing's Tom Kristensen; next up was Riccardo Zonta for Draco Engineering, followed by the second Super Nova car driven by Marcos Gueiros, the final points going to Christian Pescatori for the Durango Equipe and Christophe Tinseau driving the Apomatox car.

The 1997 Grand Prix was won by Jacques Villeneuve at the wheel of a Williams-Renault at speed of 128.443mph from the Benettons of Jean Alesi and Alexander Wurz. Fourth was the McLaren of David Coulthard from Ralf Schumacher's Jordan, with Damon Hill taking the final point in the Arrows. The fastest lap was set by Michael Schumacher as set out at the end of the chapter.

From the start of the 1998 season the Federation Internationale de l'Automobile decreed that all Formula One grids must be straight: in order to comply with this decree the Royal Automobile Club moved the start line forward at Silverstone but not, significantly, the finish line. This led to some confusion at the end of the Grand Prix which was scheduled to be run over

An aerial view of
Silverstone on Grand Prix
day 12 July 1992.
Silverstone Circuits Ltd

60 laps but was, effectively, run over 59.95 laps: it was more than a little fortunate that the timing was being taken from the finish line and not the start line as the winning car was in the pits at the end of the race and the Ferrari pit was situated between the two lines. The chequered flag is supposed to be waved at the winning car and shown to the other competitors but it was waved at the second man who thought that he had won!

Victory went to Michael Schumacher at the wheel of a Ferrari in appalling conditions. It was something of a farce, for in addition to the foregoing, the winner was penalised 10sec for passing another competitor under a yellow flag. The Stewards failed to inform the teams of their decision in the proper manner so Schumacher took his stop go penalty in the pit lane after the race was over! The Stewards later reversed their decision after watching video tapes and decided that the

Ferrari had not passed under a yellow flag. McLaren appealed to the FIA but the appeal was rejected and the results were confirmed, with second place going to Mika Hakkinen in the McLaren-Mercedes and the second Ferrari of Eddie Irvine in third spot. Next up were the Benettons of Alexander Wurz and Giancarlo Fisichella, with the final point going to Ralf Schumacher driving the Jordan-Mugen Honda. Michael Schumacher's winning speed was 107.217mph in 1hr 47min 12.45sec. Irvine set the fastest lap in 1min 26.509sec. The only other occasion when the start and finish lines have been in different places on a British circuit was at Gransden Lodge on 13 July 1947.

The 1998 Coys International Historic Festival was very special, falling as it did in Silverstone's 50th anniversary year. The sensational main event of the weekend was the re-creation of the 1948 Grand Prix: 26 cars had competed in the race and

In 2000 something very exciting occurred in the world of Historic Racing. When Lancia ran out of money and was forced to abandon Formula One in 1955, the V8 D50s were handed to Ferrari who ran them in 1956 as Lancia-Ferraris but as soon as Ferrari had something which was considered superior the D50 was abandoned and all but one of the cars were cut up. The one remaining car is in a museum and is unlikely to race again, although it was loaned for static display at the 50th anniversary meeting at Silverstone. All that was originally left of the car were some engines and transaxles, around which Robin Lodge reconstructed a Lancia D50. There has been some discussion as to whether the car should have been allowed to compete but this is not the place to do that. What matters to the enthusiast is that once more we can hear that glorious V8 in full song, as here at Silverstone in 2000, during what was to be the last Coys Festival. *Author*

no less than 17 of them were at Silverstone for the 1998 event, together with two of the original drivers — Roy Salvadori and Tulo de Graffenried. It was an unforgettable weekend and a nice touch was a reproduction of the 1948 programme contained within the programme. The final touch to the Golden Jubilee year came on the evening of 3 October, the weekend of the 50th anniversary of Silverstone's first Grand Prix, when a display of cars and aircraft was held in the centre of the circuit culminating in a spectacular fireworks display. Unfortunately, it was bitterly cold.

Victory in the 1999 British Grand Prix went to David Coulthard at the wheel of the McLaren-Mercedes in 1hr 32min 30.144sec at a speed of 124.256sec from Eddie Irvine's Ferrari and Ralf Schumacher's Williams-Supertec. Fourth and fifth places were taken by the Jordan-Mugen Hondas of Heinz-Harald Frentzen and Damon Hill, with the final point going to Pedro Diniz in the Sauber-Petronas. Mika Hakkinen set the fastest lap at 130.2mph in 1min 28.309sec.

For the final Grand Prix at Silverstone in the 20th century, the powers that be in FIA (the sport's governing body) decreed that the race would move to April and the event took place over the Easter weekend, with the Grand Prix itself being run on Easter Day. It was the earliest that the British Grand Prix had been run, but only by a few weeks, as we have seen. As matters transpired, it was not the wisest decision ever made, the English spring weather taking a hand. It rained almost continually for the best part of three weeks before the event and most of Good Friday; by Easter Saturday the car parks had virtually collapsed and were completely closed in the hope that they would recover to some degree for race day. Most of Easter Day 2000 was fine but the weather had already done its worst and many thousands of spectators were unable to get to Silverstone.

There was some comfort for British enthusiasts in David Coulthard's second successive victory in the event for McLaren-Mercedes-Benz in 1hr 28min 50.08sec from team-mate Mika Hakkinen, with Michael Schumacher third for

Ferrari. Next came the two BMW-powered Williams driven by Ralf Schumacher and British newcomer Jenson Button, Jarno Trulli taking the last point for Jordan. Hakkinen set the fastest lap in 1min 26.217sec at 133.389mph — nearly three seconds outside the lap record. On 14 May the FIA GT Championship came to Silverstone in slightly more clement conditions and victory went to Bailey and Campbell Walter driving a Lister Storm from no fewer than four Chrysler Viper GTS-Rs, with a Porsche 911 GT2 in sixth place.

From April 1997 there have been number of attempts to buy Silverstone, which the membership of the British Racing Drivers Club steadfastly resisted. Then the FIA granted the rights to the British Grand Prix to Brands Hatch. In December 1999 Octagon took over Brands Hatch Leisure Group and pursued the idea of rebuilding Brands Hatch in order to run the Grand Prix in Kent once more. However, planning permission was not forthcoming and a year later it was announced that Octagon Motorsports Ltd had come to an agreement with the BRDC to continue running the British Grand Prix at Silverstone for a further 10 years with an option for a further five years thereafter. Following this agreement there has been an announcement that a new pits complex will be built exclusively for the use of the Formula One contingent but (at the time of writing) there has been no intimation of changes to the circuit.

At the close of the 2000 season the outright lap records for the Silverstone circuits stand as follows: the 1997 Grand Prix Circuit record holder is Michael Schumacher at the wheel of the Ferrari F310B in 1min 24.475sec at 136.15mph on 13 July 1997 during the British Grand Prix; the International Circuit to Nicolas Minassian driving a Formula Three Dallara F397 Renault in 1min 14.929sec at 108.19mph on 6 April 1997; the National Circuit to Nigel Greensall driving a Formula One Tyrrell-Judd 022 in the BOSS Formula race on 28 September 1997 in 48.4sec at 121.90mph.

SNETTERTON
EAST ANGLIA'S OWN CIRCUIT

Motor racing came to Norfolk in 1951 thanks to a group of gentlemen who had the vision to see the potential in the wartime airfield at Snetterton Heath which had been home to 96th Bomb Group of the United States Army Air Force who flew B-17 Flying Fortresses. The 96th Bomb Group was part of the 45th Combat Wing which, in its turn, was part of the 3rd Air Division of the USAAF; during the war Snetterton Heath lost more than 900 aircrew and 250 aircraft — the second highest loss in the Eighth Army Air Force. RAF Snetterton Heath was built between autumn 1942 and mid-1943 but opened in January 1943 in spite of the fact that it was not yet ready for operational use. The 96th Bomb Group stayed in Britain longer than most American units, flying food to the Dutch once the war was ended before finally departing in December 1945, and the RAF left the base in 1948.

There was an undeniable need for another circuit — new ones had been built at Silverstone and Goodwood so why not here in the Brecklands? Using the perimeter track a circuit 2.71 miles in length was created that was destined to become the fastest in the United Kingdom. The far-sighted gentlemen who had the vision of seeing motor racing at Snetterton were Oliver Sear, Dudley Coram and Fred Riches, the last-named owning most of the land on which the

Only once has the RAC Rally of Great Britain ventured into East Anglia — the local farming communities in Suffolk objected to the cars in the forests disturbing the birds which they later wished to kill, so the rally never returned. The one year the rally did come to Eastern England was in 1964 when a special stage was held at Snetterton during the November event. The eventual winner, Tom Trana, is seen negotiating the Esses at speed in the Volvo PV 444, a model which Volvo did not offer for sale in the United Kingdom. *Mike Dixon*

ex-airfield stood beside the A11, approximately equidistant from Norwich and Thetford. Mr Riches was a warden of the local church and he agreed to running motor races at Snetterton on the strict understanding that no practice or racing should take place on Sundays between 10.45am and noon, and that everything should cease in time for evensong, and so it was that practice on Sundays always came to a stop between the stipulated hours with the embargo of ending in time for evensong still pertaining.

The first ever event at Snetterton was run by the Aston Martin Owners' Club who organised a sprint on the new track on

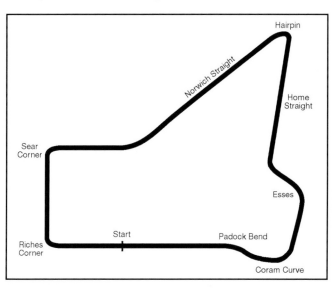

This is the original Snetterton circuit, from 1951. In terms of accuracy it is probably the best circuit map of the Norfolk track. The start line was (and still is) roughly halfway along the pit straight (though it was never so named), the first corner being the right-hand Riches Corner which is blessed with a double apex and has caught out more than one of the unwary; a short straight then led to the second right-hander, Sear Corner, which is tighter than it looks, and a further short straight took the circuit to a left flick which was never named. This led to the Norwich Straight which was a mile long, ending in the hairpin, a tight right leading to the Home Straight which was a wonderful blind to The Esses. Another short straight (which was actually taken in a curve) took the track to the seemingly endless right-hand Coram Curve and the left-hand Paddock Bend led back to the start and finish line. The lap was 2.71 miles long and at one time during the 1950s Snetterton was the fastest circuit in the country.

Right: Early Snetterton programmes had a two-colour cover of a more or less standard design featuring a line drawing of a racing car or a sports car, the meetings organised by the Snetterton Motor Racing Club being as shown here; *The Autocar* was usually the advertiser on the front cover. *Author's collection*

Below right: From two years later comes this programme for the Eastern Counties Motor Club's Eastern Counties Hundred Meeting. The 'Hundred' referred to would have been a 100-mile race over 37 laps of the original circuit, on this occasion for saloon cars; there would have been several additional races probably including the Alick Dick Trophy for Triumph TR sports cars. As was the case with so many circuits in those days, the illustration on the cover of the programme need not necessarily have implied that the car illustrated would be appearing at the meeting! *Author's collection*

27 October 1951; if the truth be told it was a race meeting in disguise as four or five cars competed at a time over two flying laps of the circuit. The principal feature of the circuit was the Norwich Straight which ran alongside the main A11 road and was just short of a mile in length, culminating in a very tight right-hand hairpin. Entry to the circuit was off the A11 or up a farm track opposite the pits; by whichever route one entered the circuit, vehicular access to the paddock was across the track which necessitated waiting for a break in on-course activity. Communication between the corners during racing was possible by way of the runways which still existed, although the least said about the fire precautions at the early meetings the better. Three of the corners are named after the people who were instrumental in the circuit's inception and creation as referred to above; the first-right hand corner after the start is called Riches which has a double apex and has caught out many of the unwary. The second right-hander is called Sear, which was followed by a short straight leading to a left-hand kink which has never officially been named. Next is the Norwich Straight leading to the Hairpin; following this is the Home Straight before the Esses (a left and right) before a short straight running into Coram Curve named after Dudley

Coram who was the starter at the first event. Coram is a long right-hand bend which tightens on itself and has also caught out many of the unwary over the years; it straightened a little for Paddock Bend, a left-hander leading on to the Start and Finish Straight.

The early circuit was marked out with sand-filled 40-gallon oil drums topped off with Christmas trees; an interesting feature was The Mound opposite the start/finish line which had been constructed by the USAAF for use by the bomber crews for gunnery practice. The Mound disappeared in 1965 when it was moved to construct the approaches to the new Bailey bridge which was erected at the Esses to ease traffic flow into and out of the paddock. The Mound was reputed to contain quite a lot of lead but no record remains of how much was found at the time of the building of the Bailey bridge. There was a footbridge at the Paddock Bend end of the pits which was later moved to the other end beyond the start/finish line; its end came one dark and stormy night when strong winds left it a mangled wreck and it has never been replaced.

As speeds gradually increased over the years it became necessary to slow the cars as they passed the pits, and a new corner was introduced after Coram in 1965; it was named Russell Corner after the great Jim Russell who had established the world's first racing drivers' school at Snetterton in the late 1950s. The new corner was much too tight and at one time the motorcycle contingent refused to use Snetterton as they could not negotiate it. Russell Bend (as it had become known) had been eased considerably by 1968; it was realigned in 1981 and 1988 and again during the winter of 1996/7.

In the early years of Snetterton each season witnessed the United States Air Force meeting and at one such, on 25 July

The early Snetterton was rather basic. This is the Esses with the outer limit of the track marked out with a barrier of wooden posts set in the ground topped off with more wood. Oliver Sear had been most pleased with the winter's work on circuit improvements until someone pointed out to him that a single-seater passing under the barrier would probably result in the decapitation of the driver. The Renault 750 is driven by John Aley, but the identity of the driver of the clearly road-going Ford Anglia is not known. *John Aley Collection*

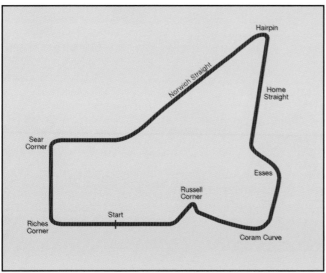

Above: If ever there was a true stalwart of club racing it was this man. At the wheel of his Jaguar 3.8 saloon Albert Betts tackles Russell Bend; he would drive the Jaguar to the circuit with the family on board, clear it out for scrutineering, practice and race it and then take the family home in it. Albert succumbed to cancer in 1996. *Mike Dixon*

Left: By 1965 speeds past the pits had increased to such an extent that unprotected personnel in the pit lane were increasingly vulnerable and the timekeepers claimed that they could not keep pace with all the cars. Something had to be done in order to slow cars down and the decision was taken to insert a new corner after Coram Curve and before the pit straight. The resultant Russell Corner was not universally popular; it consisted of a hairpin left followed almost immediately by a 90° right and the motor cycle contingent found it almost unusable. The programmes still stated the circuit length to be 2.71 miles but, clearly, it was longer than the original.

Below left: Complaints were listened to and Russell Corner was eased considerably for the start of the 1967 season, so much so that it was now called Russell Bend. Some of the original intention to slow down the cars had been lost, for speeds past the pits and timekeepers' box rose and the banking on the outside of the circuit, opposite Russell Bend, started to collect considerably more errant cars. The circuit length was still given as 2.71 miles.

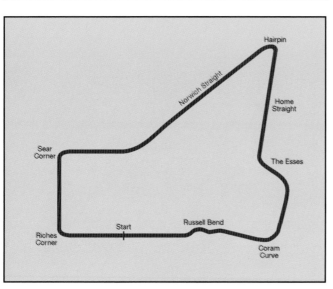

1953, the Breckland circuit first heard the scream of the BRM V16 in anger in the hands of Ken Wharton when he won the Formule Libre and the United States Invitation races. In the course of these exploits he pushed the lap record to 90.5mph. Sadly, Bobby Baird overturned his 4.1-litre Ferrari during practice and died as a result of injuries sustained; he was the first of remarkably few fatalities at Snetterton.

Long-distance racing came early to the Norfolk circuit in the late 1950s when that bible of the motor racing fan, *Autosport*, promoted the *Autosport* Championship for sports cars. The Championship was fought out on the circuits throughout the country, culminating at Snetterton in the *Autosport* Three-Hours on the weekend that British Summer Time ended. The Three-Hours was always the last race on a two- or three-race programme; it started at 4 o'clock (in true Le Mans style) with a Le Mans start in daylight and finished at 7pm in darkness; for

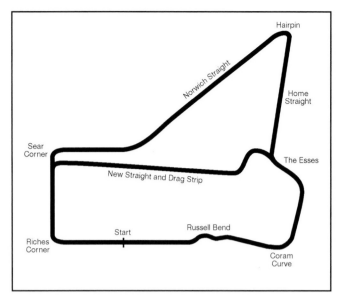

many years it was the highlight of the Snetterton year, with a fun-fair brought in for the occasion. In later years it was run in two 90-minute segments — one in daylight and one in darkness — and then as two 65-lap races in daylight. On one memorable occasion it had to be curtailed as fog descended on the circuit, making it impossible for the drivers to see where they were going; the recollection of Jack Sears negotiating Riches in a Cobra with the door held open in order to see where he was going is one which will remain with the author for many years.

In 1993, the race was resurrected by the Historic Sports Car Club as a three-hour event run in daylight for historic sports cars but, sadly, it appears that the 1996 event was the last.

The weather has always been a feature of Snetterton; being on heathland in open, flat country the wind tends to whip across with unabated strength so that summer Sundays can be very chilly but when it is hot there is no breeze at all. One year the Easter meeting was snowed off! A stalwart at Snetterton was the late Commander Philip Heseltine, who said that if you could stand in the pit lane and see the low hills to the south of

Above: Throughout 1973 rumours started to circulate that a new 'Club' circuit was to be laid at Snetterton and the start of the 1974 season proved the truth of these rumours, for a new 1.917-mile circuit was introduced. There were now two Sear Corners — one on the original circuit and one on the new. There was a new straight long enough to incorporate a drag strip, but that branch of the sport did not live long at Snetterton. The new straight ended in a left and right which became known as The Esses. The writing was on the wall for the great, original Snetterton track.

Right: The Autosport Three Hours in 1963 was also run for The Martini Rossi Trophy. This is a World Championship in action — the great Jim Clark at the wheel of the Normand Ltd (Racing Division) Lotus 23. *Mike Dixon*

Below right: The scene just before the start of the 1965 British round of the European Touring Car Championship which John Aley had brought to Snetterton. In his capacity as Clerk of the Course, John delivers his drivers' briefing on the grid before letting the pack loose for the Five Hundred Kilometres. Just below Aley's left arm is Jackie Stewart; it would have been nice if some of the drivers had at least given the impression of being interested in what he had to say to them. The grid is really full and includes works entries from Alfa Romeo, BMW and Abarth. *John Aley collection*

Right: Hotly pursued, Sir John Whitmore negotiates the original Russell Bend at the wheel of one of the Alan Mann Lotus Cortinas during the 1965 Five Hundred Kilometres of Snetterton; behind him is a Lancia Flavia Zagato entered by HF Squadra Corse, driven by Carlo Maglioli, followed by L. Bussinello at the wheel of the Jolly Club-entered Alfa Romeo Giulia GTA, with the second Alan Mann Cortina driven by Jackie Stewart in close attendance. This gaggle is brought up by the BMW 1800TI of P Koepchen and the works BMW 1800TI of Dieter Glemser. Sir John and his co-driver Alan Mann went on to win the race convincingly. The Alan Mann cars were always immaculate in their red and gold livery. *Mike Dixon*

Below right: On 12 September 1965 the final of the Autosport Championship was run as two 65-lap races starting at 2pm and 7pm. The camera cannot lie but it does not always impart the whole truth, as in this instance the author leads a pack of cars into the original Russell Bend in his Reliant Sabre (which had started life as the works development car) during the first part of the race but in truth is about to be overwhelmed. The E-Type Jaguar was entered by Red Rose Motors of Chester and driven by Brian Redman whilst the Merlyn No 43 was driven by A. L. Sargeant. The Porsche 906 was entered by John Morris and driven by him and Martin Hone (who did so much to bring motor racing to the streets of Birmingham), whilst the Lotus Elan No 3 is that of H. K. Burnand. Elan No 2 was driven by R. J. Crosfield, with Peter Beach's MG Midget alongside. The posts bearing the legend 'Lucas' are reflectors which were placed around the circuit (red on the outside, white on the inside) as guidance for the drivers during the night section of the race. This picture shows just how tight the original Russell Bend was. *Author's collection*

the circuit it was going to rain and if you could not see them it was already! One evening in the early 1960s the Commander arrived at the Clubhouse with is wife Biddy to find that Jim Russell and his team had just completed a 24-hour reliability trial in a Vauxhall at Snetterton and over a few drinks enquired whether Jim would like a cup to commemorate the feat. The offer was accepted and a tradition developed whereby the record established by Jim Russell's Vauxhall was challenged in later years. There was only one basic rule to challenge for the Commander's Cup which was that the vehicle used had to be an unmodified production saloon; the rule was later changed to allow any production car to make the challenge.

During the 1957 a young American brought his Maserati 300S to Snetterton — and wrote it off. His name was Lance Reventlow and shortly thereafter he was to make his mark upon International motor racing with the first all-American Formula One car, the beautifully prepared (but, sadly, unsuccessful) Scarab.

On Saturday, 10 October 1959 the Three-Hours was supported by just one additional event, a race for cars complying with the International Formula One with a class for Formula Two cars run over 25 laps. The race attracted entries from the Owen Racing Organisation and Team Lotus who each sent two cars, with additional Formula One entries from Jack Brabham who entered a 2.2-litre Cooper, and Tommy Atkins who entered Roy

Salvadori to drive his Maserati-engined Cooper. Bruce Halford was down to drive Horace Gould's Maserati 250F but the entry was scratched so Bruce drove one of the BRMs. The balance of the 25-car field were 1.5-litre Formula Two cars apart from Ian Raby driving a 1,720cc Cooper and David Piper in a 2-litre Lotus, these two being considered Formula One contenders. There were some interesting names in the Formula Two category: Mike Parkes drove the very pretty Fry-Climax, while André Pilette drove the Equipe Nationale Belge Cooper-Climax, Keith Greene was in the Gilby Engineering Co's Cooper and Tim Parnell drove his father's Cooper. At the time, the outright lap record stood at 98.99mph to the credit of Brian Naylor in his self-designed and self-built JBW Maserati.

There was no prize money on offer but £100 was available to the first car to set the lap record at 100mph and Raymond Mays had made up his mind that the money would go to Bourne. On the grid the BRM mechanics made great play of concentrating on Bruce Halford's P25 so that at the drop of the flag Ron Flockhart shot into the lead and held it for all but laps seven and eight when Graham Hill led in the works Lotus before expiring. The Scotsman Flockhart (who was once asked by some poor, benighted reporter if he wore his kilt when racing!) set the lap record at 103.85mph and won the race at 101.71mph. Second was Jack Brabham from Bruce Halford.

Above: As has been said elsewhere within these pages, there are rare racing cars and there are *rare* racing cars — this one falls into the latter category. Towards the end of the 2¹/₂-litre Formula One, the Maserati factory had withdrawn from racing for financial reasons and some of the staff, under the direction of Valerio Colotti, constructed a new Formula One car. The car was designed by Colotti's Studio Tec-Mec who ran it in the 1959 United States Grand Prix under the name Technica-Meccanica Maserati, but it became known simply as the Tec-Mec; it was smaller, lighter and shorter than any Maserati previously built but it came too late to be competitive (a fate which it shared with the Aston Martin DBR4 and Lance Reventlow's Scarab) for the small rear-engined cars were holding sway in Grandes Epreuves by the time it appeared. It was the final flowering of the Maserati 250F and the last Grand Prix car with any Maserati influence. In 1969 (when the car was barely 10 years old) the Archie Scott Brown Memorial Trophy Race was run for historic racing cars over 20 laps of the circuit on 21 September, and the Tec-Mec is seen here between the start line and Riches Corner driven by Tony Merrick who finished second, behind Mike Fraser driving David Boorer's Lotus 16 Climax, and ahead of Richard Bergal's Maserati 250F driven by Alexander Clydedale. Only the first two cars completed the full 20 laps of the race. The Tec-Mec was the only one built and spent a considerable time as part of the Donington Collection but early in 2000 it was purchased by Barrie Baxter and campaigned with considerable verve in historic meetings. *Richard Styles*

Below left: Circuit poster promoting the Shell-sponsored European F5000 Championship. *Author's collection/BHL*

Below right: The West Essex Car Club had the privilege of running the first race meeting on the new 1.9-mile Snetterton circuit on 24 March 1974. *Author's collection/BHL*

Below: Wearing the familiar very dark version of British Racing Green for which the Owen Racing Organisation was famous, Jackie Oliver exits the Hairpin at the wheel of his BRM P261. This was early in the 3-litre Formula One era when wings were just beginning to sprout and tyres were still treaded and had not reached the gargantuan widths which were to come later. This picture was obviously taken during private testing by the team, as the 3-litre Formula One BRM never raced at Snetterton. The wooden edifice on stilts is the commentators' box which gave the incumbent a view down the full length of the Norwich Straight and, once the cars had negotiated the Hairpin, all the way to the Esses and the start of Coram Curve. These were those happy days when Snetterton needed *two* commentators in order to keep the crowds informed of what was happening on the track. *Richard Styles*

he second works Lotus, driven by Innes Ireland, retired on the 5th lap. The winner of the Formula Two section was Chris Bristow in the Yeoman Credit Racing Team Borgward-engined Cooper from the Jim Russell-entered Cooper driven by local boy Mike McKee. It turned out to be quite a day for the Scots for the Three-Hours went to Jimmy Clark in the Border Reivers Lotus Elite, with class wins going to Bob Gerard in a Turner, W. E. Needham in an MG MGA Coupé, Dickie Stoop in his Frazer-Nash Sebring and Dick Protheroe in a Jaguar XK120.

For a number of years, John Aley was the secretary of the East Anglian Centre of the British Racing & Sports Car Club and under his aegis the European Touring Car Championship came to Snetterton to run for 500km at the circuit. The race ran at Snetterton for three years, from 1965 to 1967, but in the last of these the Championship was split, the larger capacity cars going to Oulton Park to be run as the Tourist Trophy while the -litre cars remained at Snetterton. This was the only occasion that the Abarth team cars competed in England due in no small part to the fact that John Aley drove for them!

In 1980, really long-distance racing came to Norfolk; the erstwhile competitions director of the BRSCC, John Nicol, decided that his club was quite capable of running a 24hr race and with sponsorship from the East Anglian vehicle rental company the Willhire 24-Hours was born. The early races were run for teams of production cars, be they sports or saloons, although singleton entries were accepted and these were eligible to compete for the Commander's Cup. From 1986, the race was confined to saloon cars and was a round in the Uniroyal Production Saloon Car Championship; many felt that with the exclusion of sports cars the race lost something. However, to Snetterton and the BRSCC goes the honour of

Above: Wearing his familiar No 7, Stirling Moss approaches The Esses along the Home Straight after the Hairpin on the original Snetterton circuit at the wheel of the UDT Laystall Lotus 24. The occasion was the International Lombank Trophy Race Meeting on Easter Saturday, 14 April 1962, the feature race being the 50-lap Lombank Trophy for Formula One cars which had attracted 20 entries from the cream of Formula One of the day with the exception of Ferrari. Graham Hill's BRM led the first six laps from Moss and Jimmy Clark for Team Lotus; Moss then led until lap 23, when he started to fall back, finally finishing seventh, but on the way he set the new $1^1\!/_2$-litre Formula One lap record at 104.23mph in 1min 33.6sec. It had previously been held by Roy Salvadori in a Cooper at 99.95mph but the outright lap record stood to Jimmy Clark in a $2^1\!/_2$-litre Formula One car at 105.68mph. Victory went to Clark in 1hr 20min 25.6sec at 101.09mph, from Hill. These two lapped the entire field, including the third man who was Joakim Bonnier in the Republica Venetzia Porsche. Fourth was the Gilby driven by Keith Greene, with Tony Shelly's Cooper fifth and Wolfgang Seidel sixth in his own Porsche. On the following Monday Moss suffered the crash at Goodwood which ended his Formula One career so this was the last race (before his return) in which The Master finished and, perhaps, the last photograph of him at Snetterton before his return to the sport in later life. Following some delays in getting ambulance services to scenes of motor racing accidents in 1961, the Grand Prix Drivers Association had decided to work for the general adoption of a helicopter ambulance service and this was provided for the meeting by Westland Ltd of Yeovil, entirely without charge. *Mike Dixon*

Below: As night falls on Snetterton, the competitors round Russell Bend and pass the pits during one of the Willhire 24-Hour races. *Mike Dixon*

running the longest race that has ever been staged on a permanent circuit anywhere in the world when the 24-Hours was extended to 25hrs in 1989 in honour of the Silver Jubilee of the main sponsors of the event.

The 24hr race was last run in 1994 and it is to be hoped that it will be revived in the not-too-distant future for there is something truly magical in walking down the pit lane at two or three in the morning, witnessing tired cars being worked upon by tired mechanics cajoled by fraught team managers and reflecting that this race is not yet half over.

The author well remembers a day he was flag marshalling during practice at the Second Ess on the original Snetterton when an orange Formula Ford from the Russell School appeared from under the Bailey bridge at a most peculiar angle

Below: A name that was to become familiar around the world; at the wheel of a Jim Russell Racing School Merlyn FF 1601 Emerson Fittipaldi negotiates Russell Bend in a full power slide while contesting the Les Leston Formula Ford Championship on 22 June 1969.
Mike Dixon

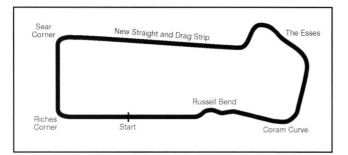

Above: From late 1980, some programmes started to show the original circuit as a dotted line with the shorter, and now permanent, circuit in solid outline. In 1981 this was Snetterton.

Right: 1983 saw another realignment of Russell Bend and the new straight at the back of the circuit had been named Revett Straight after the great Suffolk motorcycle racer, Geoff Revett.

Below right: 1990 saw another change to Russell Bend (although it would, in all truth, be more accurate to once again call it Russell Corner) and that strange name, the Bomb Hole, came into being. For the reason for this strange nomenclature, refer to page 150, but it is worth reiterating that no bomb ever fell on RAF Snetterton Heath. The circuit length was now 1.949 miles.

Bottom right: The commencement of the 1997 season saw another change to Russell (no longer Bend or Corner), and the circuit had joined in the Senna mania and named the part of the straight after the start line and before Riches Corner, Senna Straight. The 1998 Brands Hatch Leisure handbook incorrectly has the name applied to the other section of the straight after Russell and before the start and finish line. Circuit length was 1.952 miles. The apparent differences between the 1990 and 1997 circuits must be put down to cartographer's licence and not to any major rebuilding of the circuit save for the change to Russell. For the start of 1998, the grandstand at the Bomb Hole was demolished to allow for a wider run-off area, thus permitting the Interserie cars to compete at Snetterton and Armco has been put in place on the outside of the track between Riches and Sear Corners.

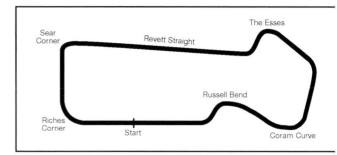

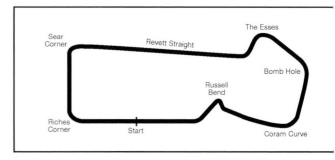

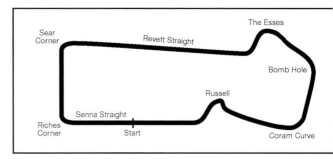

Above: This photograph was taken from the long-vanished footbridge over the track just past the start/finish line; it is the start of the Archie Scott Brown Trophy race, Shell Formula Three final on 8 October 1972. The grid (below) reads like a later 'Who's Who' of motor racing. *Mike Dixon*

60 Mike Tyrrell		57 Randy Lewis	
unknown 51 Willi Deutsch	44 R Shellard	47 Ulf Svensson	
38 Neill Ginn 21 unknown	33 Ian Taylor	54 Rudolf Dutsch	
37 Pierre Rousselot 22 Hanen Dhalquist	50 Conny Andersson	16 Bob Evans	
17 Peter Hull		63 Peter Lamplough	
4 Mike Walker 25 Jean-Pierre Jarier		12 Mike Wilds	
28 Stan Matthews 3 Rikki van Opel		40 Colin Vandervell	
5 Roger Williamson			
	15 Jones		
2 Tony Brise			

Above: Snetterton is not the warmest of places at the best of times and this is summer at Snetterton. It is 30 July 1978 and after a small shower the marshals gainfully attempt to make the circuit suitable for racing by bailing out the Esses. The meeting had to be abandoned. *Mike Dixon*

Left: The finish of the race — Roger Williamson just pips Tony Brise — both are driving GRD372s. *Mike Dixon*

Above: Following the loss of Folkingham as their test site the Owen Racing Oganisation seemed to regard Snetterton as its home circuit and the BRMs appeared to test and race at regular intervals: Peter Berthon and Raymond Mays were the power behind the original BRM concept, and here the latter looks on as work is carried out on a P44, the first of the rear-engined cars. *Author*

Below: Whilst the days of seeing a BRM contesting a Grand Prix are but a memory the marque was still alive and fighting in 1997. At the time when Peugeot was winning the World Sports Car Championship, a new BRM was built to contest the series but politics within the sport's International governing body killed the Championship and the BRM P321 sports coupé was more or less stillborn despite an investment of some millions of pounds. After lying dormant for a few years it was resurrected by Pacific Racing who fitted a Mazda engine with a view to contesting Le Mans in 1997. A few days before the great race at the Sarthe the car was taken to Snetterton for some final tests and is seen negotiating Russell Corner in the hands of Henri Toivenen. *Author*

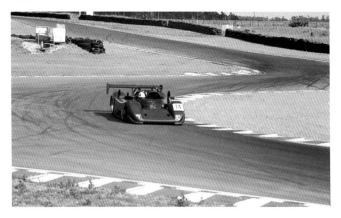

Right: The circuit from the air. At the bottom of the picture is the long, seemingly unending sweep of Coram Curve leading, after a short straight, to Russell Corner followed by the pit straight. In the top left-hand corner of the picture is Riches Corner, followed by Sear Corner and the long Revett Straight which was used for drag racing for a short time after the building of the new, shorter circuit. At the end of Revett Straight are the Esses followed by the Bomb Hole; no bomb ever fell on RAF Snetterton Heath so some explanation of how the name came about is called for. It comes from the two-wheeled contingent, some of whom used to find negotiating this part of the course somewhat difficult and parted from their machinery on a regular basis and started to call it the Bum Hole — it must be assumed that someone found this a little indiscreet and converted the name into the Bomb Hole. From here a short straight leads back to Coram Curve. The original circuit is still clear; just beyond Sear Corner is the original Sear Corner which led to the un-named left-hand flick followed by the mile-long Norwich Straight, the Hairpin and the Home Straight.

The original Esses comprised the left-hand bend after the Home Straight and the Bomb Hole. The area around the Hairpin is now occupied by Snetterton Market as witness the number of cars parked. Every year on the weekend following the last race meeting, Snetterton is given over to a weekend of fund-raising for the British Heart Foundation when members of the public come in their thousands to pay for the privilege of being whisked around the circuit in competition cars which are brought to the circuit by their owners at their own expense. This picture was taken on Heart Foundation Day 1996 and 20 cars can be seen on the circuit. Shortly after that weekend the builders moved in to transform Snetterton: the bridge over the Esses was demolished and a new one built just before the Esses, Russell was realigned once more and the pit complex and garages completely rebuilt. Behind the paddock can be seen the go-kart track. *Richard Styles*

Below: If ever a picture told a story this one does, for it encapsulates the spirit of the Willhire 24-Hour race; it is in the small hours of the morning, drivers are tired, team managers are becoming a trifle short-tempered, mechanics are approaching exhaustion, your car arrives with a problem then some idiot hangs out a sign telling you not to panic. *Mike Dixon*

Above: Then the wheel came full circle . . . not strictly true, for Spitfires never flew from RAF Snetterton Heath in active service, but on the weekend of the *Autosport* Three-Hours, organised by the Historic Sports Car Club in October 1996, David Pennell arrived in his personal transport and parked it on the grid overnight so that it would be within sight of his motorhome which was in the paddock. It was a two-day meeting and with his weekend's racing over on the Sunday morning, Mr Pennell took off in the Spitfire at lunch-time, flew a wide circle over the Norfolk countryside, made a low pass over the Revett Straight and went home. *Author*

Right: Oliver Sear's Snetterton Motor Racing Club issued annual members' badges which gained the wearer admission to all of the season's race meetings. These examples, with an outline of the original circuit, come from 1966 and 1967. *Author*

Right: Archie Scott Brown was a phenomenon whose like we shall probably never see again: born with one arm and a stump and terrible deformities to his legs which were rectified by endless painful operations manfully borne in his childhood, he became a Grand Prix driver making the mighty Lister Jaguars his own on the way. Such a man would probably not succeed today, for the nanny mentality would prevent him from racing 'for his own good'. He drove an incredible variety of cars in his career and is seen here on 25 April 1953 winning the five-lap handicap for Specials during an Eastern Counties Motor Club members' meeting at Snetterton at the wheel of the twin-cylinder 1,097cc JAP-engined Tojeiro. The hangar has long gone and the complete lack of spectator protection is quite amazing. There are some interesting cars on the public's side of the fence, not least the white Healey Duncan. *Eastern Counties Motor Club Archive/I. C. Pearce*

Right: Not too many drivers fully justify being called 'great' but Archie did. He died as a result of injuries sustained when his Lister-Jaguar crashed and caught fire at Spa-Francorchamps in Belgium. He had started his racing career at the Norfolk circuit and shortly after his death the Snetterton Motor Racing Club erected a plaque to his memory on the wall of the scrutineering building in the paddock. It reads: 'W. A. Scott Brown 1927-1958. He represented everything that was best in the sport: 71 Firsts 34 Seconds 12 Thirds'. Rarely, if ever, have truer words been worked in stone. His family presented the Snetterton Motor Racing Club with a trophy which was raced for as the Archie Scott Brown Memorial Trophy, a tradition which the East Anglian Centre of the BRSCC continues, and to this day a laurel wreath is hung upon the plaque in his memory on the occasion of the Trophy meeting. *Author*

Snetterton was purchased by Grovewood Securities in 1963 and, in company with the other Brands Hatch Leisure Group circuits (Cadwell Park and Oulton Park), was purchased by John Foulston in 1985.

Plans to build a village on the circuit at Snetterton received short shrift from the local council in the 1980s. As these words are written major work is in progress at the circuit and, after years of neglect, considerable sums of money are being spent. The Bailey bridge has been removed to be replaced by a new two-way one across the Revett Straight and the pit garages have been demolished to be replaced by new ones set further back to allow for the provision of a wider pit lane. Russell Corner has been realigned and the entire circuit has been resurfaced. During the winter of 1997/8 the grandstand at the Esses was removed in order that a wider run-off area can be provided in preparation for the arrival of the Interserie cars.

After a gap of 17 years an FIA-sanctioned race meeting took place at Snetterton again on Sunday 9 August 1998 when two 1½hr races were run for Group N cars. Sadly, there were only 14 starters, all but three of them being BMW M3s, but it is to be hoped that this will lead to the return of the 24hr race. Victory went to the only Mercedes-Benz in the race, an SLK

— the same antic was performed the next lap and the yellow flag was readied as this tyro was clearly headed for disaster. But he continued in this manner and was obviously in complete control of the situation and went on to win the first of many races — his name was Emerson Fittipaldi and the rest, as the saying goes, is history. He had come to England from his homeland with something of a reputation as a karter and became a pupil of the world's first Racing Drivers' School which was established by Jim Russell at the Norfolk circuit in May 1957 and many are the great names that have passed through its portals, not a few World Champions amongst them.

In those happy days before Grand Prix cars competed only in Grands Prix, Snetterton could usually be relied upon to run an Formula One event early in the season, the teams treating the race as a test session; BRM and Lotus were 'local' and could be counted upon to send two or three cars each.

Right: The date of this meeting is lost but the picture serves well to illustrate Snetterton in its early days: the cars are starting from a four-three-four grid, the starter stands upon what appears to be a table whilst spectators are observing from the bridge and have wandered on to the track behind the grid. The bridge and the starting point were later moved further up the track and the bridge ceased to exist one night during a storm. What is truly remarkable is the size of the crowd. The race was won by Robin Richards driving the MG MGA which is third on the grid. *Mark Lowrie collection*

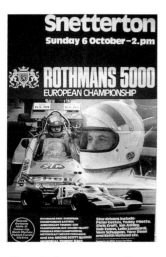

Above: Rothmans was another sponsor of the European Formula 5000 Championship.

Above right: From 1977 comes this poster for the Shell Sport International meeting for Group 8 racing cars — Formula 5000 by another name.

driven by Stephane Van Dyck and Klaus Bugler. The race marked the competition debut of the BMW Z3 in Great Britain.

History repeated itself a week later when the British Automobile Racing Club included its Supersprint Championship within the race meeting on 16 August. The event consists of competitors making a standing start from the pit lane on the out lap, covering one timed flying lap and a slowing down lap. As a competitor is on his slowing down lap, the next one starts upon his out lap — shades of the inaugural Aston Martin Owners' Club meeting back in 1951.

Sadly, major International Meetings are a thing of the past in the Brecklands, the high spot of the year being a round of the Touring Car Championship which now features a night race. The British Racing Drivers Club brings Powertour to Snetterton once a year and the circuit is regularly busy with Club car racing and motorcycles. Midweek there is the Supercar Experience when, for not too vast an outlay in view of what is on offer, one can try one's hand on the circuit (under instruction) at the wheel of a Ferrari 355, Porsche 911, Chrysler Viper or Lotus Esprit.

Having been part of Brands Hatch Leisure, the sale of the Group to Octagon means that ownership of Snetterton has once more changed, and it would appear for the better. Over the winter of 2000/1 the whole of Revett Straight has benefitted from the erection of Armco protection, as have those other parts of the circuit which were not protected.

As the new millennium starts the future is bright for Snetterton. At the close of the 20th century the outright lap record is credited to Luis Garcia driving a Reynard 95D in 59.47sec on 6 May 1996 at 118.16mph. However, as there have been some changes to the circuit since then this is not, strictly speaking, true but nothing has circulated Snetterton faster since that date. The lap record on the original circuit will stand in perpetuity and is believed to have been set by Brett Lunger driving a 5-litre Chevrolet-engined Trojan T101 on 20 April 1973 at 124.44mph in 1min 18.4sec.

Left: The original Snetterton Motor Racing Club car badge — this example showing evidence of having worked for its living on someone's radiator grille. *Author*

THORNABY
TWO CIRCUITS IN TWO YEARS

Royal Air Force Thornaby-on-Tees was constructed during the late 1920s on a site of only 34 acres and was one of the first airfields to be opened after World War 1. In January 1937 it became a fighter station and a few months before the outbreak of World War 2 it was again redesignated and became a general reconnaissance squadron. The station then had a varied career throughout the conflict.

Motor racing took place at Thornaby on only four occasions, the organisation being in the hands of the Darlington & District Motor Club who 'discovered' Thornaby and sought Air Ministry approval to race there. The first meetings took place on 6 September 1959 on a 1.9-mile circuit; for the meeting on 18 April 1960 the length had been reduced to 1.45 miles. At one of these meetings Jimmy Blumer was the star, driving the ex-Stirling Moss bob-tail Cooper. There is some evidence that one race meeting was organised by Middlesbrough & District Motor Club.

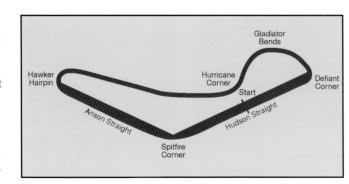

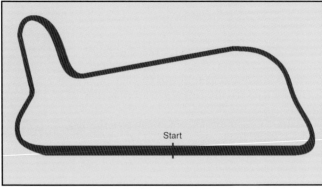

Top: This is the first circuit at Thornaby, used by the Darlington & District Motor Club. It measured 1.9 miles and was probably unique in having all of its corners named after aircraft. The start and finish line was situated halfway along the longest straight on the circuit, named Hudson Straight, on one of the runways, taking a right at its intersection with another runway on to Anson Straight, which ended at Hawker Hairpin. There then followed a straight and a gentle left to Hurricane Corner, a tight left leading to the right-hand Gladiator Bend. Defiant Corner then took competitors back on to Hudson Straight. This circuit was first used 6 September 1959, and only in that year.

Above: From 18 April 1960 this 1.45-mile circuit came into use. Rather a strange one, it used most of one of the runways, with the start and finish line almost halfway along it. The first bend was a right followed by a short straight, then a left and right and another short straight led to a 180° right which was tight but not a hairpin. The track was now running back parallel to the last straight and was of almost equal length to it, then took a 90° left on to another long straight, followed by a long right-hand bend. A further straight and a sharp right led back to the start/finish straight. It has not been possible to identify the features of the circuit by name.

Left: The programme cover from the Middlesbrough & District Motor Club's Whit Monday race meeting at Thornaby RAF station on 6 June 1960. The lines of Alan Ensoll's D-type Jaguar are not enhanced by the use of a Jaguar XK120 windscreen.

THRUXTON
HOME OF THE BRITISH AUTOMOBILE RACING CLUB

ith the loss of Goodwood in 1966 the British Automobile Racing Club was without a home, a state of affairs which could not be allowed to continue, resulting in early and strenuous activity on the part of the council of the BARC to find somewhere new for the club to rest its head. The attention of the council turned to Hampshire and the World War 2 airfield at Thruxton; efforts in 1966 proved fruitless but by October 1967 an agreement had been reached and ambitious plans laid to have the new circuit ready by 1 March 1968. But the story of Thruxton begins in 1940.

With hostilities continuing as the new decade opened, southern England and East Anglia were littered with RAF airfields but that at RAF Andover was fast becoming incapable of coping with the amount of air traffic it had to handle and a satellite airfield was required. The War Department espied the flat fields to the west of Thruxton village and purchased the required amount of land from Thruxton Manor Estate in 1940, building a three-runway airfield thereon. The new airfield opened in May 1941 — it is truly amazing what can be achieved in adversity. RAF Thruxton was in the hands of Fighter Command, part of which was 1526 Beam Approach Training Flight which was a small body of some 40 men flying Blenheims and Airspeed Oxfords and whose remit it was to train large numbers of navigators in the use of 'GEE', a revolutionary radio-location device used for

Right: The programme cover from the very first car race meeting held at Thruxton Aerodrome on August Bank Holiday Monday, 1952. Advertising from the stalwart *Motor* and a patriotic picture of two Jaguar C-types in action, but no mention of the organising club.

pinpointing targets for night-bombing over Germany. In 1941/2, the allegiance of RAF Thruxton passed to RAF Netheravon, these two stations being responsible for the Army Co-operation Squadrons of the Royal Air Force which worked with the Airborne Division towing gliders and dropping airborne troops. The units flew Whitley bombers which towed Horsa and Hotspur gliders and in June 1944 were involved in D-day with Operation 'Overlord'.

It was also in 1944 that 'Old Glory' first flew at Thruxton when the 366th Fighter Bomber Group of the United States Army Air Force based the 389th, 390th and 391st squadrons (which flew Republic P47 Thunderbolts) from the station. The Americans suffered heavy losses, as between 30 and 40 crash-landed American Lockheed Lightnings were counted at the end of the runway at one time. After D-day,

Above right: At Thruxton on 15 April 1968 Jochen Rindt awaits the start of the Formula Two race. *Fred Scatley*

Right: One of the joys of saloon car racing in the 1960s and 1970s was the invasion of the Ford Galaxies from America. Here, on 15 April 1968, two of these 7-litre monsters do battle at Thruxton; the identity of the drivers is lost in the mists of time. *Fred Scatley*

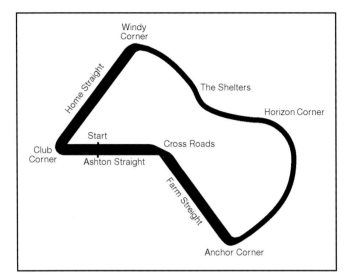

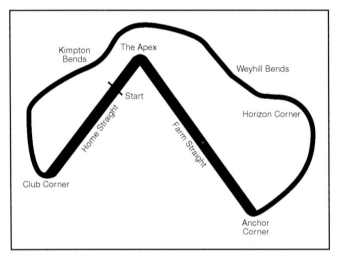

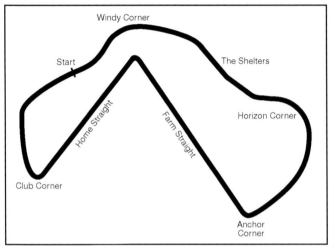

Left: A circuit map of the very first track at Thruxton which was used only once at the Bank Holiday Monday meeting in 1952. It measured 1.89 miles and bore very little resemblance to the Thruxton of today.

Below left: From 1953 onwards the circuit bears rather more resemblance to a recognizable Thruxton: this version measured 2.7574 miles.

Below: This version is from 1955 and shows the start/finish line moved to a position before a curve leading to Windy Corner.

Bottom: And so to the Thruxton of the British Automobile Racing Club as constructed in 1968, which measured 2.356 miles and is virtually unaltered today.

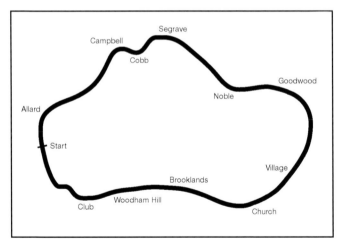

RAF Thruxton reverted to parachute training and was used to supply both aircraft and pilots to squadrons in France and other parts of Europe which had suffered losses, but as the war came to an end it was allowed to run down and finally became inactive in 1946. It then passed into private hands, soon becoming a popular motorcycle racing venue.

Bank Holiday Monday, 4 August 1952 heard the first racing car engines burst into life at Thruxton when the Bristol Motorcycle & Light Car Club and the Sporting Owner Drivers' Club jointly organised an experimental race meeting on a 1.89-mile circuit which bore very little resemblance to the Thruxton of the 1990s. The airfield had been very little used since the war and the runways were rough but it was on one of these that the start/finish line was situated on what was called Ashton Straight, very roughly in the middle of the airfield. The circuit was run in a clockwise direction and from the start ran to a right hairpin bend at Club Corner on to Home Straight, turning right again at Windy Corner (Segrave); thus far the track had been 52yd wide but it now narrowed to 50ft as it turned on to the perimeter track via a considerable step which received less than favourable comment from the competitors. The circuit now swept right and left through The Shelters (Kimpton) to

Horizon Corner (Village) then, as now, a long right-hander to Anchor Corner (Church), then turning sharp right via another step on to the runway known as Farm Straight at the end of which a left-hander turned back on to Ashton Straight and the completion of a lap.

The programme consisted of seven races; two heats and a final for Formula III, sports cars up to 1,200cc, sports cars up 1,500cc unsupercharged and up 1,200cc supercharged, sports cars up 2,500cc unsupercharged and up to 1,500cc supercharged, all of six laps except for the Formula III final which was 10 laps. The final race of the day was a 10-lapper for sports cars of unlimited capacity. Notable amongst the

On 4 August 1968 John Miles waits on the grid at Thruxton at the wheel of the factory-entered Lotus Europa in the attractive red and white Gold Leaf Team Lotus colours. Behind Miles is another Europa and behind that, what appears to be the Costin-Nathan with a Lotus 23 beside it. *Ferret Fotographics*

constructed. The first test runs were held on the following day and plans were set in motion for the first race meeting to be held on Sunday, 17 March.

Thruxton mark three has the start/finish line to the south of the circuit on a slight right bend which becomes a sharper right at Allard (named after Sydney Allard) leading to a sweeping left followed by the complex of Campbell, Cobb and Segrave (named respectively after Sir Malcolm Campbell, John Cobb and Sir Henry O'Neil de Hane Segrave, all of whom were members of the Brooklands Automobile Racing Club). There then follows a gentle right-hand sweep leading to a left-hand curve named Noble (after Richard Noble) followed by three right-handers of varying degrees of severity, named Goodwood (for obvious reasons), Village and Church. There then follows the nearest thing that Thruxton now has to a straight which is a continuous gentle left-hand bend, the apex being called Brooklands, followed by Woodham Hill and Club which leads back to the start/finish line.

Thruxton today is much as BARC laid it out in 1968, save for the fact that a chicane has been inserted at Cobb between Campbell and Segrave in order to reduce speeds somewhat. However, all has not been plain sailing for during the summer of 1970 the use of the circuit was challenged by Hampshire County Council. Following a Public Enquiry which lasted for 22 days, the Minister's decision was not announced until 1972; and when it finally came the ruling stipulated that racing could take place on only 21 days a year. Enter the NIMBY fraternity in the shape of a small number of local objectors who planned to have the use of the circuit further reduced. Fearing complete closure of the circuit, the BARC reached an out-of-court settlement which restricted use to just 12 racing days a year, a situation which still pertains today.

However, the BARC makes the most of the situation, running as a full a season as it can year on year with Formula Three and the British Touring Car Championship as the highlights. At the close of the 2000 season the outright lap record stands at 135.16mph in 1min 27.5sec to the credit of Phillipe Adams driving a Formula 3000 Reynard 91D on 26 September 1993.

entries were Roy Salvadori, Dan Margulies and Horace Gould.

Both of the organising clubs were back a year later to run a further race meeting on a circuit which much more closely resembled the Thruxton of the BARC, but still used the runways. The start/finish line was now situated on the Home Straight which was run in the opposite direction to the previous year(!) but the circuit was still run clockwise. The start was followed by Club Corner, a sharp right on to what is now the start/finish line into the Kimpton Bends (Allard) leading to a long right-hand unnamed bend and on to what, in 1952, had been The Shelters but was now called Weyhill Bends and to Horizon Corner; the circuit was now as in the previous year except that instead of turning left on to Ashton Straight it continued to a left hairpin called The Apex, on to the Home Straight and the start/finish line.

Thruxton mark two measured 2.7574 miles in length and the bumps had been eliminated. On this occasion, the programme consisted of six races over six, 10 and 15 laps to much the same format as the previous year but the standard of entries was improving, the Unlimited Capacity Sports Car race attracting three entries from Ecurie Ecosse running XK120C Jaguars. And that was the end of motor racing at Thruxton for some time but motorcycle racing continued until 1965 by which time the condition of the runways had become very poor.

Enter the British Automobile Racing Club who had chosen Thruxton as their new home following the loss of Goodwood. With a mammoth effort by all involved the ambitious deadline of 1 March 1968, which the club had set itself, was met and the new circuit using the perimeter track of 2.356 miles was resurfaced, spectator banks and marshals' posts built, telephones installed and the pits and race control buildings

Right: At the other end of the scale from the Ford Galaxies in 1968, the diminutive Fiat Abarths pawed the air as they cornered. *Fred Scatley*

Below: On 12 April 1971 Vittorio Brambilla is seen aboard a Formula Two Brabham BT30. . . *Fred Scatley*

Bottom: . . . whilst Graham Hill drove a different model of the same marque. Those happy days when the top drivers had the time to compete in other than Formula One races! *Fred Scatley*

WHITCHURCH
TWICE ONLY

ocated near Bristol, the Bristol & Wessex Aeroplane Club first flew from this airfield in 1928. It was used by the Army Transport Command during World War 2 and following the cessation of hostilities was used by British Overseas Airways Corporation, becoming Bristol Airport in 1946, for a brief period.

On Saturday, 1 August 1959 the Bristol Motorcycle and Light Car Club organised the first race meeting in conjunction with Bristol Corporation who owned the then disused airfield at Whitchurch. The meeting consisted of six races, one of which was for Formula 2 cars run under a National Permit. This race was won by H. C. Taylor in 24min 8.2sec at 66.03mph from Keith Greene and Tim Parnell, all of whom were Cooper-mounted. The fastest lap was set by Taylor in 57.4sec at a speed of 66.64mph.

The other races were for Formula III, Grand Touring cars up to 1600cc and 1601 to 2000cc, two races for sports cars up to 1500cc and over 1500cc, and production saloons. The fastest lap of the day was set by a Formula III car in exactly 53sec, a speed of 72.17mph, set by J, Pitcher. It is probable that this is the all-time lap record at Whitchurch as this may have been the only meeting held at the circuit though it is possible that another was held later in the year.

The report of the meeting in *Autosport* on 14 August 1959 speaks of indifferent weather, with only the first and last races being run on a dry track, which probably accounts for the Formula III cars being quicker than their Formula 2 brethren. The report closed with the words that Bristol Corporation had not yet decided what was to be the future of Whitchurch airfield so this meeting may well have been the only one held.

It has not been possible to obtain exact details of the configuration of the circuit but the same *Autosport* report speaks of a course 'shorter than most [but] full of interest for drivers and spectators' and the longest straight not being more than 500yd long, with a total [circuit] length of 1,870yd.

It is now the site of the Whitchurch Sports Centre.

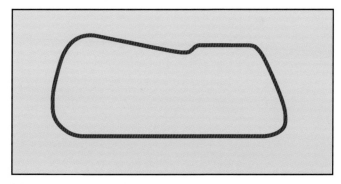

It has not proved possible to find a circuit map of Whitchurch and this one has been created by reference to contemporary reports and an aerial photograph of the airfield. The circuit length is not known but the main straight measured 600yd. The precise location of the start/finish line is not known.

BIBLIOGRAPHY

Archie and the Listers, Robert Edwards (Patrick Stephens Ltd)

Automobile Year — various years

British Grand Prix 1926-1976, Doug Nye (Batsford 1977)

Brooklands: A Pictorial History, N. Georgano (Dalton Watson)

Davidstow: A history of Cornwall's Formula One Race Circuit, Peter Tutthill (West Country Motor Books)

Forty Years of Silverstone

Racing at Crystal Palace: A History of Motorsport at London's Own Race Circuit 1927-1972, Phillip Parfitt (Motor Racing Publications Ltd)

Oliver's Mount Scarborough: 50 Years of Racing 1946-1996, Peter Hillaby and Tony Coupland (Scarborough Racing Combine Ltd and Auto 66 Club)

The Donington Grand Prix, Dave Ferns (Donington International Collection)

Wings and Wheels